Exposed Spine Sewings

MORE NON-ADHESIVE BINDING

keith a smith

Mummy,
Thank you for
always holding
me together.
Jessie xx

First Edition October 1995
First Edition, Second Printing May 1997
First Edition, Third Printing February 2002
First Edition, Fourth Printing October 2006

Published by keith a smith *BOOKS*
1115 East Main Street, Suite 219, Box 8
Rochester, New York 14609-6152

Distributed by Keith A. Smith
1115 East Main Street, Suite 219, Box 8
Rochester, New York 14609-6152
Voice message or FAX: 585 482 2496
Email orders: keith@keithsmithbooks.com
ONLINE: www.keithsmithbooks.com

Library of Congress Card Catalogue Number: 95-92103

ISBN: 0-9637682-4-7

BOOK NUMBER 170

Exposed Spine Sewings

NON-ADHESIVE BINDING

VOLUME III

keith a smith

KE⊙TH

TABLE OF CONTENTS

DOUBLE RAISED SUPPORTS with VARIOUS MEANS to CHANGE-OVER

3   ACROSS the SPINE SEWINGS

The BOOK as SEWING FRAME

5   REFERENCE

Acknowledgments

Scott McCarney, for his constant loving support.

Fred Jordan, who every Wednesday morning the past two years has gone over what I have written and drawn the previous week. Thank you, Fred.

Betsy Palmer Eldridge, for instructing me on almost seventy different stitches. I am also indebted to Betsy for her attention to every word, every stitch in this book. Thank you, Betsy.

Preface

I am not a binder.

As a book artist, I am interested in many aspects of the book. When we were students, Gary Frost told me to make books, so I did. My concern was structure of pictures. My teacher, Kenneth Josephson, taught me about group, series and sequence. Perhaps he learned it from Nathan Lyons; I am not sure. But Nathan is the only one I know who has a mastery of sequence.

After fifteen years of making books, I thought I had better learn something more than the crude binding I was putting on my books, after spending hundreds of hours imaging each of those ones-of-a-kind. Fred Jordan became my teacher in 1982.

Fred has had many students whose work is superior to mine—Todd Pattison and Gail Ferris, among them. My craft will never be on a level with theirs.

When I started this volume, Hedi Kyle told me I should devise an inexpensive sewing frame, because my reader might not be able to afford a commercial one. She told me to show means of attaching supports to boards. Almost all the other tips in this book are the ideas of Fred Jordan, from his weekly critiques. He suggested dying the supports, as well as the thread, strengthening the supports, eliminating some of my more impractical ideas and introduced me to the Dremel™ Moto-Tool. This book is also his. The traditional stitches, such as the Herringbone, Seed Pearl and Caterpillar were learned from Betsy Palmer Eldridge.

It must be stated that this book is indebted to Gary, Hedi, Fred and Betsy, and Pamela Spitzmueller, who are all trained binders. All my work is dependent upon my first teacher, Aatis Lillstrom. All I do grows out of his genius; I merely facilitate. Aatis taught me to think. He taught me to employ my previous knowledge into present explorations, and to be willing to admit my ignorance, in order to be open to learning. I respect the work of all the above mentioned, and am indebted to them...

I am not a binder; I am an explorer.

FOR FRED JORDAN III

INTRODUCTION

MORE bindings titled *EXPOSED SPINE SEWINGS* is Volume III in the series *Non-Adhesive Binding*. It is a continuation of sewings described in *1– 2– & 3–Section Sewings*, Book 169, which is Volume II of my series. These two volumes, published simultaneously in 1995, are an outgrowth of my first book on binding, Book 128, *Non-Adhesive Binding, Books Without Paste or Glue*. Book 128 will now be referred to as Volume I.

Volume I assists the beginning artist/binder with terminology and descriptions of procedure. This is followed by thirty-two simple to elaborate bindings. The book ends with a list of several hundred Sources for bookstores and dealers; distributors; guilds and organizations; periodicals; binding tools, equipment and materials; paper; services; and workshops and apprenticeships.

Volumes II and III do not address either terminology nor list sources, but only describe more sewings. If you previously have not bound books, it is recommended that you begin with Volume I, or perhaps Volume II.

Non-adhesive binding allows form to follow function in exposed spine sewings.

Volumes II and III are written with *the section* as a unit of composition. Each section is a completed unit; no sewing description extends from one section to the next.

Having each section as a completed unit comes out of my concern for those who purchase the books in sheets, unbound, as folded and gathered sections. This allows the individual to bind all, or however many sections desired as a booklet. The remainder of the book can be sewn utilizing one or more of the sewings described in either book.

Volume II presents 1– 2– and 3–section sewings. Each section, or any two or three successive sections can be sewn as samples of bindings described in this book.

It is appropriate for a book on binding to be offered in sheets. This not only affords the binder opportunity to sew; a hand-sewn manual is far easier to use. Hand-sewing the sections along, or across the spine, usually permits the book to open and to lie flat at any opened page. The reader has both hands free to sew.

ALONG THE SPINE

In Volume III, twenty-eight sewings along the spine are described.

Sewing patterns on the spine will be investigated in raised support sewings of cord, and of thread. These sewings can be flat back, or, can be rounded to improve structural stability. The spine is not dampened, hammered, or pasted, because it will not be covered.

Swelling in the back is reduced, and the rounding is slightly shaped with a hammer, taking care not to dent the paper. The book is placed in a lying press. Backing is done section by section with a dull knife, not a hammer. This is to insure an attractive paper edge to the sections, since no spine-cover is used. The boards are covered separately.

KETTLE STITCH AS (the means of by which to) CHANGE-OVER: The kettle stitch, which will be referred to as the *kettle,* is ideal as a functional means *to change-over,* that is, to alter the direction of the sewing. The path of the link and slipping under to lock allows the kettle to change direction, permitting entry in the new section on the back side of the station: it locks the sections together and climbs to the next.

When the spine is not covered, the kettle stitch becomes a decorative limitation.

BELOW: Detail of the kettle stitch. See: *LINK STITCHES,* page 25.
The *kettle stitch* will be referred to simply as the *kettle.*

HEAD

ABOVE: Prototype of The ICICLE which combines raised cord sewing with stitches on the spine. The book is rounded and backed one section at a time with a dull blade. See page 51.

The kettle stitch is replaced by climbing on a packed cord to change-over.

ENDBANDS AS (the means by which to) CHANGE-OVER: For exposed spine sewings, I have played with other means of climbing at the end of a section when sewing along the spine. One means is *endbands as change-over:* This makes use of the integrated endbands to change-over to the next section. The end, or terminal cords are placed slightly beyond the head and tail. As each section is sewn, the same thread packs and beads that area of the headband before sewing the next section.

It is critical that the square of the book protrude beyond the endband, to protect the endband from fraying. Otherwise, shelf-wear would eventually fray the endband, and compromise the entire sewing. This is one reason endbands usually are added to, rather than an integral part of, the sewing of the book.

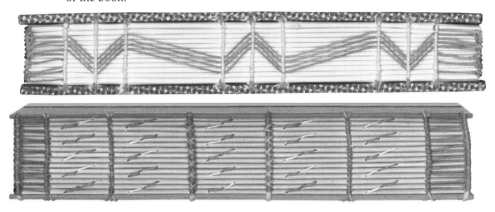

Top: An integrated endband *added to* a completed sewing. The head and tail-bands are sewn with a single continuous thread, linking the supports along the spine. Middle: Accomplished in a single sewing, the middle stations are a raised cord sewing with integrated *endbands as change-over.*

CORDS AS CHANGE-OVER: Keeping the terminal cords well within the boundaries of the boards at head and tail, I have explored solidly packing supports as a means of climbing to the next section. They help create a lovely exposed spine sewing. It also eliminates confining design possibilities of exposed spine sewings of relying upon the kettle stitch.

The SPIRAL BINDING is the name by which I refer to this particular sewing with cords as change-over. It is important to pack the cords tightly with waxed thread in lieu of a kettle stitch.

TAPES AS CHANGE-OVER:
Another means of subverting the need for a kettle stitch is sewing raised cords in combination with tapes or a continuous support. Both types of supports are used to change-over.

This is inspired by Volume II, where the investigation was sewing on continuous (paper) support. Continuous support allows a certain freedom, playing with where to change-over. There are several ideas in my head, but those investigations might become a volume in themselves; I do not present them here.

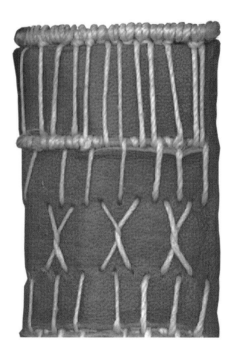

I do show two exposed spine sewings which use a combination of raised cords protruding through the continuous support of a leather spine. More than functional; the leather is decorative. Strips of leather become "tapes", more than a continuous support. The leather, with or without laced cords, attaches the side-covers.

Above: Detail of CORDS & CONTINUOUS SUPPORT I. The leather spine, itself, is used as a "tape" support-as-change-over: Slits in the leather *across* the spine allow the stitching to bulge through, for a sensuous look. See page 155.

Below: Detail of CORDS & CONTINUOUS SUPPORT II. Slits *along* the spine allow the cords to be woven through the leather, while setting up the sewing frame. Sewing proceeds on the frame, through the leather. See page 156.

ACROSS THE SPINE

- Terminal stations, and thus, their kettle stitches are eliminated: In sewing *all across,* rather than *all along,* the spine: The link stitch at *every* station climbs to change-over. These link stitches may, or may not be a kettle stitch.
- Sewing across the spine is stronger, and, a more secure sewing than along the spine.—If any thread in the two or more independently paired sewings across the spine is broken, the remaining sewings are not affected.
- The book will open flat, and remain open, at any page.
- The head and tail can be sewn across the spine. Then, in a separate sewing, the middle stations can be sewn along, or across the spine. See: *The Book as Sewing Frame,* page 273, and bottom digital scan below.

Volume III describes sixteen sewings across the spine.

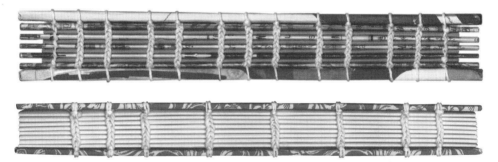

"Coptic" is not a clearly defined term. It is safer to specifically refer to such, as LINK STITCH SEWINGS. In each case, the link *stitches* at paired stations produce a double row chain *pattern* across the spine.

Top: COPTIC STITCH sewing , with a single needle along the spine, is described in Volume I on page 174. This example uses alternating size of sections for a dovetail effect at the head and tail.

Middle: The 2–Needle COPTIC SEWING II. It is one of nine "Coptics" described in this volume. All are sewn across the spine, with *single* or *double needles,* that is, either one needle, or, a needle on each end of the thread. I will refer to *single needle* as *1–needle,* and *double needle* sewing as *2–needle.*

Across the spine sewing eliminates the need for a kettle stitch. Paired stations represent one thread. The 2–Needle "Coptics" have a needle threaded at each end. Since this particular sewing has four sets of stations across the spine, it required eight needles. Yet it sews about as quickly the 1–Needle COPTIC, sewn along the spine.

Below: Head and tail sewn *all across* the spine with the 4 DOWN LINK SEWING. Afterwards, stations 3 through 7 were sewn *all along* the spine, solid packed, on raised thread supports. See page 263.

Keith Smith, 1993. CATERPILLAR sewing, used in the cover design of this volume. 23 x 15.5 x 4 cm. The sewing was devised by Betsy Palmer Eldridge.

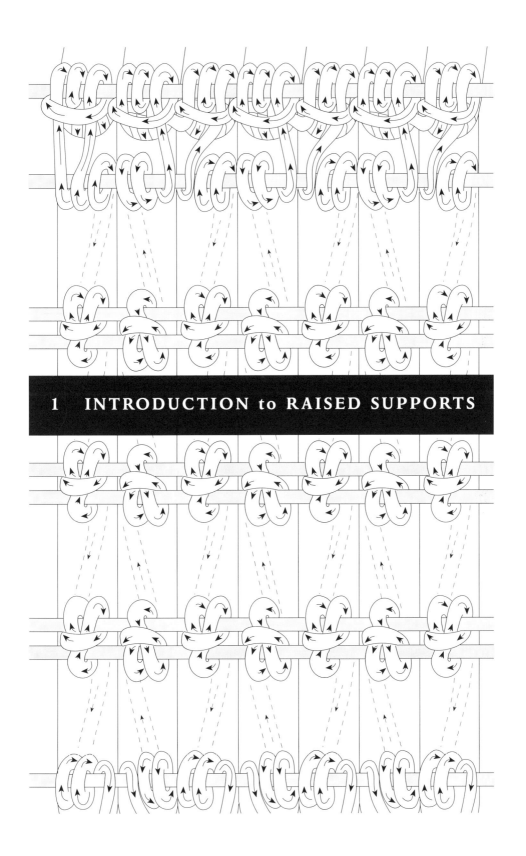

1 INTRODUCTION to RAISED SUPPORTS

MAKING A SEWING FRAME

Raised support sewings require a sewing frame.

Frances McClure, Walter Havighurst Special Collections, Miami University Libraries, said when teaching student assistants to sew without a frame, she uses a very simple devise employed by many conservators. She takes a piece of book board slightly larger than the book to be sewn, the tapes or cords are fastened in position on the back side of the board with duct or masking tape. The book board is turned over and the sewing proceeds around the dangling supports, which are tightened with a firm tug as the sewing progresses.

Hedi Kyle advised that I should demonstrate how to build a simple sewing frame. Since they are moderately expensive to purchase, you might want to construct your own, at least until you determine whether you will be sewing a good number of recessed or raised support sewings.

EXPENSE of HAND-MADE FRAME: I have very little building skills; the frame I created below and on the following page will be well within the reader's ability to construct. Expense of this frame is minimal: The carriage bolts were $1.25 each; nuts, 10¢ each; washers, 9¢. The wood was salvaged from our basement. Total cost of supplies for a frame is less than $10. See modified version of this frame on page 20.

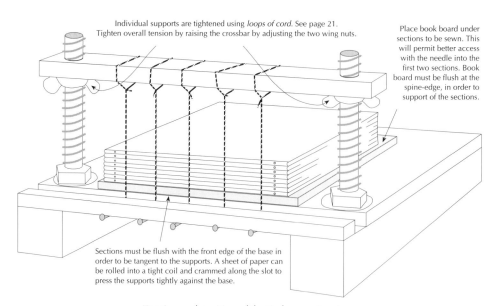

Individual supports are tightened using *loops of cord.* See page 21.
Tighten overall tension by raising the crossbar by adjusting the two wing nuts.

Place book board under sections to be sewn. This will permit better access with the needle into the first two sections. Book board must be flush at the spine-edge, in order to support of the sections.

Sections must be flush with the front edge of the base in order to be tangent to the supports. A sheet of paper can be rolled into a tight coil and crammed along the slot to press the supports tightly against the base.

Tension and position of the tied supports using
the hand-made sewing frame

SUPPLIES to CONSTRUCT SEWING FRAME A

2 2x2's $11\frac{1}{4}$" long (feet)

1 $\frac{3}{4}$" board 10 x 16" (base)

1 $\frac{3}{4}$" board 16 x $\frac{3}{4}$" (lip)

1 $\frac{3}{4}$" board 16 x $1\frac{1}{4}$" (crossbar)

nails or screws for assembly

2 8" long carriage bolts, $\frac{1}{4}$" in diameter,
   threaded to within 2" of the head

2 washers, 1 on each bolt on top of base
   before nut tightens bolt to base and foot

4 nuts: 2 nuts above the base,
and 2 wing nuts below crossbar

several 3" nails (as substitute keys)

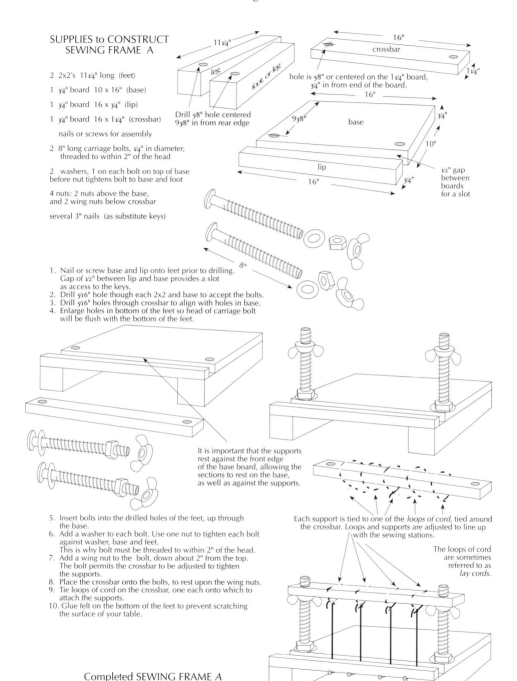

1. Nail or screw base and lip onto feet prior to drilling.
   Gap of $\frac{1}{2}$" between lip and base provides a slot
   as access to the keys.
2. Drill $\frac{5}{16}$" hole though each 2x2 and base to accept the bolts.
3. Drill $\frac{5}{16}$" holes through crossbar to align with holes in base.
4. Enlarge holes in bottom of the feet so head of carriage bolt
   will be flush with the bottom of the feet.

It is important that the supports
rest against the front edge
of the base board, allowing the
sections to rest on the base,
as well as against the supports.

5. Insert bolts into the drilled holes of the feet, up through
   the base.
6. Add a washer to each bolt. Use one nut to tighten each bolt
   against washer, base and feet.
   This is why bolt must be threaded to within 2" of the head.
7. Add a wing nut to the bolt, down about 2" from the top.
   The bolt permits the crossbar to be adjusted to tighten
   the supports.
8. Place the crossbar onto the bolts, to rest upon the wing nuts.
9. Tie loops of cord on the crossbar, one each onto which to
   attach the supports.
10. Glue felt on the bottom of the feet to prevent scratching
   the surface of your table.

Each support is tied to one of the *loops of cord*, tied around
the crossbar. Loops and supports are adjusted to line up
with the sewing stations.

The loops of cord
are sometimes
referred to as
lay cords.

Completed SEWING FRAME *A*

Crossbar can be adjusted to tighten the supports

Diagram labels:
- $11\frac{1}{4}$"
- leg
- foot or leg
- 16"
- crossbar
- hole is $\frac{5}{8}$" or centered on the $1\frac{1}{4}$" board,
  $\frac{3}{4}$" in from end of the board.
- $1\frac{1}{4}$"
- Drill $\frac{5}{8}$" hole centered
  $9\frac{3}{8}$" in from rear edge
- 16"
- $9\frac{3}{8}$"
- base
- $\frac{3}{4}$"
- 10"
- lip
- $\frac{1}{2}$" gap between boards for a slot
- 16"
- $\frac{3}{4}$"
- 8"

SUPPLIES to CONSTRUCT SEWING FRAME B

2 2x2's 11¼" long (feet)

1 ¾" board 10 x 20" (base)

1 ¾" board 20 x ¾" (lip)

1 ¾" board 20 x ¾" (crossbar)

2 2x2's 12" tall (posts)

nails or screws for assembly

several 3" nails (as substitute keys)

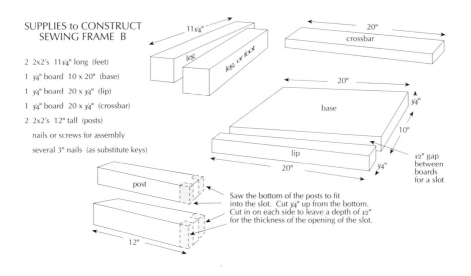

Saw the bottom of the posts to fit into the slot. Cut ¾" up from the bottom. Cut in on each side to leave a depth of ½" for the thickness of the opening of the slot.

1. Nail or screw base and lip onto feet. Gap of ½" between lip and base provides a slot as access to the keys.
2. Saw each 2x2 post to fit into slot. Glue posts into position.
3. Nail or screw through lip into posts.
4. Nail or screw crossbar onto posts.

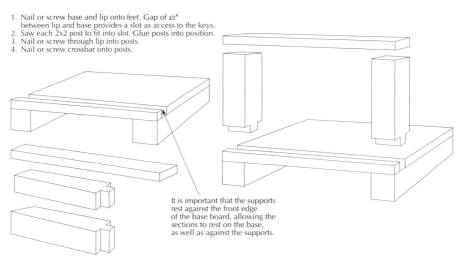

It is important that the supports rest against the front edge of the base board, allowing the sections to rest on the base, as well as against the supports.

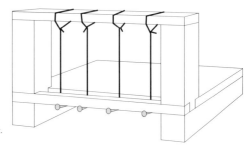

Completed SEWING FRAME *B*

Crossbar is not adjustable.
Fred Jordan modified my FRAME A to eliminate the need to drill any holes. This is more simple to construct.

HOW TO USE A SEWING FRAME WITHOUT HOOKS

LOOPS of CORD: The commercial sewing frame, keys and hooks are illustrated on the following page. Most commercial frames do not have a slotted crossbar which accepts hooks. Threaded hooks permit individual tightening of each support. Instead, *loops of cord* are tied around the crossbar, one for each support. These loops are often referred to as *lay cords.*

Tie as many loops of cord around the non-slotted crossbar as the number of supports in your sewing. Position of the loops can be adjusted along the bar to line up with the sewing stations, and, they are reusable, replacing the need for hooks.

Set the book block on the sewing frame base, and adjust the crossbar so the loops are about 3" above. This will allow enough length of the supports above the book block to attach to the boards.

Cut lengths of cord or tapes for each station. Length should be approximately 5" longer than the distance from the loop to the base. Set aside all sections, except for the first to be sewn.

For either frame on page 19 or 20, substitute keys are used. I suggest 10 penny nails. Tie each support to a nail with a slip knot, as a square knot will be difficult to untie. Leave 2" of the support dangling from the slip knot, so you will have enough length later on to attach to the boards.

Position the first nail under the base, lined up with the first sewing station. Head of the nail extends from the lip. Pull the support up through the slot, and through the loop. Pull tight and pinch the support at the loop to hold the support tight, maintaining pressure as you tie the support to the loop. Tie with an *overhand k,* releasing the pinch only after you pull up on the knot. An *overhand k* is half a square knot.

Position each successive nail. Pull the support up through the slot and tie to the corresponding loop with an *overhand k.* The partial square knot will suffice to temporarily hold the supports taut, but sufficiently loose to permit upward adjustment of the crossbar. This will individually tighten each support. Use of the inflexible square knot would result in some supports being tight, while others would sag.

Turn the nuts on the carriage bolts to adjust the crossbar slightly higher, tightening each support. Now, tie another *overhand k* on each support at the loop. This results in each support now being held by a square knot. Turn the wing nuts to raise the crossbar once again. This assures the supports will be permanently taut, and, you are ready to sew.

Use of the loops of cord eliminates the need to drill and saw a slot in the crossbar. This approach saves on cord, and the expense of hooks. It is even preferred by most binders. Substituting nails saves the expense of keys.

COMMERCIALLY AVAILABLE SEWING FRAME: If you continue to sew on a frame, you will probably want to invest in a good sewing frame. I suggest one with a slotted crossbar and hooks.

Not only is the crossbar adjustable, but individual supports can be tightened easily with the use of threaded hooks. However, that is my personal preference. On the other hand, no one considers keys a luxury, but a decided convenience.

HOW TO STRING A SEWING FRAME WITH HOOKS AND KEYS

Do not use a frame which has a dowel in front of the base, rather than a slot to accept keys. Keys save on the length of the supports, and can be more easily adjusted. Keys are more convenient than substituted nails, allowing the support to be looped, instead of tied. Keys are easier to undo after the sewing is completed, than the slip knot on the nail.

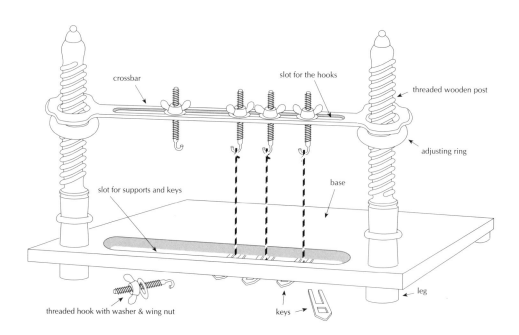

Commercially available sewing frame

Commercially available sewing frame. Each support is attached to a key, then placed beneath the slot on the base, aligned with the sewing station on the spine of the book block. The feet or legs raise the base off the table, permitting access to the keys. Each support is pulled through this slot, and tied to the threaded hook. The crossbar can then be raised to increase overall tension. Hooks can be individually adjusted to tighten each support.

For sewing supports, use 5 to 8 ply linen cord, available from any binders' supply. If sewing tapes, keep in mind the spine will be exposed.

Before measuring the length of the supports, adjust the crossbar fairly close to the top of the book block with the two adjusting rings. This will save on supports. For each support, cut approximately 6" in addition to the distance between the base of the frame and the crossbar.

1. Lay the support over the key from left to right. Allow about 1" of the support to extend on the left. Keep your left thumb on top of the support and the side of the key that is facing you.
2. With your right hand, pull the long end of the support tightly to the back of the key, and below the shorter end of the support.
3. Angle up, over the support and the left arm of the key. Pull the support snugly downward, centered on the key.

View of the key (step 3) will be the bottom. Holding the loop securely in position, turn the key upside down. Without releasing pressure on the loop, place the key under the front edge of the base of the sewing frame, close to where the first support will be positioned. Pointed edge of the keys face outward. See illustration below and on the facing page.

Reach with your free hand and pull the longer end on the support up through the slot in the base of the frame. Pull upwards with pressure, releasing your grasp on the key. Do not release pressure, or the loop will fail to secure the key against the frame. If the key falls off, repeat steps 1 through 3. Keeping constant upward tension, tie or attach the loose end of the support to the lay cord (loop), or onto a hook, if available. Leave sufficient length of supports at each end, to later attach the book block to the boards with the supports.

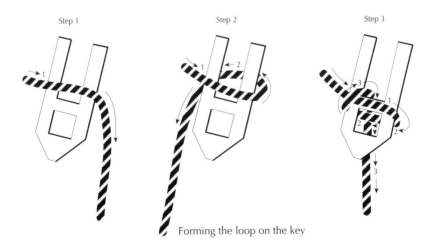

Step 1   Step 2   Step 3

Forming the loop on the key

IN ANTICIPATION OF SEWING RAISED SUPPORTS

Sewing onto supports is a great resource for sewing structures which do not require adhesives. This vast area was not covered in Volume I because it requires a sewing frame. That volume presented sewings which required little or no tools, except a bone folder, needle and a pair of scissors.

Sewing recessed supports offers little to explore, since the sewing structure on the spine is hidden, rather than flaunted.

Raised support sewing in the past was generally with the idea that the spine would be rounded, pasted and covered with leather. The curved spine would hint of the sewing only in the bulge of the supports. For those of us enamored with visible sewing structures, raised supports offers the most plentiful source of playing off tradition to create sewings which are not only functional, but rich in possibilities of design with variation in stitches. Obviously, these innovated spines will not be hidden under wrap. Examples of sewing onto raised supports will be largely limited to cords. I will explore basically two areas:

THE KETTLE STITCH AS CHANGE-OVER: The kettle stitch marks the point at which "dropping forward" will change from meaning dropping in one direction to the other. This happens at the *end* of a row of sewing, rather than at the first station of the next section.

Kettle stitch as change-over will explore sewing onto raised supports with two factors in mind: there will be no adhesives applied to the spine, and the exposed spine sewing must be an attractive pattern.

CORDS AS CHANGE-OVER: Examples of sewing raised supports continues with more examples of patterning the stitches upon the exposed spine. However, the kettle stitch will be eliminated at the head and the tail. Personally, although the kettle stitch is functional, I find it a paltry looking stitch. It is adequate, even advantageous when the spine is covered, but exposed spine sewings deserve a far better looking change-over.

Using cords to change-over is an evolution of possibilities in design. The following sewings explore this. One area is endbands as change-over.

Desire to eliminate the kettle stitch is achieved in simply abandoning sewing *along* the spine, in favor of sewing *across* the spine. Betsy Palmer Eldridge introduced this concept to me, and I find it the ultimate approach to the strongest, most durable of sewings. I will demonstrate many of these sewings Betsy demonstrated, as well as those I have made up.

LINK STITCHES with my gratitude to Betsy Palmer Eldridge

Generally, multi-section sewings are sewn lying "on the bench". In Volume I, certain sewings, such as the Buttonhole Stitch, are easier facilitated by sewing with the book upright. Booklets described in *1– 2– & 3–Section Sewings,* Volume II of *Non-Adhesive Binding,* usually are sewn easier when hand-held, standing the book on its tail.

Sewing a book, along or across the spine, proceeds on the bench. Nothing is more difficult than attempting a link sewing with the book standing. It requires painstaking effort with a curved needle. Whereas, the sewing path of that, and most other sewings are maneuvered easily sewing on the bench. In addition to sewing on the bench, sewings in Part 2 of this volume require a sewing frame.

CHANGE-OVER: Sewing along the spine requires climbing at the head or tail of a section to enter the next. Although I will show variations of Raised Support Sewings which eliminate the kettle stitch, it is by far the more common means of climbing, and it does it so easily.

Understanding the properties of these stitches is the basis for adventures with a needle. Improvisation can follow. The next several pages will show how to properly form link stitches, and explain what is gained by proper procedures. Necessarily, incomplete formation of link stitches will also be demonstrated.

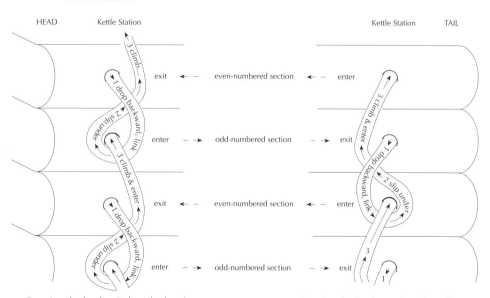

Forming the kettle stitch at the head, dropping backward to the inside

Forming the kettle stitch at the tail, dropping backward to the inside

LINK STITCH

Similar to embroidery, linking is a structure for tying together units.

The LOOP LINK EXITS and DROPS FORWARD: In sewing on the bench, exiting forward does not mean exiting always to the left of the support, or, always to the right. Exiting *left* or *right* is determined by whether you are sewing an even or an odd-numbered section. All that is necessary to remember is to *exit forward* in the direction in which you are proceeding:

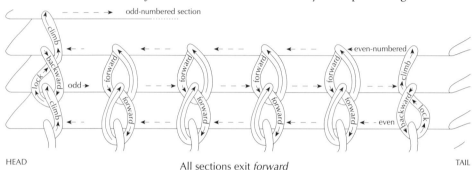

HEAD   All sections exit *forward*   TAIL
Rather than even sections "exiting left" and odd "exiting right"

In sewing any row, to form a link, exit forward (in the direction in which you are sewing). The link stitch always drops forward. The kettle stitch exits, and can drop forward. Most find it easier to exit and drop *backward,* making it easier to lock. See page 28.

In all the illustrations, the sewing starts at the head, which is on the left. This means the last section of the book is the first sewn, working from the back cover to the front.

You could start your sewings from the tail, with the tail positioned to the left. In that instance, you would start sewing from the front cover to the back, with the sections upside down.

ENTER OVER the EXIT: In linking, drop forward, slip under the last two connected sections, climb and enter *over* the exit. Practice on a sample, you will find it is simply easier than trying to enter under the exit thread.

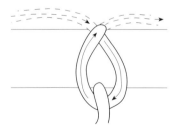

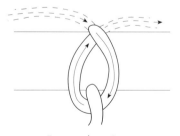

Enter over exit   Enter under exit
This is a preferred link stitch.   This is too awkward a link stitch.

The sewing diagrammed at the top of the facing page not only shows exiting forward, but also entering over the exit thread.

Similarly, in sewing raised supports, the needle exits forward of the support, loops the support, and enters over the exiting thread:

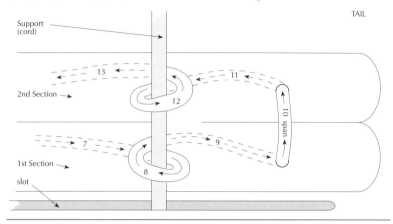

Sewing raised supports
Steps 8 and 12 enter over the exit thread. Step 10 spans to change-over.

The first section shows step 7 exiting to the right, because it is an odd-numbered section. Step 8 loops, then enters above the exiting thread. To demonstrate an even-numbered section, the second section shows step 11 exiting left. Step 12 loops, and enters above the exiting thread.

Exiting forward is a term which describes both. In sewing each section, simply keep in mind whether you are heading towards the head or the tail. Exit beyond, or *forward,* of the support.

The example above is a detail from the Basic Raised Support Sewing, which is illustrated on page 35.

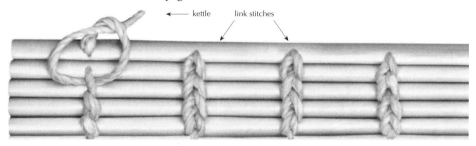

Detail of the head of the true kettle stitch, and link stitches. The kettle exits backwards, links, locks and climbs. The link stitches exit forward. See diagram on the top of the facing page.

KETTLE STITCH

In order to form a true kettle stitch, there must be three actions:

- links under
- locks
- climbs.

FORWARD OR BACKWARD DROP:
As long as it links, locks and climbs, the kettle can drop forward *or* backward.

PREFERRED BACKWARD DROP: Dropping backward to the inside is preferred, because it is easier to enter from the inside, rather than the outside, as illustrated to the right. Without opening the book, the needle is slipped between the last two connected sections at a diagonal until the point of the needle extends beyond the head. This forms

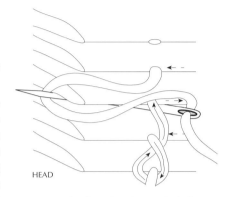

HEAD

Dropping backward to the inside, linking and locking the kettle stitch

the link. The thread is looped over the point of the needle. When the needle is pulled to adjust the tension, this forms the lock, as well as the link, all in one motion.

The kettle is the turn-around, and *change-over:* It marks the change in the direction of sewing, either towards the head, or towards the tail. In dropping backward, direction in dropping shifts; the kettle drops in the direction of the *following* section, not the current. Along any one section the links drop forward, while the ending kettle drops backwards, then climbs.

The kettle stitch at the head and the tail should look like this:

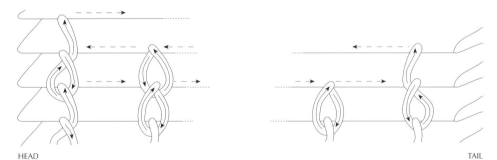

HEAD   TAIL

ideal TRUE KETTLE STITCH dropping backward to the inside, with loop/link stitch

Notice that the ideal kettle stitch at the tail is formed in the same manner as that at the head, but it is the mirror image. This is because in both instances the kettle drops to the inside.

This is a true kettle, because it links under, locks and climbs:

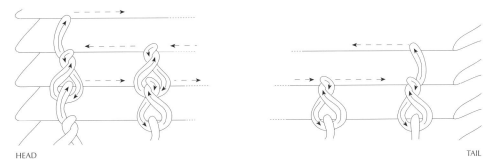

HEAD   TAIL

impractical TRUE KETTLE STITCH

However, it is extremely difficult to sew, and offers no other advantage. It is too much trouble.

In this next example, the link stitch drops backward. It laps, links, slips under, and therefore, locks. The character of this link stitch is that it is bumpy on the spine, This is a detriment for a covered spine, but can be extremely attractive in an exposed spine sewing. For non-adhesive binding, *this* impractical stitch is well worth the effort. See scan on page 130.

This is a true kettle because it links, slips and climbs:

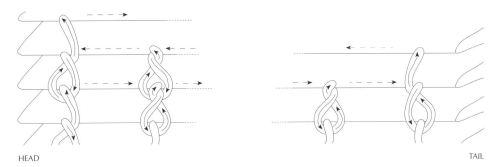

HEAD   TAIL

TRUE KETTLE STITCH with lap and slip link stitch
The kettle stitch drops backward to the inside, links, slips under to lock, climbs and enters.
See digital scan on page 130.

Since it drops forward, it is not preferred to the ideal true kettle illustrated on the facing page. This is because sewing on the bench, it is far easier to take the needle from the inside to the outside than vice versa. See illustration, *Linking and Locking the Kettle,* on the facing page.

This is the ideal true kettle dropping backward, with a lap/link stitch:

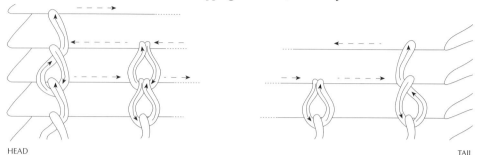

HEAD   TAIL

ideal TRUE KETTLE STITCH with lap/link stitch
See the digital scan on page 130.

In the illustration above, the link stitch is different from the ideal loop/link illustrated on pages 26 and 28. Here, the stitch laps, rather than loops. That is, it drops backward. This *U* shaped stitch laps and links, but does not lock. Therefore, it is a *slip stitch*. It should only be used with strong supports because it would easily tear out. Do not use a paper spine. Exposed spine sewings should reinforce the sections with the stations located on straps of vellum, book cloth or leather. See scan on page 130.

Notice in all the examples of link stitches, the bottom is rounded where they slip under, and are pointed at the top where they exit and enter. You can always detect the direction of the sewing, as the teardrop-shaped link stitches point towards the next section sewn.

In forming your kettles, be careful not to tighten too much, or you will pull every other section in from the head and the tail.

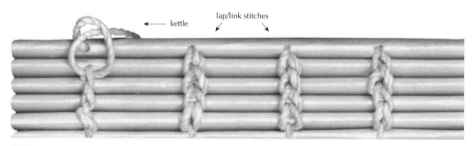

HEAD

Detail of a true kettle stitch with lap/link stitch, as diagrammed at the top of this page. The lap/link stitch should only be sewn onto straps of vellum, leather or book cloth. Otherwise, it might rip out:

Sewing proceeds forward, inside the section. It then exits backward, placing stress at the point of exit. If paper, only were used, nothing would be supporting the point of tension, except the paper, itself.

FALSE KETTLE STITCH

It is also important to show what should *not* be done. This is what the Germans refer to as a "false", that is, *incomplete* kettle stitch:

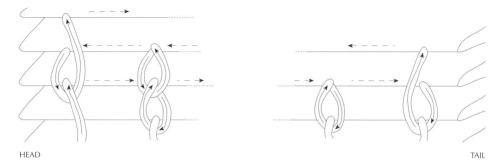

HEAD   TAIL

FALSE KETTLE STITCH

The link stitches are correct. They exit forward, loop, link, lock, and enter. At the tail, the kettle drops to the outside, links and climbs to the next section. It is a "false" kettle because it does not lock. It is impractical because the kettle drops forward, making it difficult to link under.

This is another false kettle:

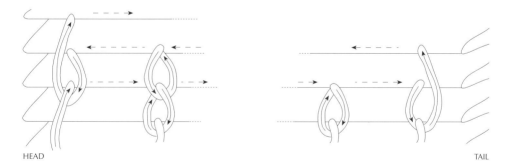

HEAD   TAIL

FALSE KETTLE STITCH

At the tail and at the head, this kettle stitch drops to the inside, links and climbs. This kettle is practical, in that it drops backward to the inside, making it easier to link under. It is a false kettle because it does not lock.

TABBING POSITIONS: Linking begins with the second section. Drop and link between the first section and the connected side-cover.

Sewing path and the linking position are followed easily by the help of two bookmarks. One is placed in the middle of the section being sewn, the other between the last two connected sections. At the end of sewing each section, the bookmarks are repositioned. At the end of sewing each section, the bookmarks are adjusted. The lower bookmark is raised the height of one section. The top bookmark is then removed from that section. The next section to be sewn is placed into position, and the bookmark is inserted as the sewing begins.

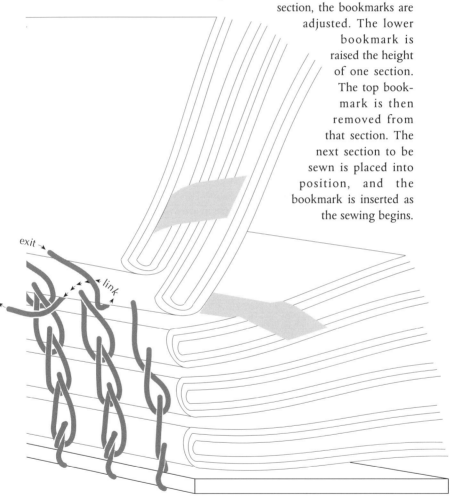

LINKING UNDER Inserting the fingers at the lower bookmark, sections are lifted increasing the gap between the last two connected sections. This accommodates easy linking procedure: Drop forward, enter between the connected sections, loop and exit. The two top sections are then lowered in place. The top section is opened at the upper bookmark, so that the needle can easily enter the section being sewn.

SEWING STATIONS FOR SUPPORTS

TRADITIONAL APPROACH: Position of the stations, number, and the proportion of the space between the supports is important. This is not only for structure, but aesthetics. This is true even in a traditional leather binding, where the raised supports are covered—the supports bulge to reveal their position on the spine.

Generally five stations are used. Larger books may require six. Small books use five, unless the spine is very tiny. Three supports plus the kettle stitches are recommended for structural integrity.

The supports are evenly spaced from the trimmed head to the kettle at the tail. Space from the (trimmed) head to the top support equals the space between the supports, whereas the space from the bottom support to the tail is larger. This suggests a base to the standing book. See the illustration on page 34.

INVENTIVE APPROACHES: In the supported exposed spine sewings described in this book, position and number of the stations should be considered, but not necessarily influenced by tradition. As long as structural issues are respected, positioning of supports can be inventive. Number of supports can exceed structural needs for purposes of design.

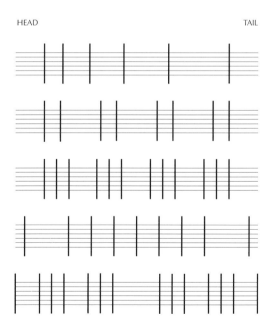

Spacing the supports

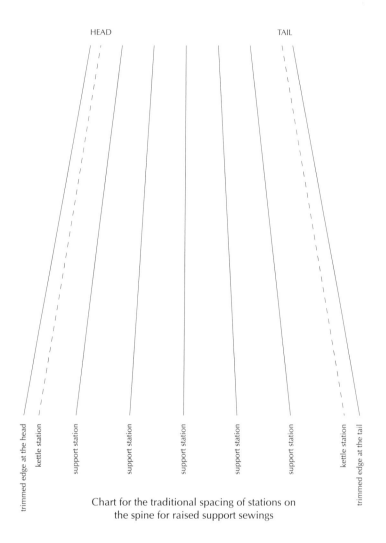

HEAD

TAIL

trimmed edge at the head

kettle station

support station

support station

support station

support station

support station

kettle station

trimmed edge at the tail

Chart for the traditional spacing of stations on
the spine for raised support sewings

A chart can be drawn onto stiff paper or card stock. Width at the top of the
chart represents the shortest spine of any book you might sew. The width at the
bottom should be more than the tallest spine.

Prior to sewing, lay an untrimmed section onto your chart. The spine is placed
horizontally, at the top of the chart. Drag the section down until the section
aligns with the markings for the trimmed head and tail. Mark the positions of
the stations on this section. Use it as a guide to mark the book block. This eliminates measuring for stations on each book you will sew.

BASIC RAISED SUPPORT SEWING

Of the variations on sewing raised support sewings, this is the most basic. Since it is so plain, it is not that attractive for an exposed spine. For covered spines, often the tie-off is on the outside, because it will not show once covered. In exposed spine sewings with no paste or glue, start the sewing inside the section to hide the tie-off. A lovely exception that flaunts the tie-off on the spine is illustrated on page 163 of Volume I. That sewing on split leather thongs is by the incomparable Gary Frost.

OUTSIDE TIE-OFF

In using a sewing frame, the end of the thread which does not have the needle is tied to the left post of the frame. This maintains tension until the tie-off. For an outside tie-off, exit station 1 of the second section, tie around the taut thread and enter the third section. Tie-off is *on the spine.* The thread to the post is clipped after the sewing is completed.

This tie-off, as well as the final tie-off can be on the *inside* of the section. This cleans up the look of any exposed spine sewing.

INSIDE TIES-OFF

FIRST TIE-OFF: To have the tie-off on the inside, start by tying the thread to the left post. Sew the first two sections. Before exiting station 1 of the second section, lay aside that needle. Untie the thread at the post. Place a second needle on it. Enter the second section. Tie-off with the other thread. Remove the second needle. Take the original needle and exit station 1 of the second section, and continue: drop backward, link, slip under, climb and enter the third section. See: *Tie-Off and the First Kettle,* diagrammed on page 55.

The FINAL TIE-OFF: After sewing the final section, complete the kettle. Enter the last station of the final section. Tie-off inside with a half hitch.

Sewn on raised cords, this is an example of the BASIC RAISED SUPPORT SEWING.

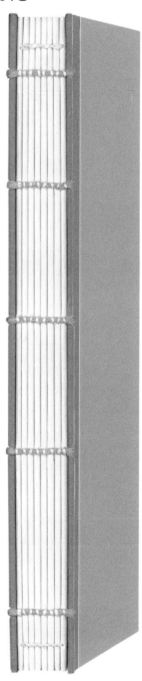

PREPARATION

Fold as many sections as desired. For purposes of diagramming, the number of supports will be limited to four, evenly spaced on the spine. The kettle stations will be set in from the head and tail approximately ¾".

PIERCING the STATIONS: Pierce the stations. Individual sections can be pierced with a bradawl. In production work, the marked book block is placed into a lying press. Stations are cut with a tenon, or backsaw, the thinner the blade, the better. For spans, it is better to pierce, rather than to saw, to avoid risking the thread slipping inside the section.

Angle in sawing the stations

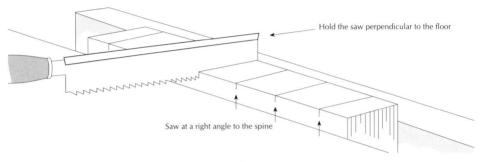

Sawing the stations

Saw only as deep until you pierce the fold of the center of the section. Sawing can be dangerous. Not sawing enough does not pierce all the folds. Excessive sawing creates a large wound. Advantages of sawing is it is faster, and, gives a straighter line than individual piercing.

String the sewing frame using a pierced section as a guide. The basic Raised Support sewing which will be diagrammed first is functional, but visually less than desired for an exposed spine. The variations which follow are specifically designed for exposed spines, to show off the sewing.

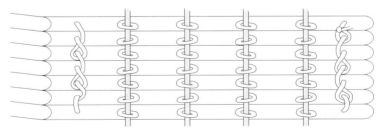

BASIC RAISED SUPPORT SEWING

SEWING PROCEDURE

Thread the needle and tie the loose end to the left post of the frame.

Sewing the First Section:

1. Enter the first section at station 1. Pull the thread to the inside until taut. Exit forward (beyond the support) at station 2.
2. Loop clock-wise around the support. Enter the same station above the exit thread, as shown in the cross-section at the right.
3. Exit forward at station 3.
4. Loop and enter above, or *over* the exit thread.
5. Exit forward at station 4.
6. Loop and enter above the exit thread.

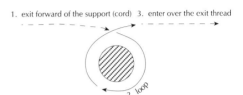

Looping the cord for
an odd-numbered section

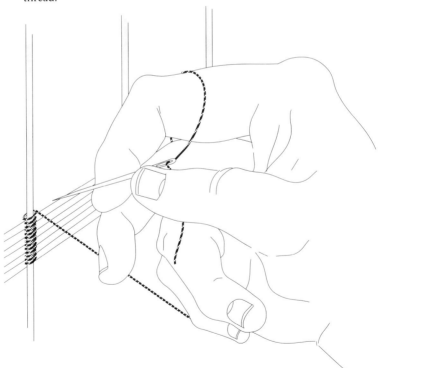

For a right-handed person: Exit forward. Keep tension on the thread with the back of the hand, on the bench. Loop, or pack the support, maintaining tension. Re-enter over the exiting thread. Tension on the thread will assure that you will not spear the support upon re-entering.

7. Exit forward at station 5.
8. Loop and enter above the exit thread.
9. Exit the kettle station at the tail.

Sewing the Second Section:

10. Set on the second section. Climb. Enter the new section at station 6.
11. Exit forward (even-numbered sections exit left of the support) at next station towards the head (5).
12. Loop counter clock-wise around the support. Enter the same station above the exit thread.

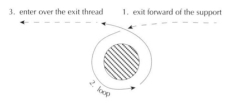

3. enter over the exit thread   1. exit forward of the support

2. loop

Looping the cord for
an even-numbered section

Repeat steps 11 and 12 at each remaining support station for the second section. After looping and re-entering station 2 with step 18, set aside this needle, temporarily. Untie the thread at the post and place a second needle on this dangling thread. Enter the second section at station 1. Tie-off on the inside at station 1 with the other thread. Remove the second needle. Clip the dangling thread, but do not cut the original sewing thread. See: *Inside Ties-Off* on page 35, and *Tie-Off and the First Kettle,* diagrammed on page 55.

Pick up the original needle. Exit station 1, step 19, with original needle. Proceed. Enter the third section with step 20.

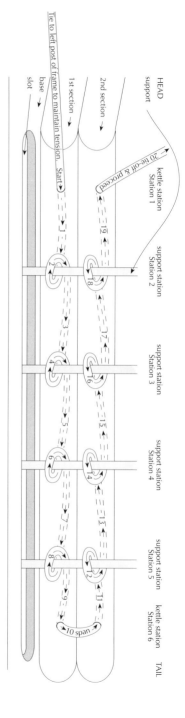

Starting the BASIC RAISED SUPPORT SEWING

Tie-off at step 20, but do not clip. Proceed with sewing. Or, tie-off inside after sewing is completed, placing a needle on the thread which is tied to the post.

HEAD

support

kettle station
Station 1

support station
Station 2

support station
Station 3

support station
Station 4

support station
Station 5

kettle station
Station 6

TAIL

Tie to left post of frame to maintain tension. Start

20 tie-off & proceed

base

slot

1st section

2nd section

10 span

Sewing the Third Section:

20. Set on the third section. Climb and enter the third section at station 1.
21. Exit forward (odd-numbered sections exit to the right of the support) at the next station towards the tail.
22. Loop the support and re-enter above the exit thread.
23-28. Repeat steps 21 and 22 for the remaining support stations until re-entering station 5 with step 28.
29. Exit the kettle station at the tail.

Sewing the Next Even-Numbered Section:

30. Set on the next section. Drop backwards (towards the head), link under the last two connected sections.
31. Climb, slip under (thread labeled as step 30). Enter the new section at the kettle station. See: *Linking and Locking the Kettle,* diagrammed on page number 28.
32 Exit forward at the next station towards the head.
33. Loop the support and re-enter above the exit thread.
34-40. Repeat steps 32 and 33 at each remaining support station for this section. After looping and re-entering station 2 with step 39, exit the kettle station at the head with step 40.

Sewing the Next Odd-Numbered Section:

41. Set on the next section. Drop backwards (towards the tail), link under the last two connected sections
42. Climb, slip under, and enter this new section at station 1.
43 Exit forward at the next station towards the tail.
44. Loop the support and re-enter above the exit thread.
45-50. Repeat steps 43 and 44 for the remaining support stations until re-entering station 5 with step 50.
51. Exit the kettle station at the tail.

Sewing the Remaining Sections: Continue, repeating the procedure for sewing and even-numbered section, then sewing an odd-numbered section until all sections are sewn. Exit the final section at station 1 or 6, depending upon whether you have an odd or even number of sections. Drop backwards, slip under the last two connected sections. Re-enter the kettle station of the final section. Tie-off the inside with a half hitch. Release the keys. Untie the cords from crossbar or hooks.

For the traditional leather binding, gluing the spine, rounding and backing, and attaching the boards would follow.

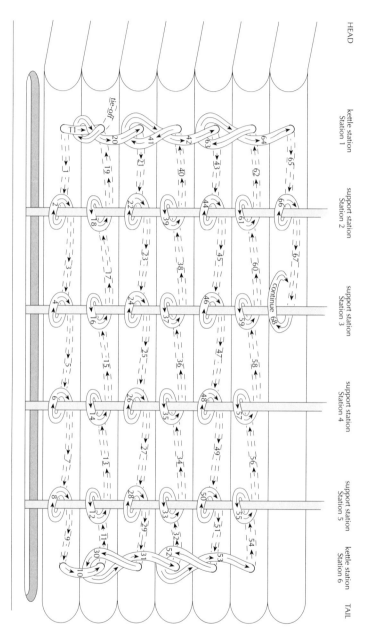

Sewing the BASIC RAISED SUPPORT SEWING

Tie-off at step 19 with T-1. See diagram on page 55.

The beginning thread is tied to the left post of the sewing frame. After the sewing is completed, and the supports removed from the frame, tie-off the beginning thread at station 1 of the second section. Tie-off the ending thread at the last station sewn. To hide the ties-off, see: *Inside Ties-Off,* page 35, and illustration of the completed sewing, at the bottom of page 36.

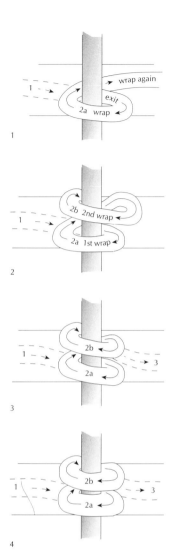

Packing the cord
Odd-numbered section, exiting forward

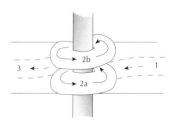

Packing the cord
Even-numbered section, exiting forward

HOW TO PACK

In the previous Basic Raised Support Sewing, the thread loops the support at each station, except for the kettle. This secures the section to the supports. However, with cords, instead of looping once and re-entering, you might "loop" around the cord two or three times before entering. This is referred to as *packing,* or as *arch sewing* Cords lend themselves to packing, being cylindrical. Packing is in a tight upward coil the height of the section, hiding the cord on the spine—a *solid pack.* See page 43 for an example of packing.

REASONS for PACKING: There are two reasons for packing. The first is functional. Packing would be recommended, even if the spine is covered. It reinforces the convex closed arch. See: *Rounding and Backing the Book,* page 45, as well as the illustration at the top of the following page. When the book is open with a concave spine, packing supports the cord. The second reason is purely for looks—it creates a lovely exposed spine sewing. All sewings in this book show off the sewing on the spine; form follows function.

DIRECTION of PACKING: If you are sewing an odd-numbered section, towards the tail, *exit forward* (to the right of the cord). Pack in a clockwise direction. .If it is an even-numbered section, sewing is towards the head, *exit forward,* (left of the cord). Packing will be in a counter-clockwise direction. See illustration to the left.

TENSION: Betsy Palmer Eldridge says that the tension varies with each sewer, like knitting. It may vary even if one person stops for a break. It is best to start and sew the entire book at once. The operative word is *snug.* Tension should not be too loose, but neither should it be too tight.

NUMBER of PACKINGS: The number of revolutions depends upon the thickness of the section and of the thread. You want the packing to equal the thickness of the section, with no bare cord showing. Do not pack more than the thickness of the section. Generally, it requires two or three times—slightly below, even with the station, and slightly above. If two revolutions is not enough, but three is too many, you can even pack 2½ times: Pack the odd-numbered sections two times, and the even, three times. It will equal out.

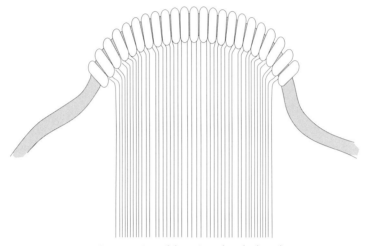

Cross-section of the spine of packed cords

Convex spine of the rounded and closed text block

Above: Cross section. Packing the cords strengthens the cord, helping to maintain the arch of the rounded book.

Below: Packing gives a flexibility to the spine, aiding the action of the opening book. And, packing opens possibilities of design for exposed spine sewings.

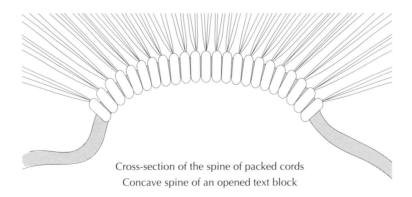

Cross-section of the spine of packed cords

Concave spine of an opened text block

RAISED CORDS WITH PACKING

This, and the previous sewing, Basic Raised Support Sewing can use any round core: cords, rolled leather-as-cord, or leather thongs as supports. For me, the previous sewing, while functional, does not serve well aesthetically, as an exposed spine sewing.

A single loop in the previous sewing leaves areas of the support visible. Solidly packing the supports, the thread covers the supports. Generally the sewing is more attractive than simply looping the support. Functionally, it is stronger.

SEWING PROCEDURE

Sew in the same manner as the previous sewing, on page 35. Instead of looping, you will pack each cord. Sewing the first section, exit forward, and pack in a clockwise movement. Use two or three packs, or revolutions until the coiled thread on the cord is the height of the section, or a little less. Re-enter over the exit thread, and continue. The change-over will be by means of kettle stitches.

Tie-off inside the section to clean up the spine. See: *Inside Ties-Off,* page 35.

On the right is an example of a RAISED CORD SEWING WITH PACKING. The beginning and ending threads are tied-off inside the sections.

A detail is shown on the left.

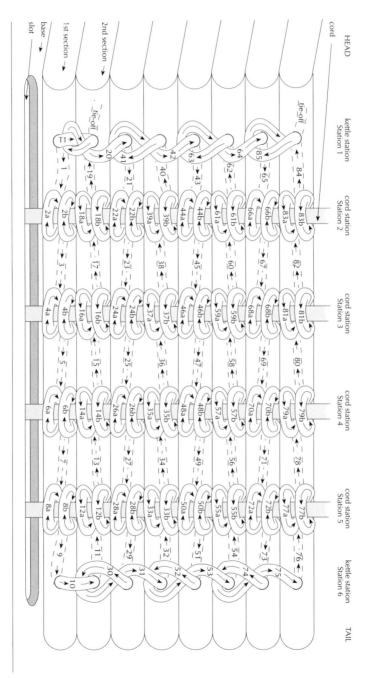

RAISED CORD WITH PACKING

For tie-off at step 19 with T-1, see diagram on page 55.

ROUNDING AND BACKING

Books created by non-adhesive binding rarely are rounded. Traditional raised or recessed cord sewing are always rounded and backed. This takes place after the book is sewn, before the spine is covered with leather.

Rounding is the process of hammering the flat spine into an arch. The constructed arch supports the pages, just as an arch supports a bridge or the brick opening in a wall for a door or window.

When the book is stored standing on a shelf, it is important that adjoining books or a bookend maintain pressure inward on both side-covers to help support the arch created by rounding the text block. Otherwise, the pages collapse, sagging in the middle. This is why it is suggested that coptic sewings eliminate the square of the book, so that the covers and the text block rest on the shelf.

Extremely thick books tend to collapse under their own weight, despite the structural support of rounding. Packing the cords reinforces them and helps maintain the arch in the rounded book.

TRADITIONAL ROUNDING: If you are going to traditionally round a book, consult a book specifically written on the subject. This is a brief explanation: After the book is sewn, the text block is jogged on the head and the spine to square it up. Against a sturdy surface, the spine is condensed in thickness by lightly tapping on the section, close to the spine-edge with the hammer.

Use dividers to measure thickness of board. Draw pencil line thickness of board on the first and last sheet with a pencil from the hinge-fold inward onto the page. Jog again. Lay boards on each end, weight on top, extend spine over edge and wheat paste spine. Let dry. Plow the foredge. Start round with hammer by placing the book on a sturdy surface. Hammer the spine to an oblique angle. Turn it over, and hammer the top half of the spine in the other direction. This starts the arc on the spine.

BACKING: Place the book in a lying press, allowing the book block to protrude only the thickness of the board. This is the amount which will be backed. With glancing blows of the hammer, gradually force the spine into an arc, and creating the shoulder. Paste gauze on the spine with wheat paste. Plow the head and the tail. Apply glue to the gauze.

Properly rounded and backed   Overly rounded and backed   Insufficiently rounded and backed   Dented   Asymmetrically rounded and backed

ROUNDING and BACKING for NON-ADHESIVE SEWINGS: Rounding is associated with gluing the spine, and thus is never considered for books without paste or glue. I have experimented with backing while devising the sewings for Part 1 of this book. Under the supervision of Fred Jordan, I have tried brushing water on the spine prior to rounding to aid in the formation of the arch. However, visually the results are unacceptable, since the surface of the paper is wilted. We tried traditional backing with the hammer, but the crisp ribbing of the folds of the sections were dented and looked beaten for an exposed spine. Fred was insistent that backing could be done, and should be done for reasons of structure. I said if the book is housed in a clam shell, or stored flat, it doesn't matter.—Needless to say, "we" persisted. Fred came up with a solution.

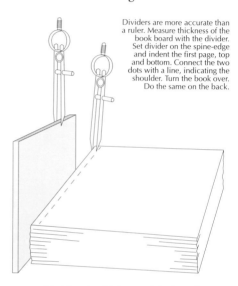

Dividers are more accurate than a ruler. Measure thickness of the book board with the divider. Set divider on the spine-edge and indent the first page, top and bottom. Connect the two dots with a line, indicating the shoulder. Turn the book over. Do the same on the back.

Marking the thickness of the board onto the book block

The thickness of the cover boards was measured with dividers. The dividers were indented from the spine, inward onto the first sheet at both ends. The same measurement was indented on the back of the text block. A fine pencil line was drawn to mark the thickness of the board to the first and last page. Start the round by distorting the book block with the hand, rather than a hammer.

Place the text block in a lying press with backing boards, with the supports on the outside. It is critical that the pencil line on both sides of the book align perfectly with the top edge of the backing boards. It tends to go out of alignment when pressure is applied to the press. Care will ensure the shoulder is precisely the thickness of the cover boards for a perfect fit. No hammer is used.

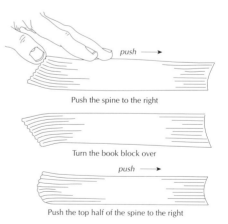

push →

Push the spine to the right

Turn the book block over

push →

Push the top half of the spine to the right

Starting the round by hand

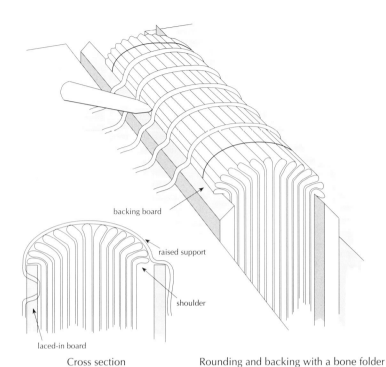

backing board

raised support

shoulder

laced-in board

Cross section   Rounding and backing with a bone folder

Backing is accomplished with a tiny bone folder or a smooth nail file, without damage to the individual folds of the sections. Width of the tool which depresses the individual folds must be able to fit between the supports, and to apply pressure right up to the edge of the supports.

Start with one half of the book block. Work with the end section first, depressing it against the backing board to form the shoulder. Then apply pressure on the next section, on towards the middle. Back the other half of the spine from the outside, towards the center. Do not attempt to accomplish the backing in one step. Proceed a second time, applying more or less pressure to each section to perfect the shape.

Attach the boards. Since I have only rounded and backed a half dozen books without paste or glue, I cannot speak of lasting success, but offer the possibility of backing to your discernment.

Simply attaching the boards can produce a *natural round,* without backing. This reduces the width of the spine *(a)* at point *b,* to nearly the width of the foredge *(c).* The boards almost will be parallel.

BUILDING A BOOK PRESS

Hardwood is needed for the two boards, so that they do not warp under pressure. Four 9" carriage bolts with butterfly nuts are needed. The bolts must be threaded withing 2" of the base. Bolts should be about 14" apart to allow books under that height to fit within.

Edges of the boards are faced with non-rusting metal strips. Screws must be counter-sunk. In this drawing, the closer edge is beveled. This permits using this edge in place of backing boards. Stand the press on its edge with the bevel facing up. Width of the book cannot extend beyond the back edge of the press, since the metal strips would indent the book block.

The opposite edge is at a 90° angle to the surface of the boards. Metal strips extend towards the gap, about half a board thickness. This side is used for casing-in. The metal edges clamp into the hinge-fold, giving a neat, permanent indentation.

I like this press because it is portable. If I am pasting, I can place a book in the press to dry, and carry it with me to Fred Jordan's, while the book is drying.

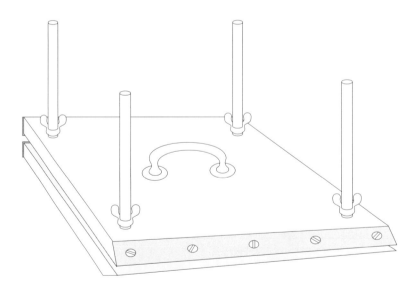

BOOK PRESS

A book press is a good early investment in your bindery. They can be purchased at a bindery supply, or, you can build one.

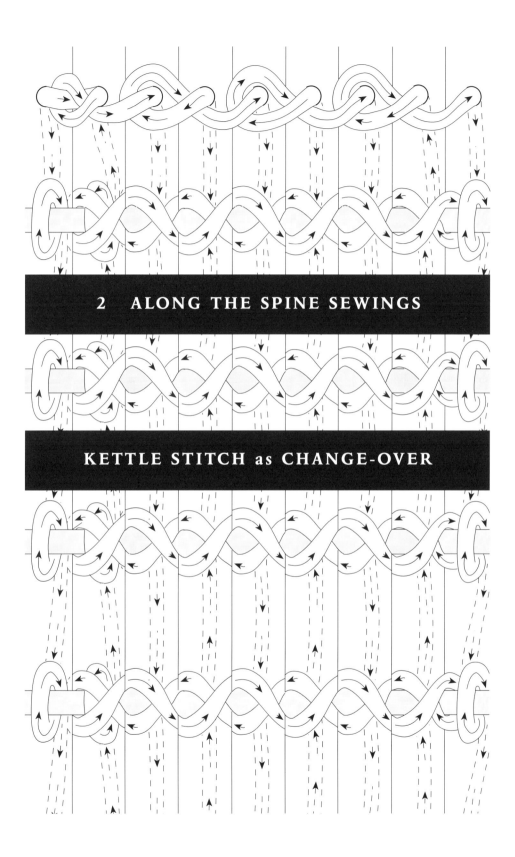

2   ALONG THE SPINE SEWINGS

KETTLE STITCH as CHANGE-OVER

DYING THE CORDS OR THREAD

Each element of the physical binding can be used not only for function, but design. Exposed spine sewings invite the use of one or more colors of thread. Strips of various colors of leather can be used as supports. When cords are employed, but not hidden by packing, I prefer dying the cords the same color as the thread, or more probably, a contrasting color.

Linen thread can be purchased in colors. Check with your favorite binder's supply. I hesitate to list a specific supplier, but since the colors of thread are difficult to find, I will list my sources: Royalwood in Mansfield, Ohio and Weaving Workshop Textile Arts Centre in Chicago. Addresses and telephone numbers are in the *Source Section* of Volume I. Each will send you samples of thread in all the colors they stock. Ask how much must be purchased in order to qualify for wholesale prices; it is not that many spools of thread.

Cords come in natural, and white. For colors, you will have to dye the cords yourself. To dye cord or thread, use a color-fast vegetable dye, such as used for fabrics and leather.

Procedure for Dying: Loop a small amount of thread or cord around two fingers. Remove the loop from your hand. Wrap around the center of the bundled thread about three times. It can then be dipped into the bottle of dye, holding onto the end of the thread. Wear rubber gloves. The thread need not unwind inside the bottle. Hold the end of the thread with one hand, and with the other, place a tissue around the thread to blot it as you slowly pull the thread from the bottle. Thread dries quickly, whereas the cord will have to be hung to dry. Approximately six feet of thread can be dyed in this manner with each dipping. Variation in coloring is slight, and probably will not be noticed once the thread is sewn.

Often I bundle the thread again, and dip it into one or more colors of dye. This can create a pleasant range of muted colors to store for future use.

Every other section of the book block was placed tightly in a book press. The exposed folds of the spine were water colored orange. The book block was re-assembled with the alternating white sections. Raw linen thread was dyed lavender for the sewings of the 2–Needle Coptic Sewing II at the head and the tail. Thread for the middle stations was dyed a grayed yellow.

THE ICICLE

The Icicle is a sewing that combines raised cord sewing with spine stitches along the spine. Kettle stitches are used as the changes-over.

Below the kettle at the head, in the illustration to the right, I have added a link stitch (Station 2). Above the tail is another link (Station 16). An additional cord is placed after the final spine stitch as a base. This cord is packed, but not linked (Station 15).

With the Icicle, the stitch on the spine laps over the cord, and then is pulled back against the spine in the linking process.

With the third section begins the dropping and linking under the cord. Dropping is always to the right, over the spine stitch. Climbing is always on the left of the cord. This results in a row of beads parallel to, and on the right side. Climbing gives a bead on the left side of the cord. See step 36a and 36b in the diagram on page 56.

This means that on even-numbered sections you will drop backward, and on odd-numbered sections you will drop forward to maintain the drop always on the "right" side of the cord.

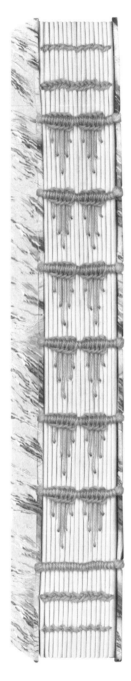

Station 1, kettle at the head

Station 2, link stitch

Station 3, 1st cord
Station 4, various size spine stitch

Station 5, 2nd cord
Station 6, various size spine stitch

Station 7, 3rd cord
Station 8, various size spine stitch

Station 9, 4th cord
Station 10, various size spine stitch

Station 11, 5th cord
Station 12, various size spine stitch

Station 13, 6th cord
Station 14, various size spine stitch

Station 15, 7th cord, packed, only

Station 16, link stitch

Station 17, kettle at the tail

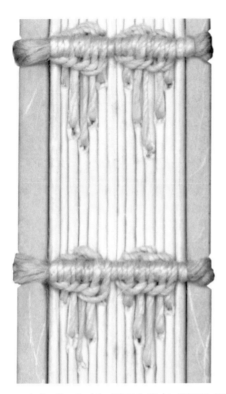 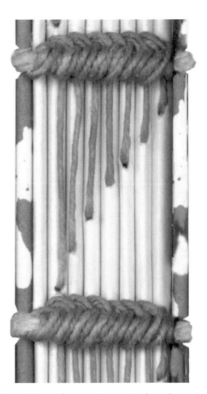

Left: Detail of the ICICLE. Right: SPIRAL BINDING, variation. These are two raised cord sewings with solid packed cords and stitches on the spine. Devised in March 1993.

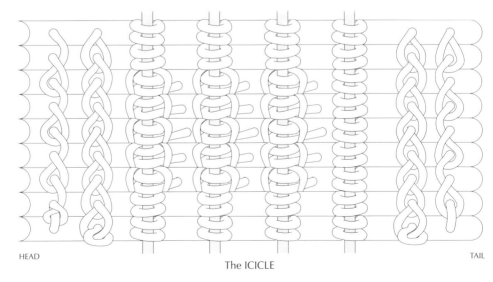

HEAD   TAIL

The ICICLE

PREPARATION

With the first two, and final two sections without spine stitches, I prefer centering the spine stitches between the hinge-folds on the spine, using the middle sections. This gives the sewing pattern of spine stitches a border. The pattern does not appear crowded on the spine.

Number of Sections: The minimum number of sections required is nine: the first two without spine stitches, five sections to form the *V* pattern of the spine stitches, and the final two sections without spine stitches. Depending upon the number of sections required in your book, you could design the Icicle to fit several number of sections.

Number of Stations: The *V*-shaped pattern of spine stitches proceeds from each cord, towards the tail, except for the final cord, closest to the tail. At that cord/station, the cord is packed, followed by the station which is linked, and finally, the kettle station at the tail.

In the diagram of the sewing stations at the top of this page, as well as in the diagram of the sewing on the following page(s), the *V*-shaped pattern will appear three times from head to tail across the spine. In the diagram at the bottom of this page, the *V*-shaped pattern appears four times, since there is an extra cord and extra stations. Determine how many cords you will need and design your spine.

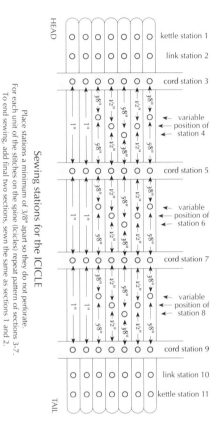

Sewing stations for the ICICLE

Place stations a minimum of 3/8" apart so they do not perforate. For each unit of the stitches on the spine (icicles) repeat pattern of sections 3–7. To end sewing, add final two sections, sewn the same as sections 1 and 2.

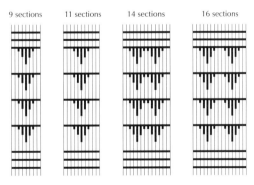

Adapting the ICICLE for various numbers of sections

Spacing the Stations: Stations for the spine stitches must be spaced so that no two stations on the same section are closer together than 3/8". With the cords a minimum of 1" apart, the middle spine stitch is 5/8", which leaves 3/8" before piercing for the following cord.

Marking the Stations: Jog the book block and mark all the stations except those for the spine stitches. Take the particular sections with the shortest spine stitches and mark those stations at once. Do the same with the middle length spine stitches, and finally, the sections with the largest spine stitches. Reassemble the book block in order.

SEWING PROCEDURE

SEWING the FIRST TWO SECTIONS: Start at the head. Sew in the traditional manner of packed raised cords. Exit forward at each cord, pack twice and enter. See *How to Pack,* page 41.

Station 2 and the next to the last station (10) are for linking. In sewing the first section, loop around a spare needle at each of these stations to temporarily maintain the anchoring loop. In sewing the second section, the spare needles are removed and the linking begins.

1-25. Sew the first two sections as diagrammed to the right. For a written description, see: *BASIC RAISED SUPPORT SEWING,* page 35.

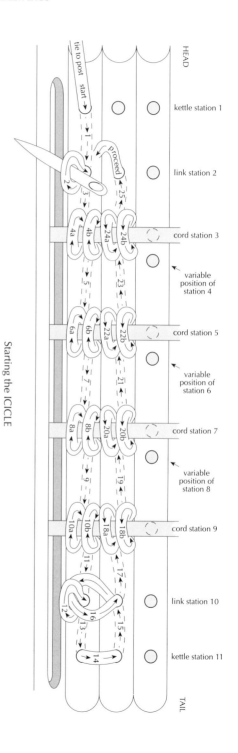

Starting the ICICLE

HEAD

kettle station 1

link station 2

cord station 3

variable position of station 4

cord station 5

variable position of station 6

cord station 7

variable position of station 8

cord station 9

link station 10

kettle station 11

TAIL

Tie-Off and the First Kettle:

26. Form the link at station 2 of the second section.
27. Re-enter the section and pause.
T1. Cut the thread tied to the left post of the sewing frame, and thread it with a separate needle.
T2. Take this needle, dangling from the first section, and enter the second section at station 1.
T3. Tie-off on the inside at station 1 with the other thread (step 27). Clip the dangling thread, and remove the spare needle. The tie-off is hidden on the inside.
28. Exit backward at station 1 of the second section.

Sewing the Third Section:

Set on the third section.
29a, b. Drop backwards. Link (under thread marked T1) between the first and second section.

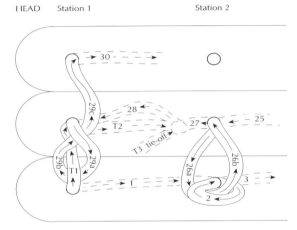

Tie-off and the first kettle stitch

This inside tie-off is rather elaborate, but worth the effort. Follow steps 26, 27, 1T, 2T, 3T, then steps 28 and 29.

29c. Slip under (the thread marked 29a) to lock. Climb and enter the third section at station 1.
30. Exit at station 2.
31. Drop forward, link under, climb and enter.
32. Proceed to station 3, the first cord.
33. Exit backward (to the left) of the cord), Lap over the cord in a horizontal movement. Proceed to the spine stitch station (4). Enter.

NOTE: In sewing odd-numbered sections, pack up high enough so that the icicle stitch is *centered* on, and parallel to, the fold of that section.

34. Retreat to the previous cord/station. Exit forward (to the right)
35. Pack once, clockwise.
36. After looping behind the cord, drop forward (to the right). Link under the last two connected sections. Climb and enter, carefully adjusting the tension of both the drop and the climb. Do not pull tightly, but allow the drop and the climb to be visible arcs. This starts the beading pattern on each side of the cord.

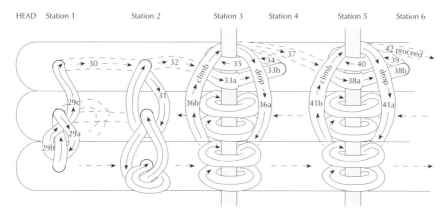

Sewing the third section of the ICICLE

Sewing the Remainder of this Odd-Numbered Section:

37-41. Proceed on the inside to the next cord/station. Repeat steps 32-36 at each cord station until you come to the final cord.

Step 47   (if four cords are used, step 52 if five cords). Exit forward at the final cord, (station 9 if four cords are used).

48. Pack clockwise once or twice as needed. Enter.

49. Proceed to the linking station (10). Exit.

50. Drop forward, link under, climb and enter.

51. Proceed to the tail. Exit at the kettle station.

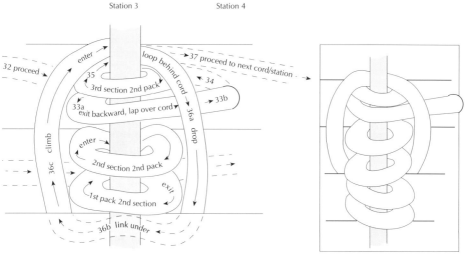

Detail of sewing the third section

Packing and beading will appear more like this.

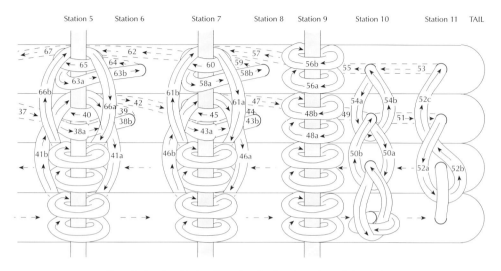

Completing the third and starting the fourth section of the ICICLE

NOTE: Pack odd sections higher than the even. This is so that on the even-numbered sections, the icicle stitch exits and remains at the center of, and parallel to, the fold as it proceeds to pack the support. Otherwise, the icicle stitch would have to drop at an angle to pack. Take care to keep the icicle stitches centered on the fold.

Sewing the Next Even-Numbered Section:

52. Drop backward and link under.
Set on the next section. Slip under to lock. Climb and enter.
53 Exit at the next station towards the head (10).
54. Drop forward, link under, climb and enter.
55. Proceed to the next station (9).
56. Exit forward. Pack once or twice counter-clockwise as needed to bring the packing to the height of this section. Enter.
57 Proceed past the spine stitch station to the next cord/station. (7) and exit forward (to the left).
58. Lap over the cord, and retreat back to the spine stitch station (8). Enter.
59. Proceed to the cord station (7), again. Exit backward (to the right).
60. Pack once clockwise.
61. After looping behind the cord, drop backward (to the right) and link under the last two connected sections. Climb and enter. Adjust both the drop and the climb.

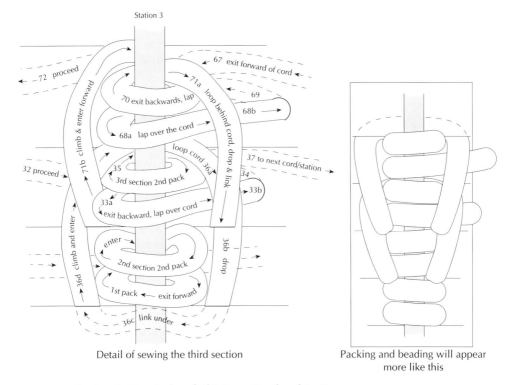

Detail of sewing the third section

Packing and beading will appear
more like this

Sewing the Remainder of This Even-Numbered Section:

62-66. Proceed on the inside to the next cord/station. Repeat steps 57-61
     until you finish sewing all the cords. You will finish the final cord and
     enter with step 71, if four cords are used.

72. Proceed on the inside to station 2. Exit.

73. Drop forward, link under, climb and enter.

74. Proceed to the head. Exit at the kettle station. Set on the next section.

75. Drop backward, link, slip under. Enter the next section at station 1.

Sewing the Remaining Sections: Sew the odd-numbered sections the same
as the third section. Sew the even-numbered sections the same as the
fourth section.

Rather than trying to remember whether you exit forward or backward at
the cords which are beaded, it is easier to keep in mind that both the odd
and even-numbered sections *exit to the right*. All sections drop to the right
and climb to the left of the cord.

You might try sewing the Icicle and always exit and drop forward. This
will give you an alternating pattern of beading. However, I prefer the
beading as described, exiting always to the right.

Kettle Stitch as Change-Over

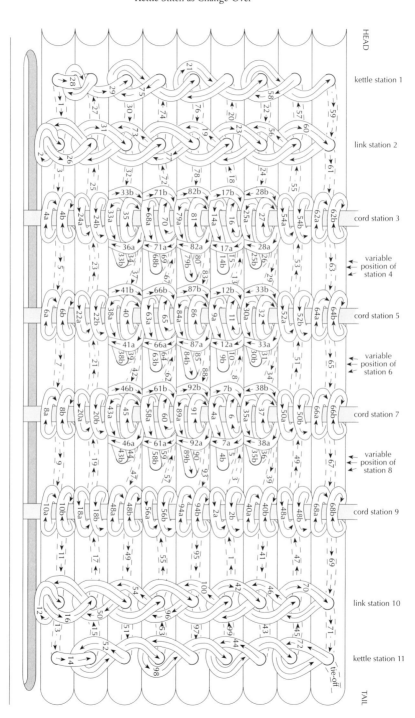

THE ICICLE

Step 28: For the tie-off and first kettle, see page 55.

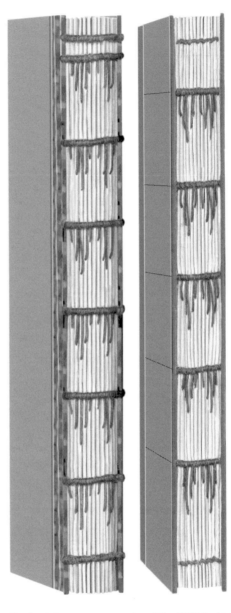

On the right are two examples of the ICICLE which have been backed with a bone folder. See page 47. The example in the center uses Packed Cords as Change-Over. See page 74. The other two employ a kettle stitch.

1–SECTION *X*

This loop-link sewing is on a single raised support. The *X* formed along the section upon each support is the height of one section. This is because it exits forward, angles and drops one section, links under, angles and climbs one section to re-enter the same station.

The *X* is striking on the spine. Unlike packing, the support is bare between the *X*'s. You might want to dye the supports prior to use. See page 49.

The first two sections are sewn looping, but not linking the support. If the linking process started before the third section, you would link under the the entire book block. When the supports are then removed from the sewing frame, these links can ride up, becoming loose, since they are not held firmly in place, sandwiched between two sections. The final section is sewn with a second loop, after looping and linking the support forms an *X*. This is for symmetry in appearance, not for function.

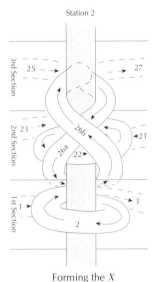

Forming the *X*

Step 26 exits forward, drops at an angle, links under, climbs at an angle, and enters on the back side of the support.

As you link under, form the shape of the first leg of the *X*. After you enter, form the remainder of the *X* before proceeding.

SEWING PROCEDURE

Thread the needle and tie the loose end to the left post of the frame.

1-22. Sew the first two sections as diagrammed on the page 62, the same as basic Raised Support, more clearly described on page 38. After looping at station 1 of the second section, enter the section with step 22, if five supports are used.

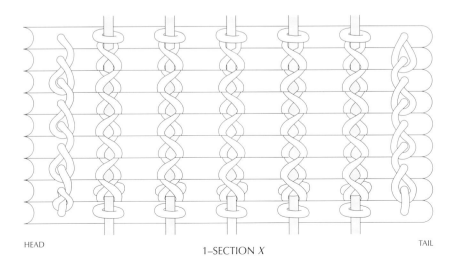

HEAD   1–SECTION *X*   TAIL

T1. Temporarily lay aside this needle.
Untie the thread from the post, and
attach another needle. With this
needle, enter station 1 of the second section.

23. Tie-off. See: *Inside Ties-Off,* page
35, and *Tie-Off and the First Kettle,*
diagrammed on page 55. Discard
this second needle. Clip the dangling thread. Pick up the original
needle.

24 Set on the third section. Exit backward at station 1 of the second section with the original needle. Drop,
link, slip under and climb to form
the first kettle. Enter the third section at station 1.

25. Exit forward at station 2.

***Forming the First* X:** In forming the *X,*
or *figure 8,* it is important to exit forward and to enter from the back side
of the support. This prevents tearing
the paper, strengthening the sewing.

The first leg of the *X* must be positioned when adjusting the tension after
linking. It tends to lay low, and horizontal. Upon re-entering, adjust the
tension, for the second half of the *X,*
centering it on on the support.

26a. Exit forward, angle backwards as
you drop, link under.
26b. Angle as you climb and enter on
the back side of the support.

***Remaining Support-Stations for the
Third Section:*** Repeat steps 25 and 26,
until you are on the inside at the kettle
station (step 33).

34. Set on the fourth section. Form the
kettle at the tail.

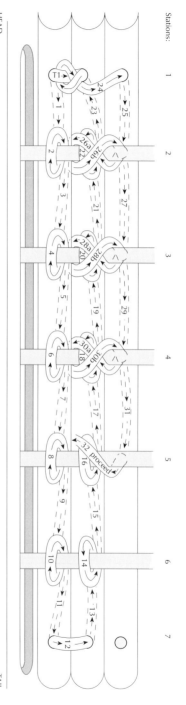

Starting to sew the 1-SECTION X

The X is formed by dropping, linking and climbing one section

Sewing the Remaining Sections: As you exit each support/station, repeat steps 25 and 26, always exiting forward and re-entering on the back side of the support. The final section is sewn differently.

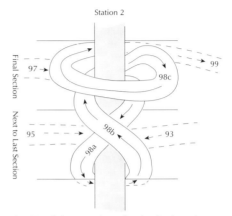

Forming the *X* and the extra loop for the final section

Sewing the Final Section: Set on the final section. Form the kettle stitch, entering this section. Exit forward at the first support/station. Drop backward, link under, angle and climb to the back side of the support, but do not enter the station. This has formed the *X* on the support. Now, proceed behind the support, and loop the support 360°. If it is an odd-numbered section, loop in a clockwise movement, and enter. If it is an even-numbered section, loop counterclockwise, then enter the support/station.

Proceed to the next support/station and repeat the pattern of forming the *X* by looping, linking. Continue by looping around the support before entering. This makes the final row of loops on the support symmetrical to the row of loops which begin the first section.

After all the support/stations are sewn, proceed to the final kettle station. Form the kettle, and re-enter the final station. Tie-off on the inside with a half hitch.

> The 1–SECTION *X* Sewing on a single raised support, drops and climbs by one section, as opposed to the 2–SECTION *X*, page 65, which drops two. With the excessive amount of linking, it is important to use thin thread and thicker sections to avoid bulk-up. Otherwise, the spine will expand thicker than the foredge.

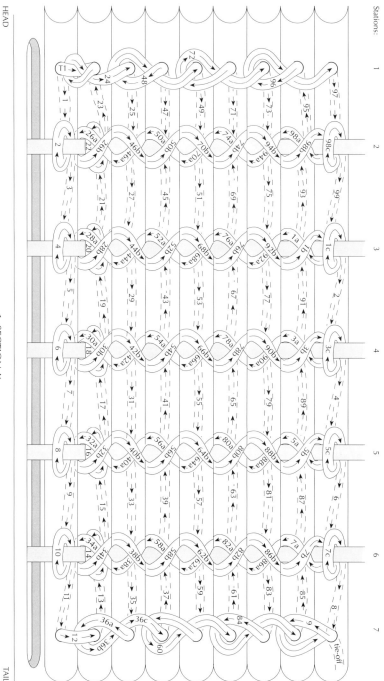

1-SECTION X

The X is formed by dropping, linking and climbing one section.
After Step 99, numbering returns to single digits.

HEAD

TAIL

Stations:

2–SECTION *X*

The *X* formed along the section upon each support in this loop-link sewing is the height of two sections. It is more readable than the previous single-section loop-link, referred to as the 1–Section *X*.

In this sewing, the *X* changes from texture, or, perhaps pattern, to a recognizable letter form. The first three sections are sewn looping the support 360° in the manner of the Basic Raised Support sewing. There is no dropping or linking. If the linking process started before the fourth section, you would link under the the entire book block. When the supports are then removed from the frame, these links can ride up, becoming loose.

At the end of the sewing, the final section drops, links under and climbs to form the final *X*. Before entering, the support is again looped, 360°. This is to obtain symmetry with the first section, rather than for function.

This sewing requires an even number of sections—two sections to start, and pairs of sections for each row of *X's*.

Right: The 2–SECTION *X*. This particular example uses a kettle stitch. For a detail of this sewing with endbands as changeover, see page 69.

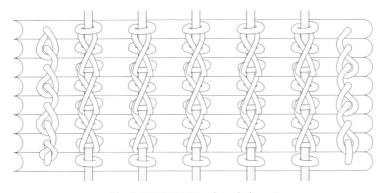

The 2–SECTION *X* is a loop-link sewing.

SEWING PROCEDURE

1-35. Start at the head. Sew the first three sections as diagrammed, the same as for the basic Raised Support sewing.

36. Add fourth section. Form the kettle at the tail.

37. Exit forward of the support at station 6.

38a. Loop the support, but do not enter.

38b. From forward of the support, drop back, dropping two sections to link under.

38c. Climb and enter from back of the support.

39 Proceed to next station. See the diagram at the top of the facing page.

Remaining Stations: Sew remaining stations of the fourth section in same manner as steps 37 and 38. Proceed to station 1, the kettle station. Form the kettle stitch, and the fifth section and enter.

Sewing the Next Odd-Numbered Section: All odd-numbered sections are sewn as a basic Raised Support sewing: exit forward, loop the support and enter. Do not drop or link. After all the support/stations have been sewn, proceed to the kettle station at the tail, which is station 7. Set on the next even-numbered section. Exit backwards. Drop *one* section, link under. Slip under to lock, climb and enter the new section.

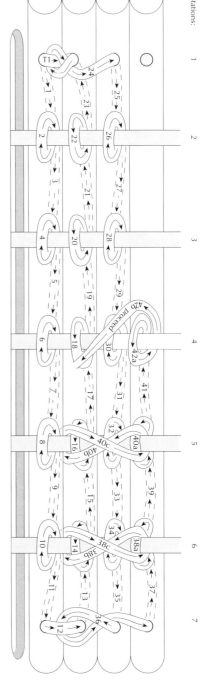

HEAD

TAIL

Starting to sew the 2–SECTION X

The X is formed on the even-numbered sections, only:
Drop at an angle, link and climb at an angle two sections and enter.

Stations:

Sewing the Next Even-Numbered Section: Proceed to station 6. Sew the same as the fourth section: Exit forward of the support. Loop, but do not enter. Drop back, link under, climb and enter from the back. Sew next odd-numbered section.

Final Section: With the final section, exit forward of the support, but do *not* loop at this point. First form the *X*: Drop back, dropping two sections to link under. See step 86a in the diagram at the bottom of this page as well as on the following.

86b. Climb to the back of station 6 of the final section but do not enter.

86c. Pass behind the support to the forward side. Loop the support in a counter-clockwise motion. Enter. This places the final loop above the *X*, so that it appears symmetrical to the loop and first row of *X's* at the beginning of the sewing.

87. Proceed to station 5.

Remaining Stations: Sew remaining stations of the final section in same manner as steps 85 and 86. After all support/stations are sewn, proceed to station 1, the kettle station. Form the kettle stitch. Re-enter station 1 of the final section. Tie-off. See illustration on the following page.

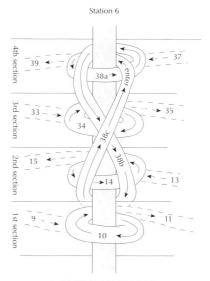

2–SECTION *X* SEWING

Starting to form the *X's*:
The first drop, link and climb is with the fourth section: Step 38a exits forward, loops behind the support. Step 38b angles and drops two sections, links under, and 38c climbs and enters.

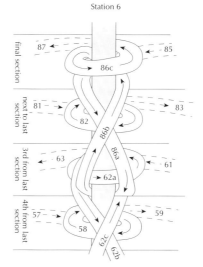

2–SECTION *X* SEWING

Starting to final section:
Step 86 a & b drops, links and climbs to form the *X*.
Step 86c loops the support prior to entering.

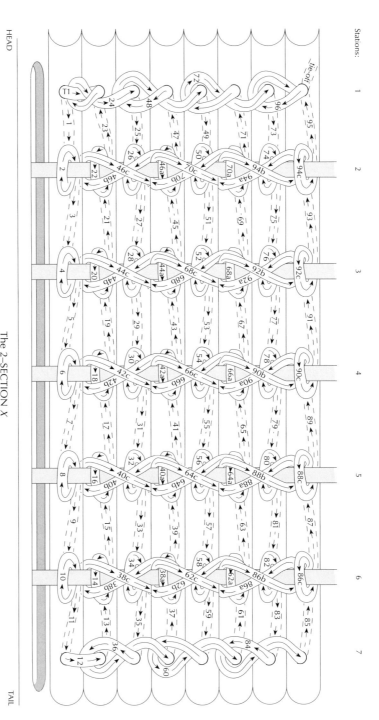

The 2-SECTION X

The X is formed on the even-numbered sections, only:
Drop two sections at an angle, link and climb at an angle two sections and enter.
The 360° loop around the support is formed prior to the X starting with section 4, and for all remaining even-numbered sections except for the last. With the final section, the X is formed, then the 360° loop is added as the ending of the sewing.

HEAD

TAIL

Stations: 1   2   3   4   5   6   7

Above: Detail of the head of a 2–SECTION *X* Sewing which uses *Endbands as Change-Over,* rather than the kettle stitch. See page 133.

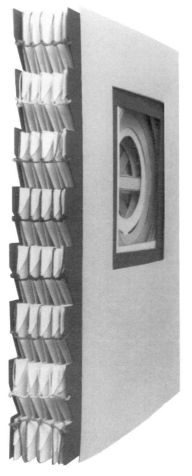

To the left and above: Keith Smith, Book 171, 1994. The cut paper and digital drawings represent my birthday greeting to Scott McCarney. With a saw-tooth spine, and slit and folded pleat, the sewing for this concertina was devised specifically for his book.

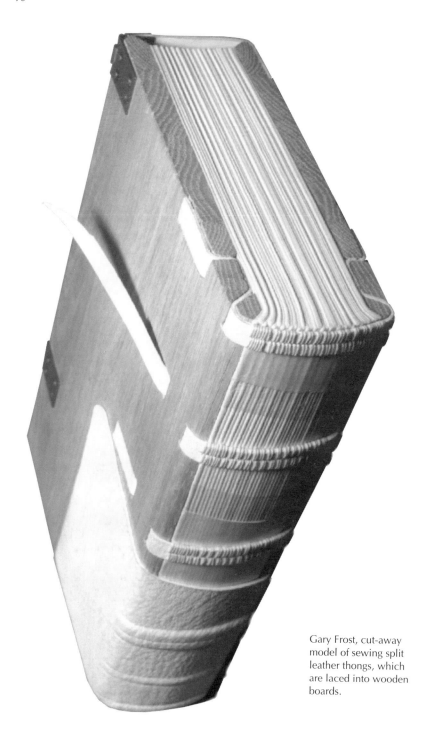

Gary Frost, cut-away
model of sewing split
leather thongs, which
are laced into wooden
boards.

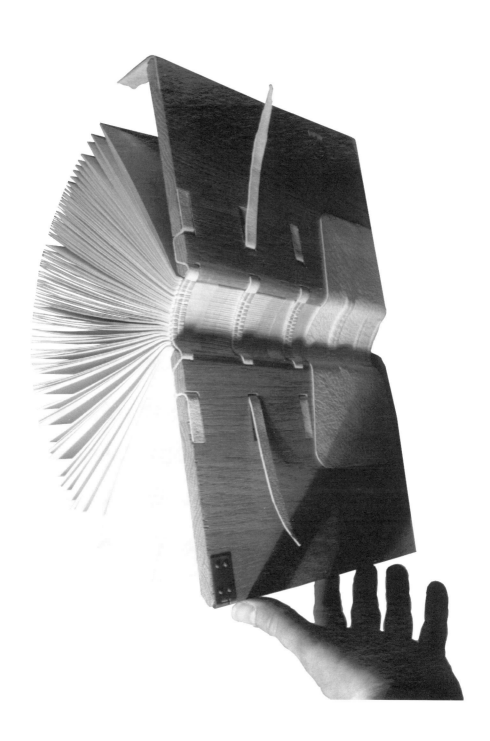

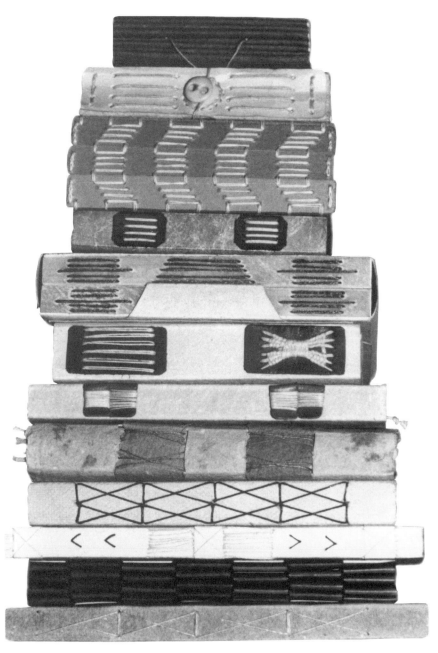

Hedi Kyle, Prototypes with sewing variations from the Conservation Lab at the American Philosophical Society, Philadelphia, PA. 11x 9 to 18 x 14 cm.

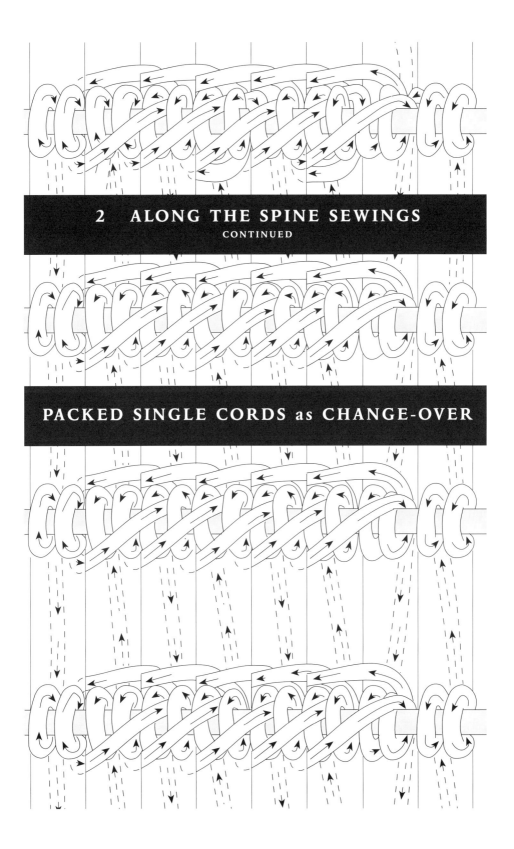

2 ALONG THE SPINE SEWINGS
CONTINUED

PACKED SINGLE CORDS as CHANGE-OVER

CLIMBING BY PACKING

Traditionally, in sewing raised supports, the kettle stitch is employed to climb from one section to the next; it also locks the sections together at the head and the tail. However, in non-adhesive binding, I almost always make use of an exposed spine sewing. The kettle stitch is not that exciting in appearance. More, it can interrupt the design of the stitches created for an exposed spine.

In sewing raised supports, cords lend themselves to packing, as they are ideally a cylindrical shaft.

To climb by other means than the kettle stitch, I have played around with sewing the endbands as part of the sewing along the spine. A cord is placed at the head and the tail, or slightly beyond the spine. This has advantages and drawbacks, and will be discussed in the following group of raised support sewings where I utilize endbands to change-over.

In addition to endbands, I have experimented with *climbing by packing* cords at the head and the tail as the means of change-over. Unlike end-bands-as-change-over, cords are set in from the head and the tail about 3/8", to where the kettle stations would have been placed. Placement and dimensions of the cords are design elements. See digital scans on the facing page. Keep in mind the strength needed in plying threads as supports.

To achieve a climb, I pack the cord, lay on the new section, and continue to pack until the new section is entered from the back side. This gives the strength of packing, with a clean look to the sewing without a kettle stitch. A more complete description is on the following page(s).

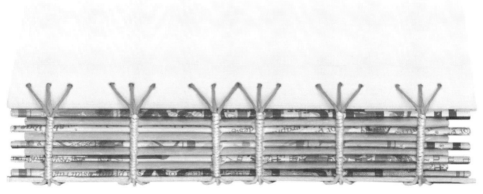

LOOP PACK WITH CLIMBING PACK Ends of 6-ply cord can be separated into three 2–ply cords after the sewing is completed. Each is threaded on a needle and sewn to the board. Threads can be plied as supports, then individually sewn to the board. Notice the even-numbered sections are smaller, giving a dove-tail effect on the spine at the head and the tail.

LOOP PACK WITH CLIMBING PACK

This is a basic raised cord sewing with packing, (page 43) except this sewing does not have a kettle stitch. This sewing climbs by continuing to pack the cords at the head and the tail to the height of the next section, then enters the new section. For information on *How to Pack*, see page 41. The look of the spine is streamlined; it is subtle elegance. Many of my variations proceed from this structure.

Three examples of the LOOP PACK WITH CLIMBING PACK. Top: At some stations #18 thread is strung as supports, at others, 4–ply cord. Middle: At each station, an increasing number of threads, 1, 3, 5 and 7, are plied and strung as supports. This patterns a progression in the size of the solid pack supports. Bottom: Uniform size supports of 6–ply cord are used.

PREPARATION

Sewing Stations: The kettle stations are replaced by cord/stations. Instead of four cords and two kettle stations, there are six cord/stations.

SEWING PROCEDURE

Sewing the First and Second Sections: Set on the first *and* the second sections. Open the second section.

1. Start on the inside of the second section. Exit backward at station 1. Pack *downward,* clockwise, two to four times to cover the cord the thickness of the second and the first section. This will be the only time packing is in a downward direction, except at the end the sewing. Enter the first section on the back side of the cord at station 1. Dangling thread inside second section will be tied-off with step 21 upon completing sewing of the second section.

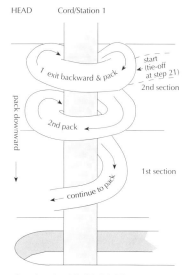

Starting the LOOP PACK WITH CLIMBING PACK

Set on the first and second sections. Begin inside the second section. Exit and pack counter-clockwise.

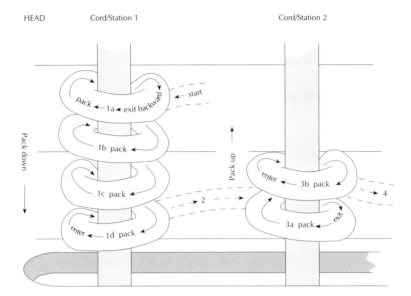

HEAD   Cord/Station 1   Cord/Station 2

Starting the LOOP PACK WITH CLIMBING PACK

Pack *downward,* counter-clockwise, from the second to the first section and enter to connect the two sections at the head.

Pack upward at all times for the remainder of the sewing, except at the final station of the final section.

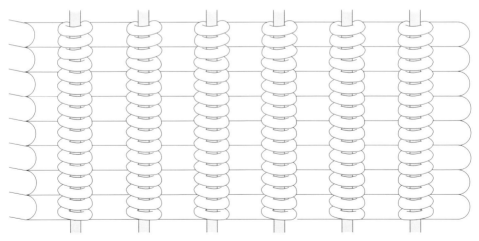

LOOP PACK WITH CLIMBING PACK

It is critical to maintain a tight pack with waxed thread to insure this structure without a kettle stitch.

2. Proceed to station 2, inside first section.
3. Exit forward of the cord. Pack clockwise two or three times. Re-enter the first section at station 2.
4. Proceed to station 3.
5. Exit forward of the cord. Pack clockwise two or three times. Re-enter.
6. Proceed to station 4.
7. Exit forward. Pack clockwise two or three times. Re-enter.
8. Proceed to station 5.
9. Exit forward of the cord. Pack clockwise two or three times. Re-enter.
10. Proceed to station 6. Since this is the point of the change-over, exit backward, just as exiting backward at a kettle station.
11. Pack counter-clockwise, probably four to six times, until the thread is the height of the second section. Enter the second section on the back side of the station at the tail (6).
12. Proceed to the next station (5).
13. Exit forward. Pack counter-clockwise two or three times. Re-enter.
14-19. Repeat steps 12 and 13 to sew all the remaining cord/stations on the second section, except for the one at the head.
20. Proceed to the cord/ station at the head (1).
21. Tie-off with the dangling thread, but do not clip.

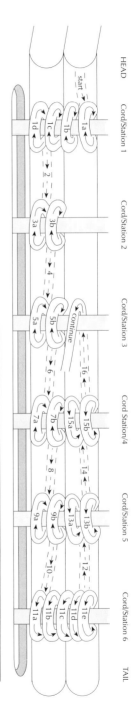

Sewing the first two sections of the LOOP PACK WITH CLIMBING PACK

At stations 6 and 1, exit backward to change direction of the packing in order to enter the new section on the back side of the cord.

Sewing the Third Section: Set on the third section.

22 Exit backward at station 1 of the second section. Pack clockwise probably four to six times, until the thread is the height of the third section. Enter third section on the back side of the cord at station 1.

23. Proceed to station 2.

24. Exit forward. Pack clockwise two or three times. Re-enter. Keep the total number of packings on this second cord the same number of packs thus far on the first cord. It is important when packing any section that all cords have accumulated an equal total number of packings.

25-30. Repeat steps 23 and 24 to sew all the remaining cord/stations on the third section, except for the one at the tail.

31. Proceed to the cord/ station at the tail (6).

Sewing the Fourth Section: Set on the fourth section.

32. Exit backward at station 6 of the third section. Pack counter-clockwise, four to six times, until the thread is the height of the fourth section. Enter the fourth section on the back side of the cord/station at the tail (6).

33. Proceed to the next cord/station.

Continue to exit forward, pack twice and re-enter, until all cord/stations of the fourth section are sewn, except for the one at the head. Proceed to the head. Exit backward. Set on the next section. Pack clockwise four to six times until the thread is the height of the fifth section. Enter on the back side of the cord.

Sewing the Remaining Sections: Continue in this manner. At stations 2 through 6, exit forward, pack two or three times. Re-enter. At the head and the tail, exit backwards, set on the next section. Pack four to six times and enter the new section.

Diagram to end the sewing is illustrated on page 80.

NOTE: Since the kettle has been eliminated, connection of the sections at the head and tail are dependent upon the packing. Pack tightly, and use waxed thread for a tight sewing.

Packed Single Cords as Change-Over

LOOP PACK WITH CLIMBING PACK

Exit backward at the head and the tail to change direction of the packing in order to enter the new section on the back side of the cord. At the final station, exit forward, pack downward. Tie-off inside the next to last section.

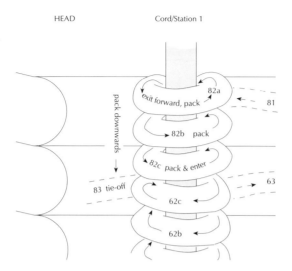

HEAD   Cord/Station 1

pack downwards

82a
exit forward, pack   ← — — 81
82b   pack
82c pack & enter
83 tie-off   → 63
62c
62b

Ending the LOOP PACK WITH CLIMBING PACK
Exit forward at the final station. Pack downward from
the last to next to last section. Enter and tie-off.

To Finish the Sewing: Proceed to the final cord/sta-
tion, whether at the head or the tail. Exit *forward.*
Pack *downward,* forming a coil from the final section
towards the next to last section. If it is at the head,
the packing will be counter-clockwise. If the final
section is an of an odd-number, you will exit forward
and pack in a clockwise movement towards the next
to last section. Pack tightly.

Enter the next to last section. Tie-off on the inside
with a half hitch. This connects the final section to
the next to the last.

LOOP PACK, PACK CLIMB WITH BEAD results in a
pleasing exposed spine sewing, eliminating the need
for a kettle stitch. Description begins on page 81.

LOOP PACK, PACKED CLIMB WITH BEAD

The previous sewing has the simplicity of packed cords. Nothing else interrupts the look of the spine, since the kettle is eliminated in favor of climbing by packing. This sewing, Loop Pack, Packed Climb with Bead, decorates the spine a little more by adding a bead on each side of the cords. More, it is a sturdier sewing, locking together the sections. See the digital scans on page 74, 75, and, on the facing page.

PREPARATION

Sewing Stations: Preparation is the same as for the previous sewing. The kettle stations are replaced by cord/stations. Instead of four cords and two kettle stations, there are six cord/stations.

SEWING PROCEDURE

Sewing the First and Second Sections:
Steps 1-21. The first and second sections are sewn identically to the previous sewing. See pages 75 through 77.

With the third section, after exiting and packing, the thread drops, links and climbs, resulting in beads. These appear flanking, and perpendicular to the packing. At all cord/stations, except at the head and the tail, exit *forward* and pack, prior to linking. At the head and the tail, exit *backwards.*

Detail of the sewing LOOP PACK, PACK CLIMB WITH BEAD. See the facing page for a digital scan of this sewing.

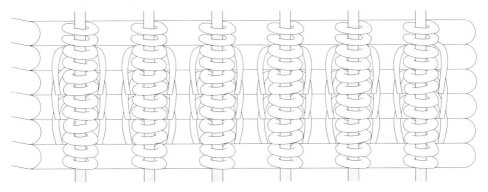

LOOP PACK, PACKED CLIMB WITH BEAD

22. Exit backward of the cord. Set on the third section. Pack clockwise as many times as necessary until the thread is level with the third section.

23a.   With the final pack, proceed behind the cord. Drop towards the tail. Link under between the first and second sections.

23b. Climb. Enter station 1, third section, on the back side of the cord.

24. Proceed to station 2.

25. Exit forward. Pack clockwise two or three times until the cord is level with the section.

26. With the final pack, proceed behind the cord. Drop on the forward side. Link under. Climb on the back side. Enter station 2.

27-35. Repeat 24-26 to sew the remaining cord/stations of the third section, except for the station at the tail.

36. Proceed to station 6.

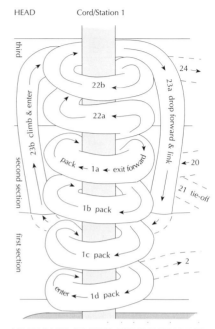

LOOP PACK, PACKED CLIMB WITH BEAD
Starting the third section

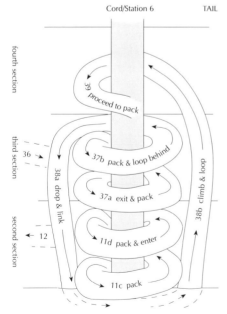

LOOP PACK, PACKED CLIMB WITH BEAD
Starting the climb to the fourth section

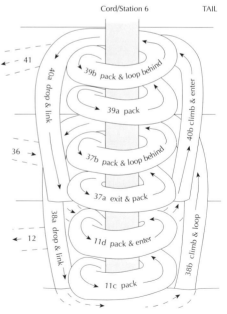

LOOP PACK, PACKED CLIMB WITH BEAD
Completing the climb to the fourth section

Sewing the Fourth Section:

37. Exit backward of the cord. Set on the fourth section. Pack counter-clockwise twice. Loop behind the cord.

38a. Drop towards the head. Link under between the first and second sections.

38b. Climb and loop behind the cord.

39. Pack counter-clockwise until the thread is level with the fourth section. Raise the marker between the sections to in between the second and third sections. Refer to *Tabbing Positions,* page 32.

40a. Drop towards the head. Link under between the last two connected sections (second and third).

40b. Climb. Enter the new section (4th) at the station at the tail (6).

41. Proceed to the next cord/station (5).

42. Exit forward. Pack counter-clockwise as many times as needed.

43a. Drop towards the head. Link under between the last two connected sections (second and third).

43b. Climb and enter.

44-52. Continue, repeating steps 41-43 at each cord station, except the one at the head.

53. Proceed to the head. Exit backward at station 1.

54. Set on the fifth section. Pack clockwise two times. Loop behind the cord.

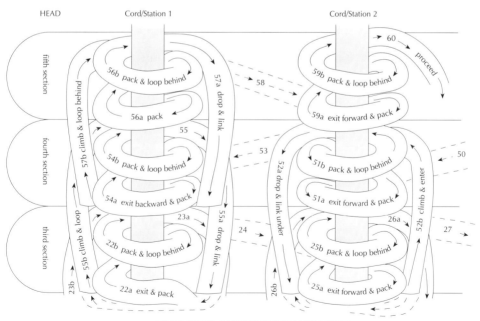

LOOP PACK, PACKED CLIMB WITH BEAD
Climbing at the head

55a. Drop towards the tail. Link under between the last two connected sections (second and third).

55b. Climb and loop behind the cord.

56. Pack clockwise until the thread is level with the fifth section. Raise the marker to in between the third and the fourth sections.

57a. Drop towards the tail. Link under at the new marked position (between the third and fourth sections).

57b. Climb and enter the new section (5th) on the back side of the cord.

Sewing the Remaining Sections: Continue in this manner. sewing the odd-numbered sections similarly to the third. Sew the even-numbered section like the fourth.

After packing the cord at the final station of the next to the last section, drop, link under, climb, but do not enter. Set on the final station. Loop behind the cord. Pack and enter. Proceed to each station. Exit forward, pack and enter.

Exit backward at the final station. Pack, enter and tie-off with a half hitch.

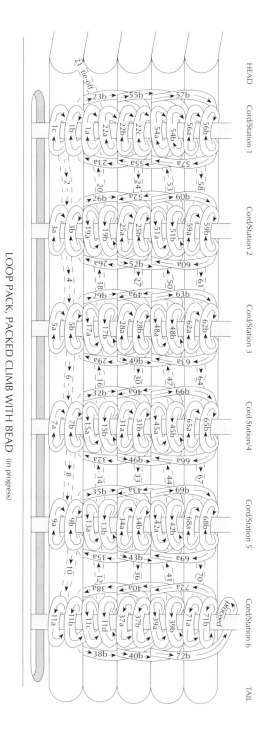

LOOP PACK, PACKED CLIMB WITH BEAD (in progress)
The final section does not link, to be symmetrical with the first section.

Left: An example of the prototype for THE SPIRAL BINDING.

Second from left: Pattern of the angled climb alternates. This variation, SPIRAL BINDING, *Alternating Climb,* is described on page 97.

Two books on the right: These are another variation of the Spiral, which I refer to as SPIRAL BINDING WITH SPINE STITCHES. This sewing is not described in this book.

THE SPIRAL BINDING

In playing around with packing the cord as change-over, I wanted to improvise some sewings which would utilize the cord, but not as an end-band change-over. Connecting one section to another with the cord set in slightly from the head and the tail posed different problems. Connecting the sections was now more closely related to using the traditional kettle stitch:the changeover comes at the end of the row with the cord at the head or tail.

After composing *Loop Pack With Climbing Pack,* page 75, I quickly found the sections would be held together stronger at the head and the tail if I dropped and linked under before entering the next section. See previous sewing. Dropping creates a pattern of beads on one, or both sides, of the cords.

Climbing is another variable for possibilities of design. To climb at an angle yields a pattern I could not resist calling the *Spiral Binding.*

PREPARATION

The sewing procedure will describe only five raised cords for purposes of space in the diagrams. I suggest a minimum of six cords, four in the middle plus one each set in from the head and the tail for the change-over.

Fold the sections and pre-pierce the stations.

TABBING BETWEEN SECTIONS: Linking is elaborate in this sewing. Tabs help. Refer to *Tabbing Positions,* page 32.

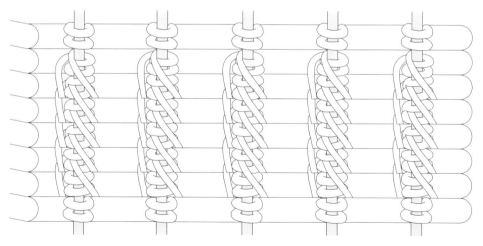

THE SPIRAL BINDING

Step *e* is the point to raise the location of the tabs, and thus, the linking, one section higher. The third section links under between the first and second sections. With step 26e linking begins between the second and third sections for the remainder of this section, as well as for all of the following section at step c. Step 34e marks the point to start linking under between the third and fourth sections.

The complete diagram of this sewing is on page 96.

SEWING PROCEDURE
Sewing the First and Second Sections:
1-15. See diagram to the right. The first and second sections are sewn the same as for *Loop Packed with Packed Climb.* To begin the sewing, you might want to refer to text and diagrams on pages 75-77.

It is critical that the cords are tightly packed and that the thread is waxed. Otherwise, without a kettle, the structure could be compromised.

Number of packings depends on the thickness of the section and the thread. The illustrations always show two packings, but it will vary with each book from one to four packings in order to build the thread to the height of the section.

Since the angle of the climb is always towards eleven o'clock (\) and never towards one o'clock (/), packing is always counter-clockwise for both the odd and even-numbered sections.

16. Proceed inside the second section to station 1.

17. Tie-off with the dangling thread, but do not clip.

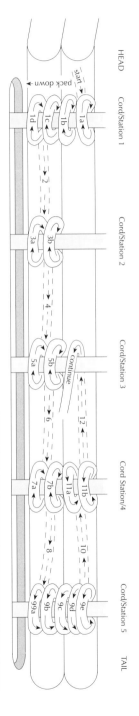

Sewing sections 1 and 2 of THE SPIRAL BINDING

At station 5 of the first section and station 1 for the second, exit backward to change the direction of the packing in order to enter the new section on the back side of the cord.

HEAD

Cord/Station 1

Cord/Station 2

Cord/Station 3

Cord Station/4

Cord/Station 5

TAIL

Sewing the Third Section:

18a. Set on the third section. Exit forward at station 1 of the second section. Pack once counter-clockwise.

18b. Pack counter-clockwise again, or as many times as needed.

18c. As you proceed behind the cord, drop on the outside. Link under between the last two connected sections (the first and second).

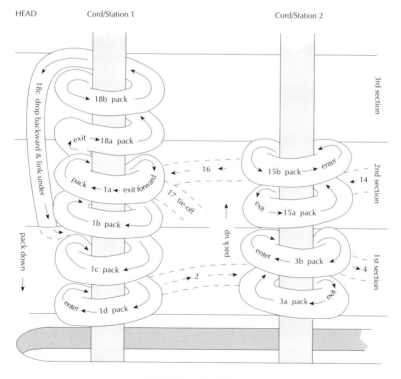

THE SPIRAL BINDING

Ending the second section

18d. Climb at an angle (\) to the back side of the cord. Enter the third
section at station 1 on the back side of the cord.
19. Proceed to station 2.

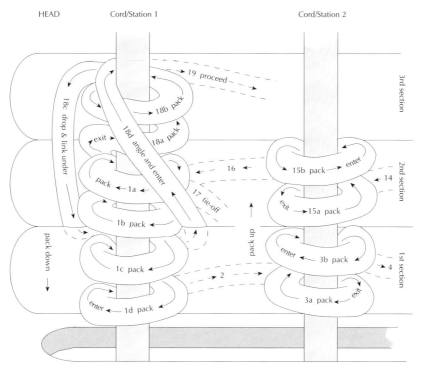

THE SPIRAL BINDING
Starting the third section

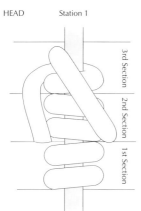

The first bead and spiral will appear
more like this.

ODD-NUMBERED SECTIONS: All cord/stations for odd-numbered sections will exit backwards. Pack one to three times counter-clockwise. Drop on the back side and link under. Angle (\) and re-enter the same station on the back side of the cord.

20a, b. As just stated, exit backwards. Pack counter-clockwise as many times as needed.

20c. As you proceed behind the cord, drop on the back side of the cord. Link under between the last two connected sections.

20d. Angle (\) to the back side of the cord. Re-enter the (third) section on the back side of the station (2). Each time as you enter, catch the thread on the inside (step 19) to lock threads. This is *not* shown in the diagrams.

21-24. For the remainder of the cord/stations for this odd-numbered section, except for the cord at the tail, repeat steps 19 and 20.

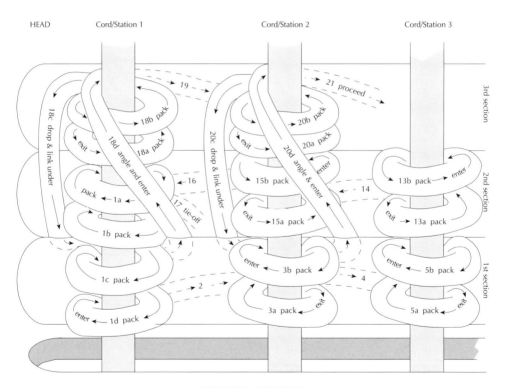

THE SPIRAL BINDING

Sewing an odd-numbered section
Steps 18b and 20b: Pack as many times as necessary.

CHANGE-OVER at the TAIL:

25 Proceed to the cord/station at the tail.

26a, b. Exit backwards. Set on the next even-numbered section. Pack
counter-clockwise as many times as needed.

26c. As you proceed behind the cord, drop on the back side of the cord.
Link under between the last two connected sections.

26d. Angle (\) to the back side of the cord.

26e. Do *not* enter the station. Loop behind the cord from the back to the
outer side. Drop on the outside and link under, but *not* between the
last two connected sections. Link under between this (3rd) and the
previous (2nd) section.

26f. Climb on the back side. Lap in front, then loop behind the cord to
form a packing. See diagrams on the following page.

26g. It may be necessary to pack a second or third time in order to bring
the thread to the height of the new section.

26h Drop on the back side. Link under the last two connected sections.

26i. Angle (\) from the outer side to the forward side of the new section.

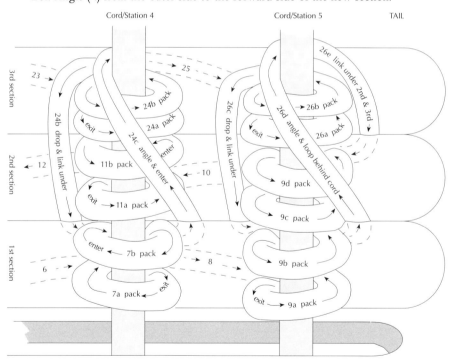

THE SPIRAL BINDING

Change-Over at the tail.
Steps 24b and 26b: Pack as many times as necessary.

Adjust tension after linking to form the bead. Enter the new even-numbered section on the forward side of the cord (station 5). After exiting station 4. make sure the angled thread at the tail lays on top of the previously angled thread. The bottom of the angled thread tends to want to rise to a more horizontal stitch.

Sewing the Fourth Section:

27. Proceed to station 4.

EVEN-NUMBERED SECTIONS: All cord/stations for even-numbered sections will exit forward. Pack once to three times counter-clockwise. Drop on the forward side and link under.

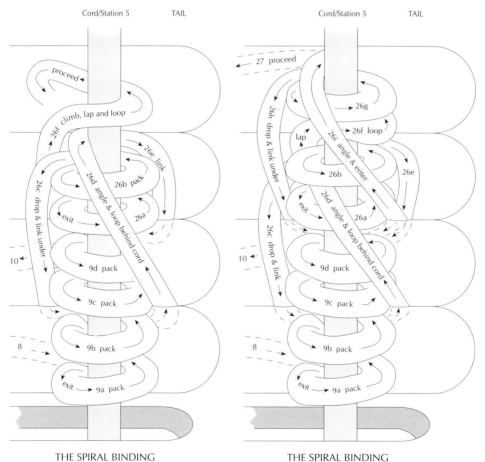

THE SPIRAL BINDING
Beginning the change-over at the tail.

THE SPIRAL BINDING
Completing the change-over at the tail.
Starting an even-numbered section.
Steps 26b and 26g: Pack as many times as necessary.

Angle (\) and re-enter the same station on the forward side of the cord. This will maintain the continuity of the bead formed by the drop always to the left of the cord, and the angle (\) always aiming towards eleven o'clock.

28a, b. As just stated, exit forward. Pack counter-clockwise as many times as needed.

28c. As you proceed behind the cord, drop on the forward side and link under between the last two connected sections.

28d. Angle (\) to the forward side of the cord. Re-enter on the forward side of the station (4).

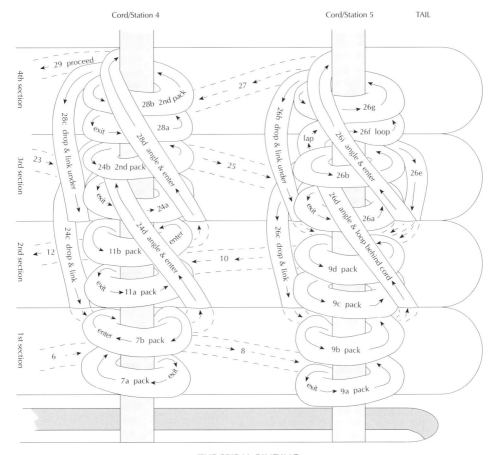

THE SPIRAL BINDING

Steps 27 and 28: Sewing an even-numbered section.
Steps 24b, 26b, 26g and 28b: Pack as many times as necessary.

29-32. For the remainder of the cord/stations for this even-numbered section, except for the cord at the head, repeat steps 27 and 28.

CHANGE-OVER at the HEAD:

33. Proceed to the cord/station at the head.

34a. Exit forward at station 1. Set on the next odd-numbered section. Pack once counter-clockwise.

34b. Continue to pack as many times as needed.

34c. As you proceed behind the cord, drop on the outside. Link under between the last two connected sections.

34d. Angle (\) to the outside of the cord.

34e. Do *not* enter the station. Loop behind the cord from the back side to the forward side. Drop on the forward side and link under, but *not* between the last two connected sections. Link under between the top (4th) and the previous (3rd) section. Change the position of the tab which marks the position of where to link under to between the third and fourth sections. This will be the point to link under for step 34h and all step *c's* for the fifth section.

34f. Climb on the outer side. Lap the cord, then loop behind as the first pack.

34 g. Pack counter-clockwise again, if needed.

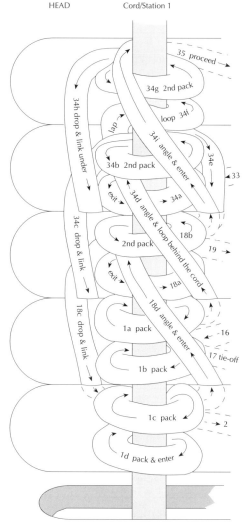

THE SPIRAL BINDING
Change-Over at the head.
Steps 28b and 34g: Pack as many times as necessary.

34h. Drop on the outer side and link under.

34i. Angle (\) from the inside to the back side of the new section. Make sure the angled thread lays on top of the previous. Enter the new even-numbered section on the back side of the cord at station 1.

Sewing the Remaining Sections: Sew the remaining odd and the even-numbered sections as previously described, until completing the next to last section.

Sewing the Final Section: Depending upon whether your book has an odd or even number of sections, you will complete the next to last section at either the head or the tail. After packing, dropping and linking, climb at an angle with step d at the final station for the next to last section. See step 58d in the diagram on the following page. (Climb, but do not enter.)

58e, f. Set on the final section. Pack counter-clockwise as needed. Enter the final section at the tail if an even number of sections. Enter at the head if your book has an odd number of sections.

58g. Proceed to the next station. Exit *forward,* whether it is an even-numbered or an odd-numbered section.

58h. Pack as many times as needed. Enter.

Continue to sew the remainder of all the cord/stations in this manner, until the final cord.

66a, b. Exit forward at the final cord. Pack downward, from the top of this section towards the next to the last.

67. Enter the next to last section. Tie-off with a half hitch.

The complete illustration for the sewing is on the following page.

Detail of the change-over at the head for the SPIRAL BINDING

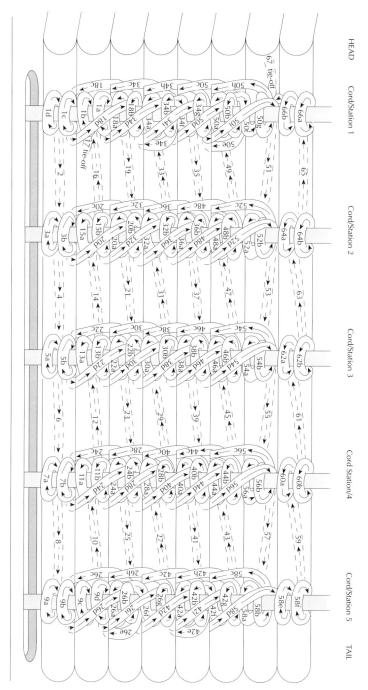

The SPIRAL BINDING

SPIRAL BINDING *Alternating Climb*

In the previous sewing, the Spiral Binding, all cords have an angled climb which points at an angle (\) from 4 to 10 o'clock: \ \ \ \ \.

Spiral Binding, Alternating Climb differs with every other cord having the climb from 8 to 2 o'clock: \ / \ / \. This is accomplished by keeping track whether to exit forward, or, to exit backward at each station so as to maintain an angled climb (\) at all odd-numbered cord/stations, and an angled climb (/) at all even-numbered stations.

SEWING PROCEDURE

It will be less confusing if you sew an example of the previous sewing before attempting this one. The principle in sewing is the same as for the previous sewing. The difference is whether to exit forward or backward at each station, beginning at the end of the second section, in order to have the proper direction in the angled climb:

EVEN-NUMBERED SECTIONS, ODD-NUMBERED STATIONS: Exit forward, pack counter-clockwise. Drop behind the cord towards the head. Climb (\) at an angle, enter on the forward side of the cord.

EVEN-NUMBERED SECTIONS, EVEN-NUMBERED STATIONS: Exit backwards, pack clockwise. Drop behind the cord towards the tail. Climb (/) at an angle, enter on the back side of the cord.

ODD-NUMBERED SECTIONS, ODD-NUMBERED STATIONS: Exit backwards, pack counter-counter-clockwise. Drop behind the cord towards the head. Climb (\) at an angle, enter on the back side of cord.

ODD-NUMBERED SECTIONS, EVEN-NUMBERED STATIONS: Exit forward, pack clockwise. Drop behind the cord towards the tail. Climb (/) at an angle, enter on the forward side of the cord.

Final section is sewn with packed cords, only, with no drops or climbs, similar to The Spiral Binding. A digital scan of this sewing is on page 85.

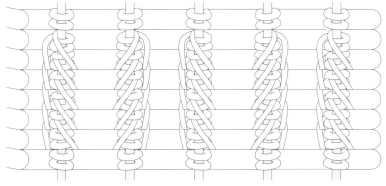

SPIRAL BINDING *Alternating Climb*

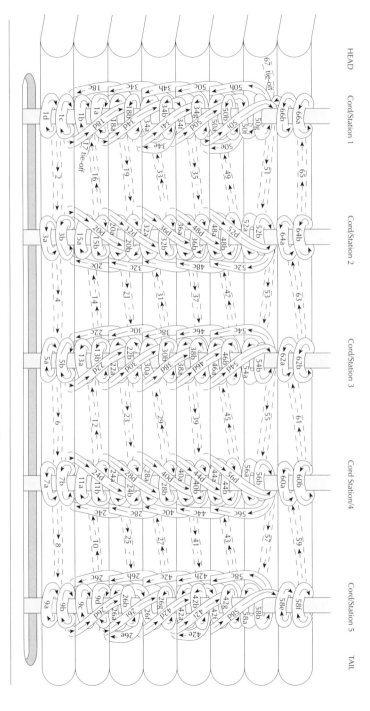

SPIRAL BINDING   *Alternating Climb*

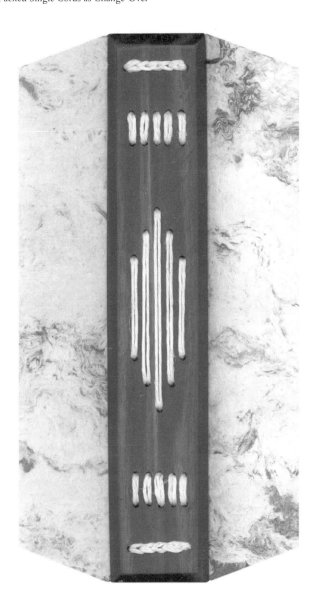

Left: Example of SPIRAL BINDING *Alternating Climb.*

Right: Michele Powers, LANGSTITCH und KETTENSTITCH,
as described on page 142, Volume I. The ebony spine was
drilled for sewing stations. Sewn at Penland, Session 2, 1995.
14.5 x 13 x 1.5 cm.

WOVEN SPINES

PART of SEWING the SECTIONS:
Playing with sewing raised cords, I
wanted to explore woven threads on
an exposed spine. The sewing to the
right, Pack & Weave, creates the
diagonal threads as part of the structure: as the cord is packed, the
thread then drops at an angle and
links under the adjacent support. It
then angles to return to that cord to
continue on to the next.

Sewing the odd-numbered sections
place angled (\) threads across the
spine. Even-numbered sections add
threads angled (/) in the opposite
direction.

PART of SEWING the ENDBANDS:
Other woven spines are achieved by
adding the weaving after the book is
sewn, while sewing the endbands.
See: *Endband Woven From Head To
Tail,* pages 113 through 127.

The headband is started, and sewn
only the width of one or two sections. Then, the thread weaves along
the spine to begin the tailband. The
thread then snakes along the spine
to the head to continue the headband. Traversing the spine to alternately complete the endbands, the
path back and forth produces the
woven spine.

Description of that particular integrated endband begins on page 111.

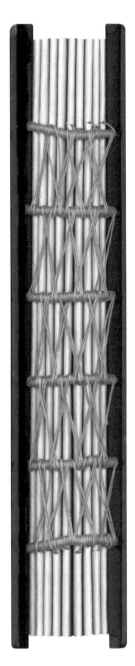

Michele Powers, PACK & WEAVE,
sewn at Penland, Session 2, 1995.
Supports are sandwiched between lam-
inated boards. 22.6 x 15.4 x 3.2 cm.

PACK & WEAVE

Exposed spine sewings look better when the kettle is eliminated. Packing offers possibilities of design. These are expanded with linking. To explore the permutation possibilities, I explored angling, then linking under.

In this sewing, angling always in the same direction distorts the spine:

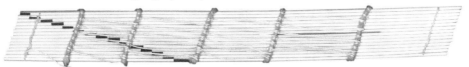

Above: This is an undesirable attempt at packing, angling, then linking under: The odd-numbered sections drop forward and angle. Even-numbered sections drop backward and angle, keeping all the diagonal threads parallel. Since the angled threads are in one direction (\), and, so is the tension; the book block is distorted.

Right: This detail shows a correct sewing, where the direction of dropping at an angle is alternated with each section (\ / \ / \ /) This is achieved by always

dropping forward at an angle. Tension is counter-balanced; the book block is not distorted.

Other photographs of the Pack & Weave are on pages 100 and 166.

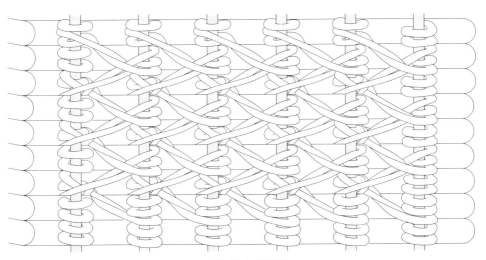

PACK & WEAVE

PREPARATION

As in any of these raised cord sewings containing excessive linking, use thin thread and wax it. The sections are each preferably configured as an octavo or duodecimo, rather than a quarto. This will lessen the number of times necessary to link under.

Pierce as many cord/stations as desired. Set in the cords at the head and the tail approximately ⅜ to ½" for climbing, in lieu of kettle stations.

SEWING PROCEDURE

Sewing the First Two Sections: The first two sections are sewn identically to the Loop Pack With Climbing Pack. See page 75-77.

1-19. Set on the first two sections. Sew identically to the Loop Packed with Packed Climb.
20. Proceed to the head.
21. Tie-off with the dangling thread with a square knot. Do not clip the longer thread.

Sewing the Third Section: Set on the third section.

22 Exit backwards. Pack clockwise to the height of the third section, less the width of one thread. Loop behind the cord.
23a. Drop at an angle towards the tail.
23b. Lap the second cord. Link under between the first and second sections, coming out *over* the thread (step 23a).
24. Climb at at angle towards the head. Lap the cord at station 1, just above the packed threads. If the thread is now the height of the third section, enter station 1 of the third section on the back side of the cord. If the thread is not the height of this section, pack clockwise as many times as needed prior to entering. Place a tab inside this section, and another tab positioned between the first and second sections to facilitate linking under. See *Tabbing Positions,* page 32.
25. Proceed to station 2.
26. Exit forward at station 2. Pack clockwise, proceeding behind the cord.
27a. Drop at an angle towards the tail.
27b. Lap the cord at station 3. Link under between the first and second sections.
28. Come out over the thread (27). Climb at at angle towards the head. Lap the cord at station 2, just above the packed threads. If the thread is now the height of the third section, enter station 2 on the back side of the cord. If the thread is not the height of the third section, pack clockwise as many times as needed prior to entering.

Packed Single Cords as Change-Over

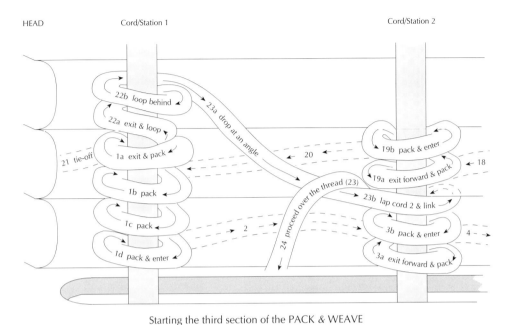

HEAD   Cord/Station 1   Cord/Station 2

Starting the third section of the PACK & WEAVE

Step 22: Exit backward the second section. Pack counter-clockwise to the height of the third section, less one thickness of thread.

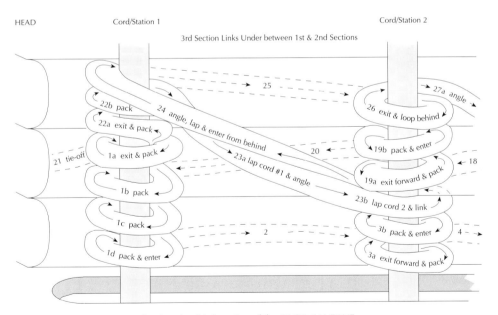

HEAD   Cord/Station 1   Cord/Station 2

3rd Section Links Under between 1st & 2nd Sections

Starting the third section of the PACK & WEAVE

Step 23: Drop at an angle, lap and link under cord 2 between the first and second section.
Step 24: Climb at an angle and lap cord 1. Enter the third section back of the cord.

Sewing the Remainder of the Third Section: Repeat steps 25-28 to sew cords 3 through 5. Step 40 will climb at an angle towards the head, and enter station 5 on the back side of the cord.

41. Proceed to the tail.

Sewing the Fourth Section: Set on the fourth section.

42. Exit backward at station 6. Pack counter-clockwise to height of fourth section, less the thickness of one thread.

43a. As you loop behind the cord, drop at an angle towards the head, lapping the cord at station 5.

43b. Link under between the second and third sections.

44. Come out over thread 43, but under threads 39 and 40. Climb at an angle. Lap the cord at the tail. Enter station 6 of the fourth section on the back side of the cord.

45. Proceed to station 5.

46. Exit forward at station 5. Pack once counter-clockwise, looping behind the cord.

47a. Drop at an angle towards the head, lapping the cord at station 4.

47b. Link under between the second and third sections.

48. Come out over thread 47, but under threads 35 and 36. Climb at an angle. Lap the cord at station 5. If the thread is now the height of the fourth section, enter station 5 on the back side of the cord. If the thread is not the height of the fourth section, pack counter-clockwise as many times as needed prior to entering.

Sewing the Remainder of the Fourth Section: Repeat steps 45-48 to sew cords 4 through 2. Step 60 will climb at an angle towards the tail, and enter station 2 on the back side of the cord.

61. Proceed to the head.

Shanna Leino, 4–DOWN LINK SEWING, New England Workshop, 1995, at Haystack Mountain School of Crafts. (actual size) This inventive and whimsical first sewing is a joy to see: Position and range of density of stations, and the X's in the center from the angled climbs between paired stations reveal a creative binder. See page 263 for the 4–DOWN LINK SEWING across the spine.

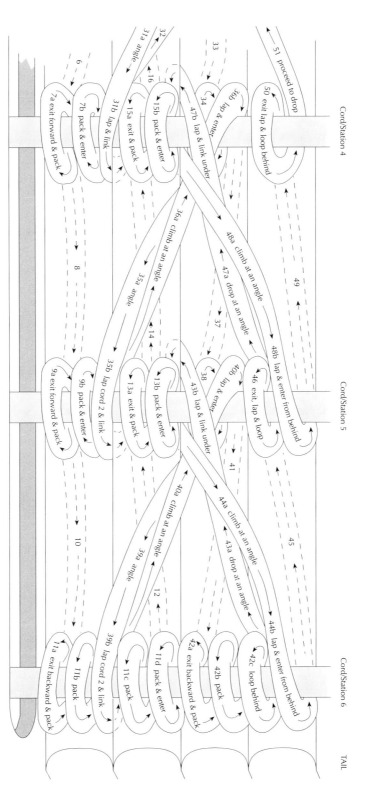

Sewing the fourth section of the PACK & WEAVE

Cord/Station 4

Cord/Station 5

Cord/Station 6

TAIL

51 proceed to drop
50 exit lap & loop behind
49

7a exit forward & pack
7b pack & enter
31b lap & link
15a exit & pack
15b pack & enter
47b lap & link under
34
36b lap & enter
33
32
31a angle
16
6

48a climb at an angle
47a drop at an angle
37
48b lap & enter from behind

36a climb at an angle
35a angle
35b lap cord 2 & link
14

9a exit forward & pack
9b pack & enter
13a exit & pack
13b pack & enter
43b lap & link under
38
40b lap & enter
41
46 exit, lap & loop
45

44a climb at an angle
43a drop at an angle
44b lap & enter from behind

40a climb at an angle
39a angle
39b lap cord 2 & link
12
10
8

11a exit backward & pack
11b pack
11c pack
11d pack & enter
42a exit backward & pack
42b pack
42c loop behind

Sewing the Fifth Section: Set on the fifth section. Raise the tab one section, so that it slips between the third and the fourth sections as a marker.

62a-d. Exit backwards at station 1. Pack clockwise past the fourth, to the height of the fifth section, less one thread.

63a. As you loop behind the cord, drop at an angle towards the tail, lapping the cord at station 2.

63b. Link under between the third and fourth sections. Make sure the needle passes under the diagonal threads labeled as steps 59 and 60.

64. Come out over thread 63. Climb at an angle. Lap the cord at the head.

65. Proceed to station 2.

66. Exit forward. Pack clockwise to the height of the fifth section, less one thread.

67a. As you loop behind the cord, drop at an angle towards the tail.

67b. Lap the cord at station 2. Link under between the third and fourth sections.

68. Climb at an angle towards the head. Lap the cord at station 1. Enter station 1 of the fifth section on the back side of the cord.

69- 80. Sew the remainder of the cords for this section, except at the tail, the same as for the second cord. Follow steps 65 through 68.

81   Proceed on the inside of the section to the tail.

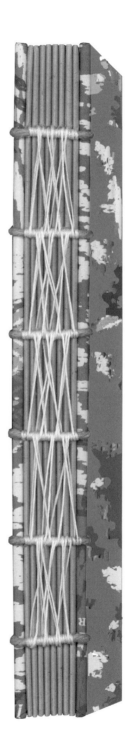

Example of the PACK & WEAVE

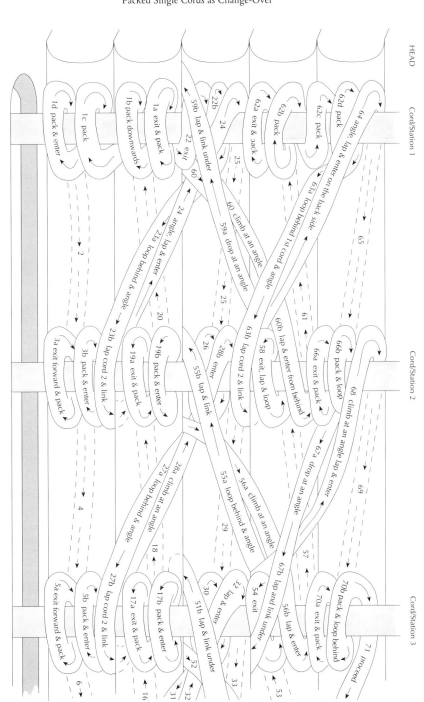

Sewing the fifth section of the PACK & WEAVE

HEAD

Cord/Station 1

Cord/Station 2

Cord/Station 3

Sewing the Next Even-Numbered Section: Set on the next section. Raise the tab one section, so that it slips between the next higher layer as a marker (between the fourth and the fifth sections).

82. Exit backwards at station 6. Pack counter-clockwise to the height of the present, as well as the new odd-numbered section, less one thread.

83a. As you loop behind the cord, drop at an angle towards the head, lapping the cord at station 5.

83b. Link under between the fourth and fifth sections.

84. Come out over thread 83. Climb at an angle. Lap the cord at the tail.

85. Proceed to station 5.

86. Exit forward. Pack counter-clockwise to the height of the section, less one thread.

87a. As you loop behind the cord, drop at an angle towards the head, lapping the cord at station 4.

87b. Link under between the fourth and fifth sections.

88. Come out over thread 87. Angle and lap the cord at station 5. Enter station 5 on the back side of the cord.

89-100. Sew the remainder of the cords for this section, except at the head, the same as for the fifth cord. Follow steps 85 through 88.

101. Proceed on the inside of the section to the head.

Sewing the Next Odd-Numbered Section: Set on the next section. Raise the tab one section, so that it slips between the next higher layer as a marker. Sew in the same as the previous odd-numbered section. Add the next even-numbered section, as sew the same as the sixth section.

Continue in this manner until all sections are sewn. In sewing the final section, pack once after the angled climb. See steps 43c, 47c, 51c, 55c and 59c in the illustration on page 110. This final pack on the edge of the spine will protect the angled thread from slipping on the cord, once the book is removed from the sewing frame.

Upon entering the final station, tie-off on the inside with a half hitch.

NOTE: A Variation of the Pack *&* Weave, called Isolated Pack *&* Weave is described on page 174. It appears again on page 180.

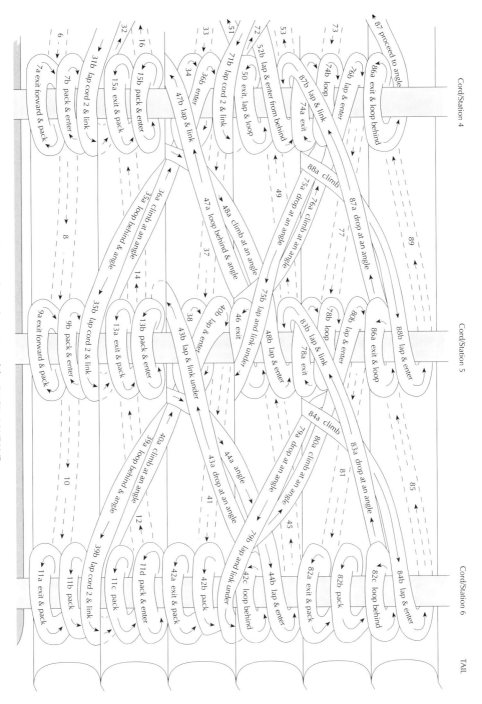

Sewing the sixth section of the PACK & WEAVE

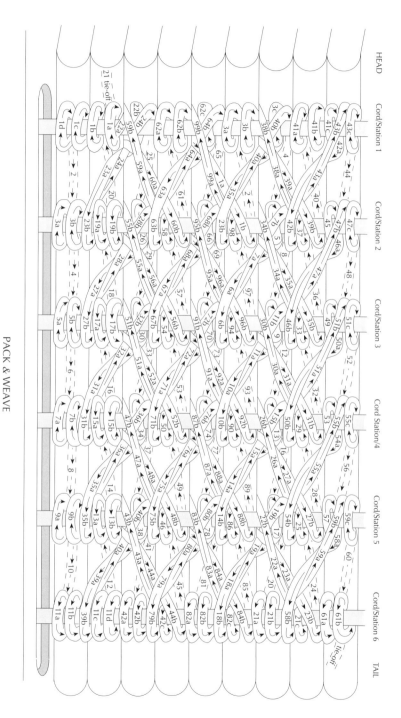

PACK & WEAVE

After step 99, numbering returns to single digits.

Above and below: Hedi Kyle, *Anaphanda,* 1984. Unsupported concertina with shaped pages. The folios are sewn in the valleys of the pleat. One-of-a-kind. 21.5 X 17.8 X 2.5 cm.

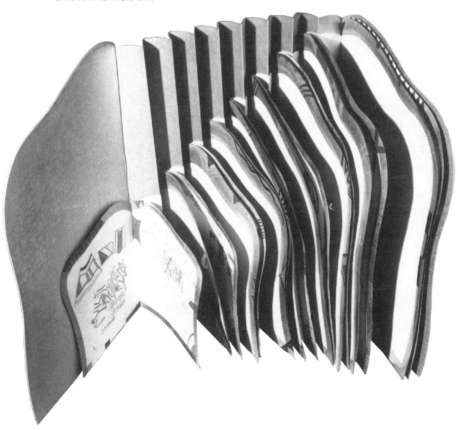

Above: Hedi Kyle, *Alphabet Panorama,* 1989. Found text in a one-of-a-kind flag book. This popular type of binding is one of many devised by Hedi Kyle. Closed, 21 x 12.6 cm. Opens to 252 cm.

Below: Hedi Kyle, *From A to Z,* alphabet concertina 1989. Edition of 65, four color offset flag book. 31.5 x 16.5 x 2 cm.

ENDBAND WOVEN FROM HEAD TO TAIL

HEADBANDS and TAILBANDS: Traditionally, after a raised support sewing is completed, a headband and tailband are each sewn separately. This book will not describe traditional endbands added. Other textbooks are entirely devoted to the subject. I will describe the *integrated* endband.

After devising the Pack & Weave, I consequently experimented with sewing the endbands with a single thread. This can be done *as* the sections are sewn, that is, *along with* a raised support sewing, or, afterwards, *added to* a raised support sewing:

An *integrated endband* can be sewn at the head and the tail, *along with* sewing the sections as a raised support sewing: The headband is sewn to the first section, only. Then the first section is sewn with a raised support sewing. The tailband is then sewn onto the first section with this single, continuous thread. The second section is added; the tailband is sewn. Continuing, the raised supports of the second section are sewn. Then the headband of the second section is sewn. The process of simultaneously sewing the endbands along with creating a raised support sewing with a single thread is explored in the following chapter, *Endbands as Change-Over.*

An added *integrated endband* can be sewn at the head and the tail, *added to* a completed raised support sewing. First, sew a Basic Raised Support Sewing, page 35, or Raised Cords with Packing, page 43. Then, a new thread starts the headband, packing and beading approximately the width of one section. The journey of the thread from end to end, head to tail, and back proceeds in a zig zag along the spine. At each end, a small portion of the endband is sewn, before reversing to the other end The thread links under the supports on its way, building up a criss-cross pattern. The single sewing forms an endband at both the head and the tail, with a woven spine denoting the trips back and forth. The weaving is decorative, not structural, as with the Pack *&* Weave. See pages 115-117 for designs. The sewing description begins on page 115.

The advantage of a spine weaving added to, rather than sewn along with, the sections is that it adds a second color and a different weight of thread to the exposed spine. If you desire endbands of two or three colors, you can plan a weaving across the spine that incorporates the additional color(s). Or, the extra colors can remain at the head and the tail, while only one or two colors of thread traverse the spine. The patterning of designs and necessary itinerary await your travel plans. I might add, I eagerly await your explorations in this area.

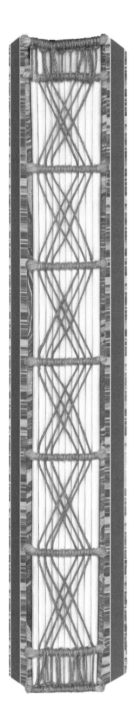
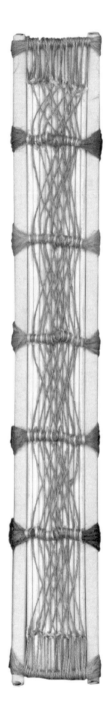
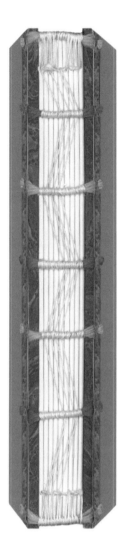

These are my first attempts of sewing an Integrated Endband a*dded to* a raised support sewing. In this second sewing, a single thread moves back and forth in a zig zag along the spine, linking under the supports. This single thread alternately sews part of the headband, then, part of the tailband, as the zig zag proceeds back and forth along the spine, linking under, and sometimes packing the supports. This adds an extra color thread in the pattern of the packing.

INTEGRATED ENDBAND
Added To A Raised Support Sewing

The following is my limited exploration, to introduce you to the possibilities:

PREPARATION

First, sew a Basic Raised Support Sewing, page 35, or Raised Cords with Packing, page 43. The Integrated Endband is a separate sewing, adding the endbands at the head and the tail, while decorating the spine with the connecting threads.

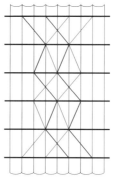

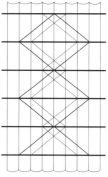

8 Sections with 6 Cords

8 Sections with 6 Cords

THE DESCRIBED DESIGN: On page 118 one design is diagrammed. It requires the raised cord sewing to have 7 cord/stations, and 10 sections. The principle for the endband sewing is the same for any other design.

CUSTOM DESIGNS: You can design a zig zag for your spine with any number of cords and sections. Draw it out on a sheet of paper before you attempt to sew it. Longitudinally, the angled threads of the zig zag on the spine link under the cords. Latitudinally, the linking transpires in the slits between the sections. At the right, and on pages 116 and 117 are options you might consider:

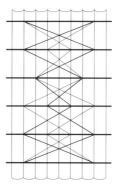

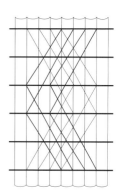

8 Sections with 6 Cords

8 Sections with 6 Cords

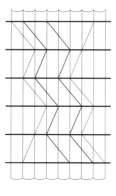

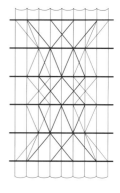

8 Sections with 6 Cords

8 Sections with 6 Cords

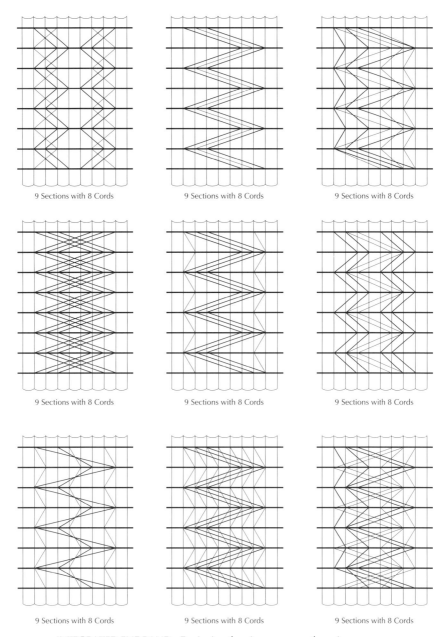

9 Sections with 8 Cords

9 Sections with 8 Cords

9 Sections with 8 Cords

9 Sections with 8 Cords

9 Sections with 8 Cords

9 Sections with 8 Cords

9 Sections with 8 Cords

9 Sections with 8 Cords

9 Sections with 8 Cords

INTEGRATED ENDBAND: Designing the zig zag across the spine

Each of these designs use two colors of thread, represented here by line thickness. This will allow two colors in designing your beaded endbands, as well.

The Added Integrated Endband

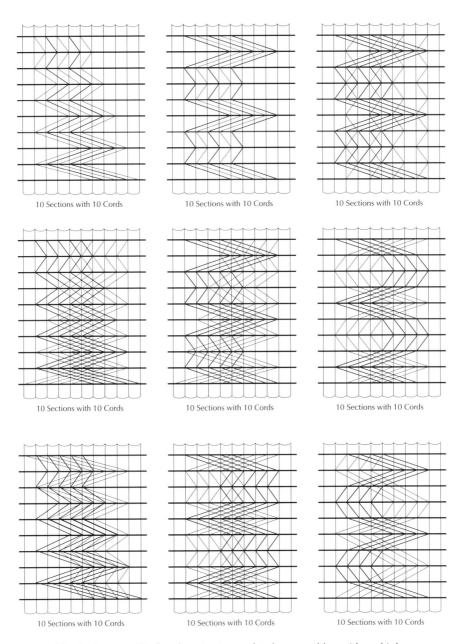

10 Sections with 10 Cords   10 Sections with 10 Cords   10 Sections with 10 Cords

10 Sections with 10 Cords   10 Sections with 10 Cords   10 Sections with 10 Cords

10 Sections with 10 Cords   10 Sections with 10 Cords   10 Sections with 10 Cords

After the Integrated Endband sewing is completed, you could consider a third
sewing (not illustrated). This would be an embroidery or macramé on the spine.
Additional color/s of thread would be "woven", using the zig zag sewing as a
loom.

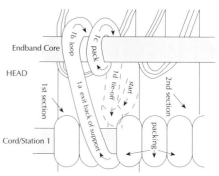

Starting the headband

SEWING PROCEDURE

Prop the book upright. Better, place the book in a book press (see page 48) with the spine exposed. Stand the press upright, freeing both hands for sewing.

1a, 1b. Start inside the first section. Exit station 1. Lap the cord. Set on the cord (core) for the head-band. Let it rest across the edge of the sections. Length of the core can extend onto the front and boards, where later it might be laced-in.

1c, 1d. Pack core clockwise once. Tie-off on inside at station 1.

2a. Proceed on the inside of the section to the head.

2b. Lap the headband core.

2c. Form spine bead by looping the vertical threads 1a, 1d, and 2a.

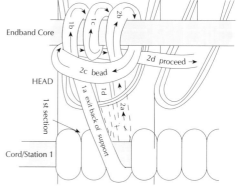

Packing and beading

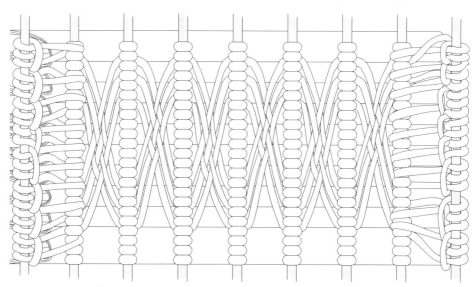

The INTEGRATED ENDBAND *added to a Raised Support Sewing*

Drawing of the zig zag design which is described beginning on page 118. Photograph of this spine is on the far left of the photo on page 114. The procedure is easily adapted to whichever zig zag spine design you might wish to sew.

Do not pull tightly. Allow the bead to be slightly loose. For uniform beads, form all with the same pressure.

2d. Proceed across top edge of the section. This forms another bead, on the other side of the endband core, seen from a top view of the book.

ENDBAND PATTERNING: All future packing is to the center of the section. If three packings is too much, you can pack two and a half times by alternating with three packs and bead, then two packs and bead. This may better fit the width of your sections:

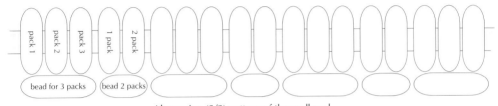

Alternating (3/2) pattern of the endband
View from either side, spine or foredge, since the beading is on both sides.

Step 2d passes under the endband core, so it does not lap. Drop on the outside of the spine, and link under cord 1 at the crack between the first and second section. This anchors the thread. You could pack here. See the Variations, page 127.

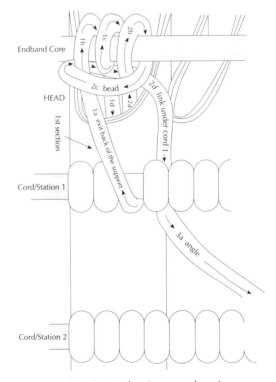

Step 3 starts the zig zag on the spine.

Make sure the endband cord rests on the sections. It is raised higher in the diagram in order to show the steps.

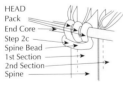

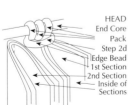

Bead both sides of the end *core,* either a cord, or rolled leather core.

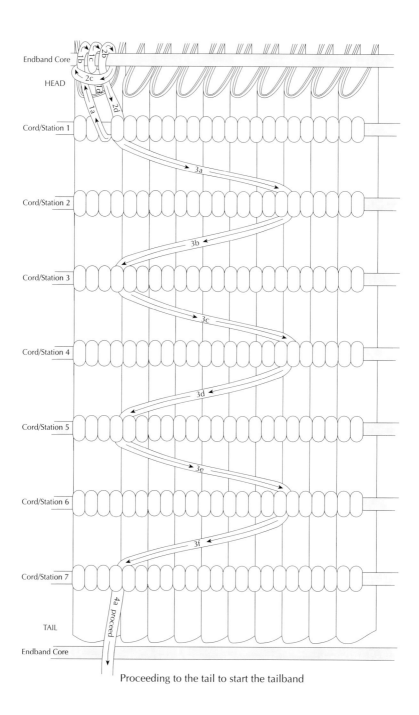

Proceeding to the tail to start the tailband

STARTING the ZIG ZAG DESIGN:

3a. The zig zag design begins with step 3a

•*Along the spine,* link under each successive cord that is part of your design.

•*Across the spine,* the point at which the linking transpires is the point on the cord which is the crack between any two sections.

3a-3f. In forming the zig zag for this *described design,* every cord is linked.

The position is the crack between the first and second sections, alternated with linking between the seventh and eighth sections. See the facing page.

4a, 4b. Set on the core for the tail-band. Lap the core. Pack once counter-clockwise.

ANCHORING the TAILBAND: 4c. Proceed inside the first section. Exit station 7 forward of the core. Reverse to lap core 7. Lap and loop the endband to anchor, in lieu of a kettle stitch in a traditional sewing. You will anchor inside every section, after packing to the center of section.

5a, 5b. Lap and loop the end core. Proceed horizontally, backward across, and in front of base of section to form the spine bead.

5c. Loop thread 4a. Advance beyond the packing to form the bead on other side of the core.

5d. Lap and loop the end core.

6a, 6b. Pack counter-clockwise to center of the second section.

6c. Proceed inside the second section.

6d. Exit forward of cord 7. Reverse to lap cord 7, proceed to tail. Lap and loop the end core.

6e. Proceed horizontally, backward across, and in front of the base of the section to form the spine bead.

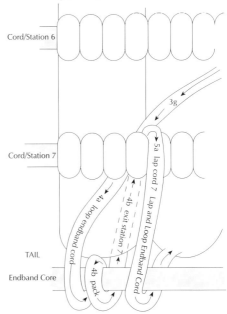

Starting the tailband

Steps 4b-5a anchor the tailband to cord 7, just as traditional endbands anchor to the kettle stitch.

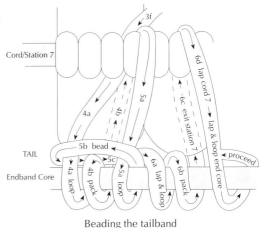

Beading the tailband

6f. Loop threads 5a and 6d. Advance beyond the packing. This forms the bead on other side of the end core, between the core and the tail edge.

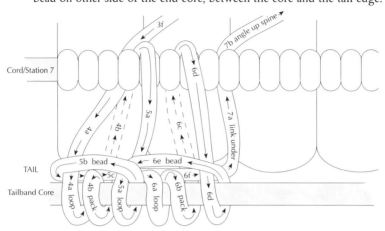

Tailband for the second section

Pack to the center of each section, and anchor before beading.

7a. Proceed to cord 7, passing under the end core, so that you do not lap it. Link under cord 7, between the second and third sections.

7b. Angle to cord 6. Link under between the eighth and ninth sections.

7c-7g. Continue to zig zag on the spine, towards the head, linking at each lower numbered cord. The odd-numbered cords are linked between the second and third sections. The even-numbered cords are linked between the eighth and ninth sections. With step 7g, cord 1 is linked.

8a. Lap and loop the headband core adjacent to the last packing.

8b, 8c. Pack the core clockwise to the center of the second section. Proceed inside the section to anchor.

8d, 8e. Exit forward of cord 1. Reverse direction to lap it. Proceed to head. Lap and loop the end core. Form the spine bead by proceeding horizontally, backward across, and in front of the edge of the section to form the spine bead.

8f. Loop thread 8a and 8c. Advance beyond the packing. This forms the second bead for this packing, on the other side of the end core.

9a, 9b. Lap and loop the endband core. Pack clockwise to the center of the third section.

9c. Proceed inside the section to anchor. Exit forward of cord 1.

9d, 9e. Reverse direction to lap cord 1. Proceed to head. Lap and loop the end core. Proceed horizontally, backward across, and in front of the edge of the section to form the spine bead.

9f. Loop thread 9c and 9d. Advance beyond the packing. This forms the second bead for this packing, on the other side of the end core.

The Added Integrated Endband

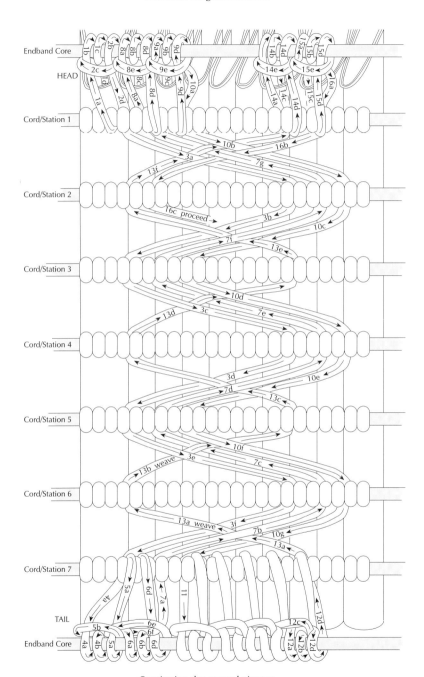

Continuing the second zig zag

The second zig zag weaves through the first for strength.

10a Proceed to cord 1, passing under the end core, so that you do not lap it. Link under cord 1, between the third and fourth sections.

10b. Angle to cord 2. Link under between the ninth and tenth sections.

10c-10g. Continue to zig zag on the spine, towards the tail, linking at each higher numbered cord. The odd-numbered cords are linked between the third and fourth sections. The even-numbered cords are linked between the ninth and tenth sections. With step 10g, cord 7 is linked.

This completes half of the zig zag design on the spine. The other half of the zig zag is a mirror image of this. It starts at the tail between sections 7 and 8, alternated by linking between 1 and 2.

11. To get to the starting point of the zig zag, continue to pack and bead the tailband: Pack to the center of each section. Anchor and form the beads. Repeat until you anchor inside the eighth section.

12a, b. Exit section 8 at the tail. Lap and loop the tailband core. Pack.

12c. Form the spine bead, looping thread 12a. Advance beyond the packing to form the bead on the tail edge.

12d. Lap and loop the end core. Proceed to cord 7. Link under between sections 7 and 8.

13a. The second zig zag now begins. The odd-numbered cords are linked between the seventh and eighth sections. The even-numbered cords link between the first and second sections. As you cross the threads from the first zig zag, weave in and out to secure the long stitches on the spine. Proceeding to cord 6, go over, under, over. Alternate by going under, over, under, when proceeding to cord 5. Proceed in this manner. Cord 1 is linked between the seventh and eighth sections with step 13f.

14a, 14b. Lap and loop the end core. Pack to center of eighth section.

14c, 14d. Proceed inside the eighth section. Exit forward at station 1. Reverse direction, passing cord 1. Lap and loop headband core.

14e. Form the spine bead by proceeding horizontally, backward across, and in front of the edge of the section to form the spine bead. Loop threads 14a and 14c.

14f. Advance beyond packing to form the second bead.

15. Proceed on the spine. Lap and loop the end core. Pack, anchor and form the beads.

16. Proceed to cord 1. Link under between sections 8 and 9. Zig zag, linking the even-numbered cords between sections 2 and 3. The odd-numbered cords are linked between 8 and 9.

17, 18. Form the tailband for sections 9 and 10. Proceed on the spine to link cord 7 between sections 9 and 10. See diagram on page 126.

19. Complete the zig zag across the spine by linking the odd-numbered sections between sections 9 and 10, and the even-numbered cords between sections 3 and 4. The zig zag ends with step 19f linking under cord 1 between the ninth and tenth sections.
20. Lap and loop the end core. Pack to the center of the tenth section. Anchor inside the section. Exit forward of cord 1. Reverse direction. Lap and loop the end core. Form the beads and tie-off inside section.

The remainder of the headband must be sewn. Start inside the fourth section. Exit forward of cord 1. Reverse direction. Lap and loop the end core. Pack to center of the fourth section. Proceed inside. Tie-off at station 1 to anchor. Exit and bead as usual. Continue sewing the headband for sections 5 through 7. Tie-off inside the seventh section.

COLOR VARIATIONS: Endbands present an opportunity to introduce color(s). You can match, complement, or contrast with colors in the threads, paper stock, decorative papers or leathers.

With traditional sewing of endbands, sometimes two or three threads are used to form the packing and beading. In sewing this integrated endband, the packing and beading could introduce a second, and even a third color. The additional color thread(s) could be carried along the endband cores, leaving the zig zag monochromatic .Or, periodically, the additional color(s) could proceed on the spine, while the original color is carried along the endband core. You would have to play with the procedure.

This is not an example of the single endband sewing, but it is related. The book was first sewn with a basic RAISED SUPPORT SEWING, page 35. Each cord is then packed and beaded with embroidery thread. The sewing on each cord starts inside the first section, and is tied-off inside the final one. The bead alternates on each side of the cord, as it advances a section, to start the packing between the following two sections. The embroidery packing covers areas of the bare cord, creating a solid pack, but allowing the original raised cord thread to appear intermittently across the spine. It really dresses up a basic sewing.

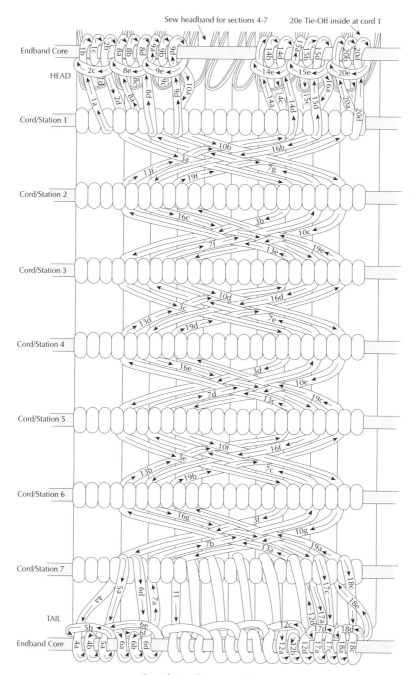

Completing the second zig zag.

Now sew the headband for sections 4 through 7.

VARIATIONS OF THE INTEGRATED ENDBAND

- Rather than the first sewing being Packed Raised Cords, sew as a Basic Raised Cord. This leaves the cord exposed across the spine. The second sewing, the Integrated Endband is sewn in a contrasting color. In addition to linking the zig zag, pack the cord *once* before angling to the next cord. This holds the zig zag design tightly in place. In addition, it gives a lovely spine: the cords are intermittently bare, with "stripes" of the sparsely spaced packing in alternating colors from each sewing. I suggest the same weight thread for both sewings. See: *Dying The Cords Or Thread,* page 49.

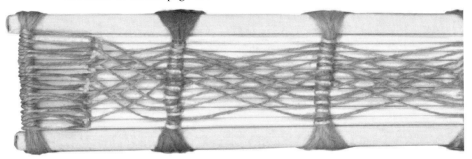

Prototype for Variation of the INTEGRATED ENDBAND: The plain appearance of the BASIC RAISED SUPPORT SEWING is salvaged by packing when linking the zig zags with the second sewing of the INTEGRATED ENDBAND. The second sewing is a different color. This enables the resulting solid packed cords to be patterned in alternating colors. Or, you could have one pack of the first sewing, then three of the second, to fill in as a solid pack, in a 3:1 pattern across each cord.

- A third variation would be to sew a Basic Raised Support Sewing. Then, the second sewing, Integrated Endband is sewn in a contrasting color. In addition to linking the zig zag, pack the cord *as many times as necessary* to completely cover the cord between the first and second sections. Then, angle to the next cord. Again, pack as many times as necessary to fill in the space between the packing. After all the zig zags of your design are completed, you may want to go in an pack any bare spaces on each of the cords. This will yield cords predominately packed in the color of the endbands, punctuated by a single loop denoting each section from the raised support sewing.
- A fourth variation is similar to the previous. In the first sewing, pack more than once, but only enough to cover 50% of the cord across the width of each section. With the second sewing, when linking with the zig zag, pack to fill the remaining bare spaces on the cords. This will yield alternating colors of a solid pack across each cord. ...I haven't tried it yet, but it *will* be stunning!

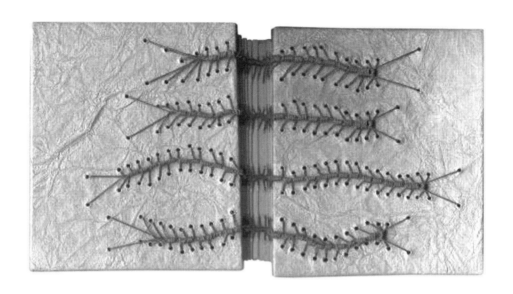

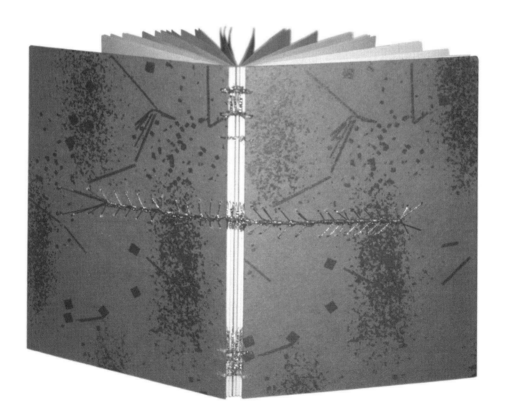

OPPOSITE PAGE, TOP:
Kathy Wyatt Thiele, untitled Caterpillar
sewing with across the spine Coptic
sewing at the head and tail. November
11, 2001. 12.6 x 16.5 cm.

Kathy learned the sewing from reading
Exposed Spine Sewings. She emailed an
enclosure shown here.

OPPOSITE PAGE, BOTTOM:
Penny Carey–Wells, untitled, 2000.
Caterpillar sewing, paper, metallic
thread. 20 x 15 cm.

LEFT:
Adéle Outteridge, *Long, Thin
Caterpillar Book,* 2000, one-of-a-kind.
6 x 31 cm.

Penny and Adéle made their books at
TAFTA/Textile Fibre Forum workshop,
April 2000, in Mittagong, Australia.
Scott McCarney and I were guest
teachers.

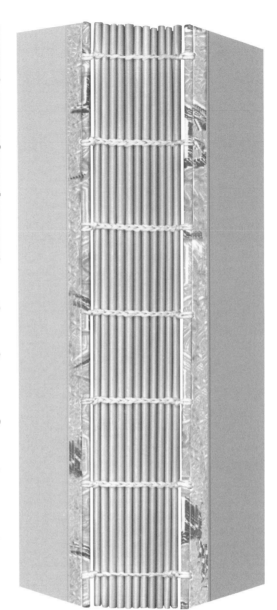

On the left is a "Coptic" single needle Link Sewing along the spine, which utilizes a true kettle stitch, with a lap and slip link stitch that is difficult to sew. For
the sewing path, see the diagram at the bottom of page 29. Cut commercial
paper sections alternate with hand–made deckled paper.

On the right is another unsupported sewing. This "Coptic" single needle Link
Sewing along the spine uses the ideal true kettle stitch to change-over at the
head and the tail. All other stations use a lap/link stitch, sewn onto vellum
guards. The sewing path is diagrammed at the top of page 30.

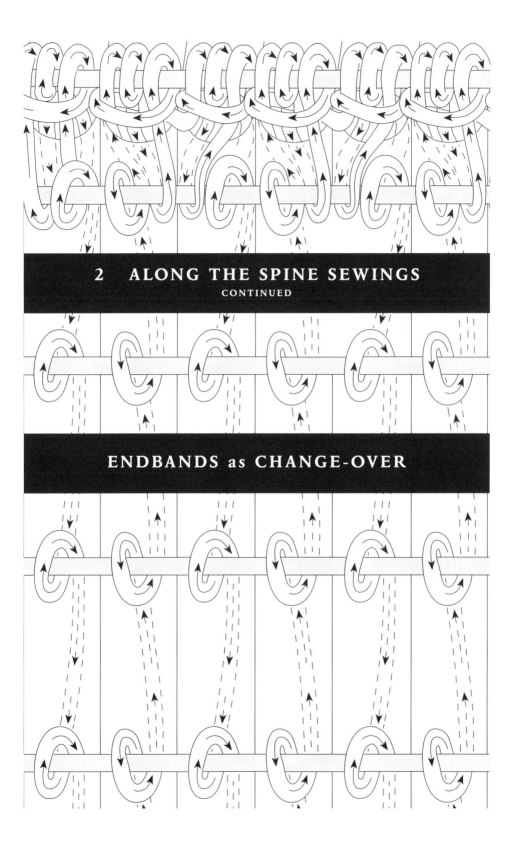

2   ALONG THE SPINE SEWINGS
CONTINUED

ENDBANDS as CHANGE-OVER

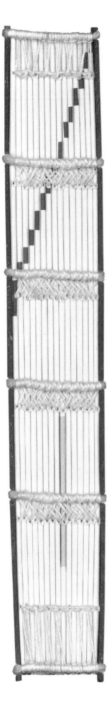

Left: PACKED CORDS *With Integrated Endbands And Ties-Down*. The *ties-down* are the stitches on the spine that extend in from the endband to the next station to anchor the endband. See page 149. On the left, the ties-down anchor into the section. On the right, they link under a support. Additional stations for the sewing on the left allow for angled threads to form a decorative *X* pattern extending from the packed supports.

Right: 2–ply thread raised sewing. It is sewn PACKED CORDS *With Integrated Endbands*. See page 141. The middle supports are sewn with the 2–SECTION *X*. See page 65.

ENDBANDS AS CHANGE-OVER

In the late 15th century, the endbands were often sewn as part of the raised support sewing. However, this practice was abruptly discontinued about 1530 when the result of wear became obvious: sliding the book on and off the shelf wears the leather on the tail. When the threads in the tail-band eventually break, the entire sewing of the book is compromised—a major design flaw. Be forewarned of this literal Achilles' heel.

HEAD and TAIL as CHANGE-OVER: With this caution, I present these non-adhesive raised support sewing variations to you. It is not that dangerous a structure. If your book will have little use, or be stored in a book box, rather than directly on the shelf, it should enjoy a long life. This binding is no less practical than *Long Stitch through Slotted Wrapper Cover*, and the other various link/stitch bindings or the *Buttonhole Stitch* which I described in *Non-Adhesive Binding*, Volume I. In those instances, as well, in sewing back and forth along the sections, the thread wraps around the head and tail to change directions for sewing the following section.

The raised support sewings in this chapter do not employ a kettle stitch as the means of changing the direction of sewing. Instead, an extra support is placed at the head, or slightly beyond, and another support at the tail. These two supports are not sewn as raised supports, but as endbands.

The endbands are sewn as an integral part of the single sewing across the spine. The headband is started, then the first section is sewn raised supports, except for the final support. It is sewn as the tailband. The second section is added. More of the tailband is sewn, and the second section raised support sewing proceeds to the head. At the end of the second section, the headband is continued. The third section is placed on. The headband is sewn for that section, before changing direction in sewing the third section.

In diagramming bindings with endbands as change-over, I assign the supports at the head and the tail a sewing station number. They are not pierced sewing stations, but what I refer to as *passive stations*. Numbering this position at the head, and at the tail, makes for easy reference in the drawn illustrations.

In the previous sewing, the Integrated Endband, *Added to a Raised Support Sewing*, page 115, the endband was sewn separately, *after* the sections were sewn. In the next chapter, Endbands As Change-Over, the sewings described use a single sewing: A single thread, sews the endbands simultaneously while proceeding with a raised support sewing.

BASIC RAISED SUPPORTS
With Integrated Endbands

PREPARATION

Sewing Stations: There are seven sewing stations. Five are pierced stations for raised supports. Two additional "stations", which are *not* pierced, are the supports at the head and tail for the endbands. The support (cord) at the head is referred to as station 1, followed by the five pierced stations with supports. The cord at the tail is called station 7.

Position the cords at stations 1 and 7 slightly beyond the book block, so that the endbands are not flush with the head and tail.

Packing: Supports at the head and the tail are packed solidly, as these are the endbands. The supports at the other stations can be looped once, or packed solidly, as described on page 141.

This is an example of the Basic Raised Supports *with Integrated Endbands.* Navy and cream threads were plied as supports, to be tied into the boards. Since the middle supports are not a solid pack, a dotting of the colors of the supports can be seen on the spine.

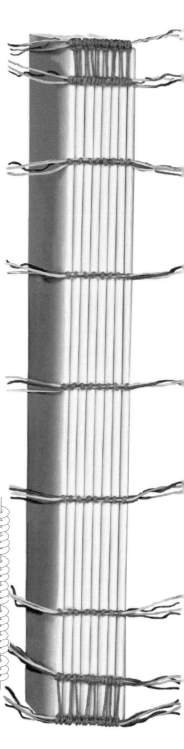

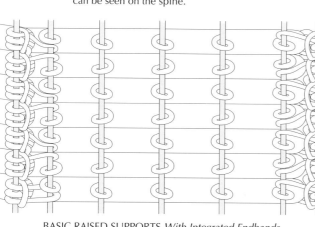

BASIC RAISED SUPPORTS *With Integrated Endbands*
This is a single, continuous raised support sewing with endbands as change-over.

SEWING PROCEDURE

Starting the First Section and Endband:

1a. Set on the first section to be sewn. Start on the inside of the first section. Exit station 2 towards the tail, leaving two inches of thread on the inside. Lap cord 2. Lap, loop cord 1.

1b. Pack once or twice clockwise.

1c. Proceed inside. Tie-off at station 2.

1d, 1e. Proceed to the head. Lap, loop cord 1.

1f. Drop and slip under threads 1a, 1d and 1c to form the spine bead.

1g. Climb, proceed inside the section. Exit forward at station 2.

2. Lap and loop cord 2 and enter on the back side of the cord, if the headband is the width of the first section.

*Optional, for step 2, if the headband needs to be expanded to the width of the first section: Lap cord 2. Lap and loop cord 1. Pack. Drop and slip under thread 2a to form the bead. Proceed inside the section. Exit forward at station 2. Loop cord 2. Enter on the back side.

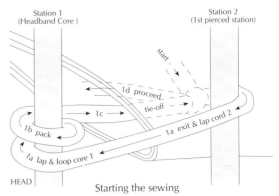

Starting the sewing

I generally pack once, (not shown) after exiting at station 2 (step 1a), prior to proceeding to the core at the head. Step 1c ties-off at station 2.

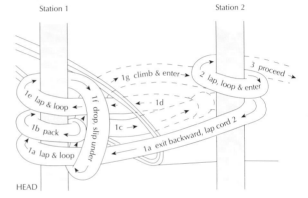

Forming the headband for the first section

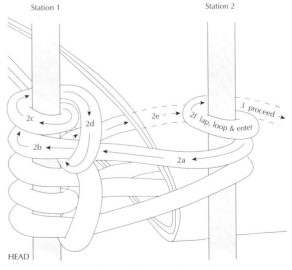

Optional packing and beading for headband if a thicker section or thinner thread is used

Sewing Supports 3 -5:
Sewing all sections at stations 3 through 5 will proceed in the usual manner of
sewing raised supports. See:
Basic Raised Support Sewing,
page 35.

However, if you wish all
supports to be solidly
packed, see *Raised Cords
With Packing,* page 43, as
well as *Packed Cords With
Endbands,* page 141.

Instead of a kettle stitch, the
supports 1 and 7 use the
endbands as change-over.

Anchoring of the headband
is by looping the support at
station 2. Similarly, the tailband is anchored to the support at station 6.

Detailed descriptions of
how the endbands are
anchored to the supports at
stations 2 and 6 are illustrated on page 137, 138
and 139.

Completing the First Section, Starting the Second:

10   Exit forward at station
        6. Loop cord 6, and
        enter station 6 on the
        back side.
11a. Proceed on the inside
        to the tail. Lap and loop
        cord 7.
11b. Pack once or twice
counter-clockwise.
11c. Proceed inside the first
section at the tail to anchor
the tailband.

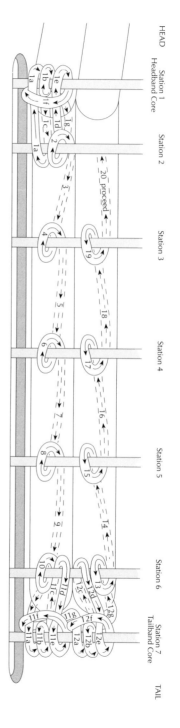

Starting the sewing of the BASIC RAISED SUPPORTS *With Integrated Endbands*
This diagram utilizes the BASIC RAISED SUPPORTS Sewing for the middle stations. See page 35.

11d, 11e. Exit forward at station 6. Lap cord 6. Proceed to the tail. Lap and loop cord number 7.

11f. Drop, slip under threads 11a and 11c to form the bead.

11g, 12a. Climb. Lap and loop cord 7, tangent to thread 11e.

12b. Pack counter-clockwise once or twice.

12c. Proceed on the inside the second section to anchor the tailband.

12d, 12e. Exit forward at station 6. Lap cord 6. Proceed to the tail. Lap and loop cord number 7.

12f. Drop and slip under threads 11a and 11c to form the bead.

12g. Climb and enter the second section at the tail. This anchors the tailband.

13. Exit forward at station 6. Loop and enter station 6 on the back side of the support.

14. Proceed on the inside towards the head.

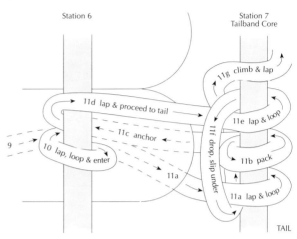

Starting the tailband for an odd-numbered section

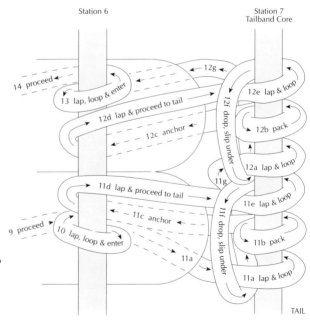

Change-Over at the tail

Forming the tailband from an odd to an even-numbered section.
Step 11a marks the change in direction of packing from the odd, to the next even-numbered section.

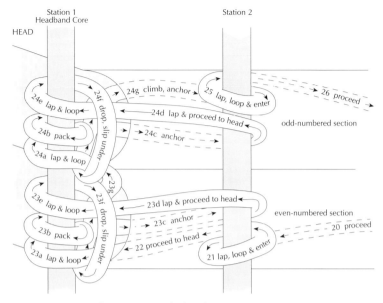

Change-Over at the head

Forming the headband from an even to an odd-numbered section.
Step 23a marks the change in direction of packing from the even, to the
next odd-numbered section.

Continuing the Sewing: The sewing continues in the manner of sewing basic Raised Supports or Raised Cords With Packing, for the even-numbered sections, from station 5 towards the head to station 3.

At the head, the change-over from sewing the even to the odd-numbered section is always accomplished in the same manner. This creates a uniform pattern of packing and beading the headband. See diagram above for sewing stations 2 and 1 of the even-numbered section, then proceeding to sew stations 1 and 2 of the following odd-numbered section.

Stations 3 through 5 of the odd-numbered section is then sewn

At the tail, the change-over from sewing the odd to the even-numbered section is accomplished in the same manner. See diagram above for sewing stations 6 and 7 of the odd-numbered section, then proceeding to sew stations 7 and 6 of the following odd-numbered section.

The following page gives the complete diagram of this sewing. After completing the endband for the final section, proceed inside the head, or the tail, depending upon the number of sections sewn. Tie-off on the inside at the next station.

Change-Over at the Head and the Tail:
The tailband is the change-over from sewing an odd, to an even-numbered section. It is marked by reversing the direction of the packing for the final cord of the odd-numbered section, and for all in the following even-numbered section, except cord 1. Likewise, the cord at the head marks the point at which packing reverses direction. With cord 1 on each even-numbered section, packing becomes clockwise. It continues to be clockwise for all stations of the following odd-numbered section, except the cord at the tail. That cord marks the change-over to counter-clockwise packing.

Two-Sided Beading: Just as with the Single Endband Added To Raised Supports, page 115, endbands in this sewing have two-sided beads: the drop creates the *spine bead,* always labeled as step *f.* The bead facing the foredge is formed by slipping under and climbing. It is referred to as the *inside bead,* and is always labeled as step *g* in the diagrams on page 135 through 154.

Improvised Sewing: As a general rule, I think that in an exposed spine sewing, packed cords present a lovelier spine than a basic raised support sewing. To decorate the spine of this sewing, I might add an additional non-structural sewing to the spine. This could be a second color improvised packing, and/or linking, along and across the cords. The supports might eventually be solidly packed. If not, I would dye them a different color(s) prior to starting the sewing. —What can you come up with?

If you were to solidly pack the BASIC RAISED SUPPORTS *With Integrated Endbands,* it would be the next sewing described, PACKED CORDS *With Integrated Endbands,* which is shown on the right. See Page 141.

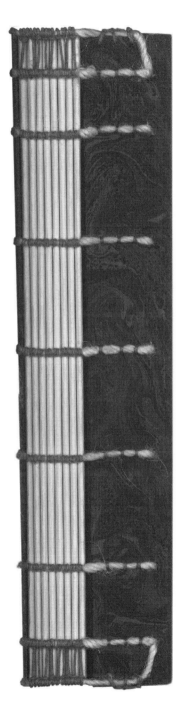

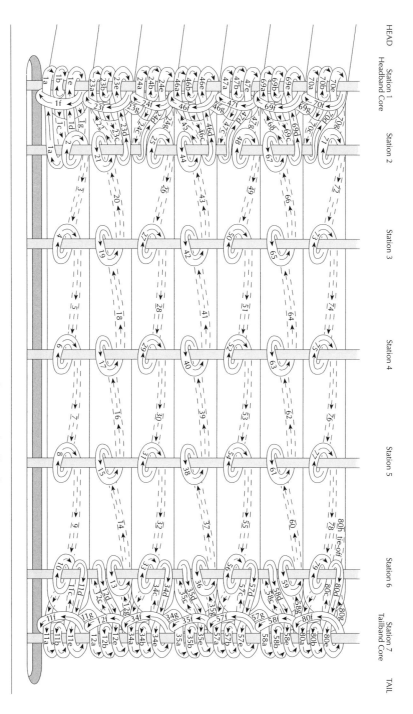

BASIC RAISED SUPPORTS *With Integrated Endbands*

PACKED CORDS *With Integrated Endbands*

This sewing is a variation of the previously described, Raised Supports *With Integrated Endbands,* page 134. In this sewing, raised cords are used at stations 3 through 5, so that those supports can be easily solidly packed. This makes for a nicer looking spine, as well as a structurally superior one.

PREPARATION

Set-up is the same as for the previous sewing. There are seven stations. Five are pierced stations, plus the unpierced stations, which are the cords at the head and tail. These are for the change-over, by means of sewing the endbands to proceed from section to section.

Detail of PACKED CORDS *With Integrated Endbands.* See page 139 for digital scan of entire spine. The endbands are part of the continuous sewing, and make a lovely means to change-over. Square of the boards must extend beyond endbands to avoid wear, fraying the tailband, compromising the entire sewing.

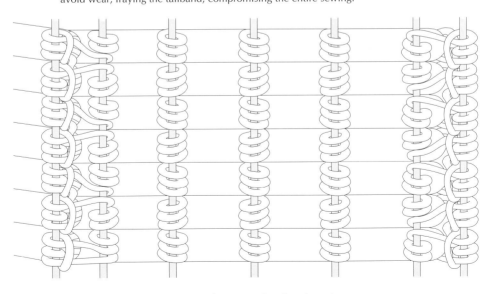

PACKED CORDS *With Integrated Endbands* to change-over

SEWING PROCEDURE

1a. Start on the inside. Exit forward at station 2. Reverse direction, and lap the headband core 2. Proceed to the head. Lap and loop the core.

1b. Pack once clockwise.

1c. Proceed inside the section. Tie-off at station 2.

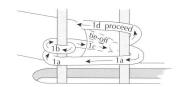

Step 1c ties-off at station 2.

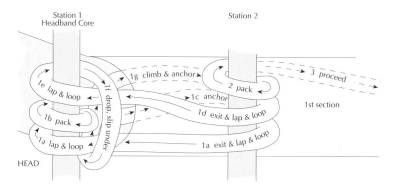

Starting the sewing
Forming the headband for the first section

1d. Exit forward at station 2. Lap cord 2. Proceed to the head.

1e. Lap the core at station 1.

1f. Drop and slip under threads 1d and 1a to form the spine bead.

1g. Climb. Proceed inside the section to anchor.

2. Exit forward at station 2. Loop and enter station 2 on the back side of the cord.

3. Proceed to station 3. Exit.

Sewing Supports 3 -5: Stations 3-5 for all sections are sewn in the usual manner of raised cords which are solidly packed. See: *Raised Cords With Packing,* page 43, See: *Two-Sided Beading,* page 139.

To turn-around and to *change-over* at the tail see the description at the top of the following page. The following even-numbered section is sewn with pack cords. At the head, to change-over to the next odd-numbered section, see diagram at the bottom of page 143.

Endbands as Change-Over

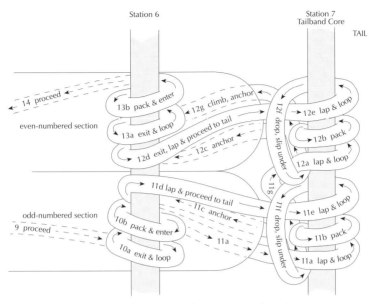

Change-Over at the tail

Forming the tailband from an odd to an even-numbered section
Step 11a marks the change in direction of packing
from the odd, to the next even-numbered section.

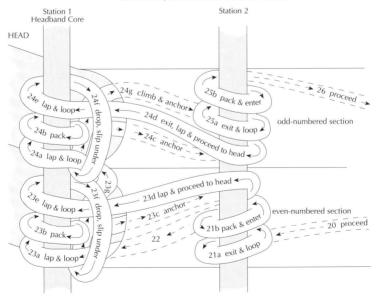

Change-Over at the head

Forming the headband from an even to an odd-numbered section
Step 23a marks the change in direction of packing
from the even, to the next odd-numbered section.

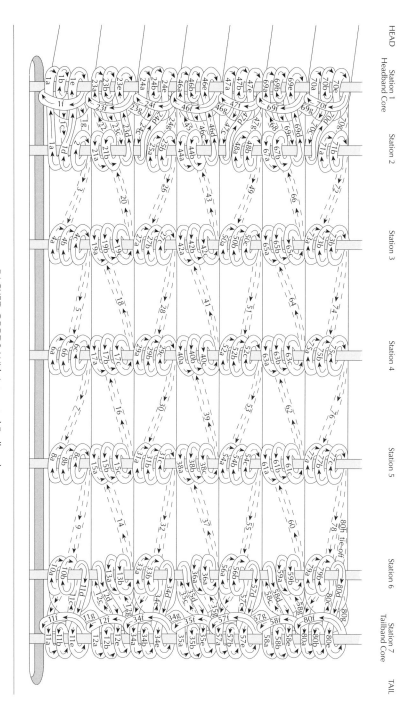

PACKED CORDS *With Integrated Endbands*

Pamela Spitzmueller, *Another Copper Book,* 1992. Copper book pleat-cover, copper supports and sewn with copper wire. 11.3 x 20.4 cm.

PACKED & BEADED CORDS
With Integrated Endbands

This sewing is a variation of the previously described, *Packed Cords With Integrated Endbands,* page 141. The difference is that in this sewing, the cords at stations 3 through 5 are not only solidly packed, they are linked. This suggests beading along the top and bottom of cord 3 through 5, perpendicular to the packing.

To sew cords 3 through 5, refer to the sewing *Loop Packed, Packed Climb With Bead,* page 81. The final section has no linking at cords 3 through 5. This is for two reasons: to appear symmetrical to the first section, and to secure the links at the hinge-fold.

To start the sewing, and to sew the stations at supports 1, 2, 6 and 7. Refer to Packed Cords *With Integrated Endbands,* page 141.

With all the linking, you might want to use a thinner thread so that the spine is not swelled larger than at the foredge.

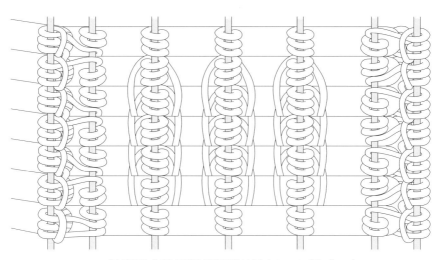

PACKED *&* BEADED CORDS *With Integrated Endbands*

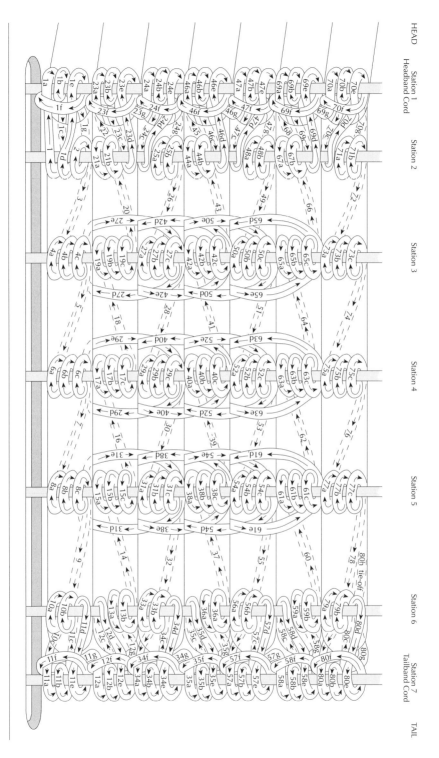

PACKED & BEADED CORDS *With Integrated Endbands*

Station 1
Headband Cord

Station 2

Station 3

Station 4

Station 5

Station 6

Station 7
Tailband Cord

TAIL

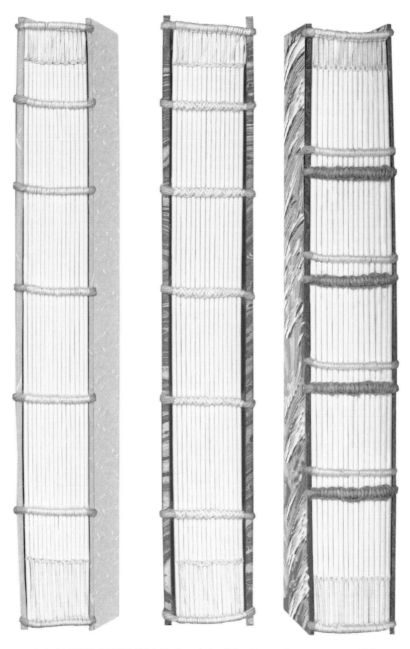

Left: PACKED CORDS *With Endbands And Ties-Down.* See page 149. Middle: PACKED CORDS *With Integrated Endbands And Ties-Down,* with additional 2–SECTION *X* sewing, described on page 65. Right: First sewing is PACKED CORDS *With Integrated Endbands And Ties-Down.* A second sewing was added, using a different color thread. It is LOOP PACKED, PACKED CLIMB WITH BEAD. See page 81.

PACKED CORDS
With Integrated Endbands And Ties-Down

This sewing is a variation of the previously described, *Packed Cords With Endbands,* page 141. The difference is that in this sewing the ties-down anchor into the section, at stations 2 and 8, rather than linking under a support. A kettle station, but not a kettle stitch, is implied: Station 2 is placed in from the head approximately ⅜" to ½". Station 8 should be placed about ½" to ¾" in from the tail.

TIE-DOWN: A *tie-down* is the anchor stitch which extends from the end-band core to the next station in on the spine, with or without a support. In this sewing, neither station 2 or 8 are for supports, as in all the previous sewings in this chapter which use endbands to change-over. See the digital scans on the facing page. See page 132 to compare a sewing with ties-down that link under a support, and one that anchors without a support.

Ties-down can be explored as an element of design— reminiscent of traditionally sewn separate headband and tailband which anchor under the kettle stitch, but then are hidden when the spine is covered.

PREPARATION
Sewing Stations: There are nine sewing stations. Five pierced stations are for cords. Two additional stations, without cords, are placed ½ to ¾" in from the head and tail. These are to anchor the tie-down. This makes a total of seven pierced stations. The two non-pierced stations simply denote the position of cores for the head and tailbands.

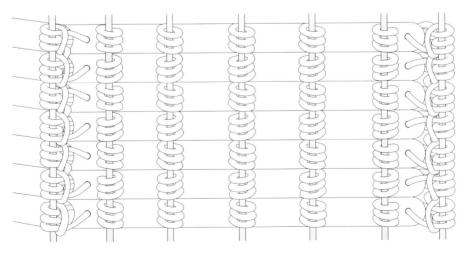

PACKED CORDS *With Integrated Endbands And Ties-Down*

The core at the head is station 1. Station 2 is in from the head about ½".
Stations 3 through 7 are at the cords along the length of the spine. Station
8 is about ¾" in from the tail. The core at the tail is station 9.

You may want to position the cores at stations 1 and 9 slightly beyond the
book block, so that the endbands are not flush with the head and tail.
Make sure the boards extend beyond the endbands to protect them.
Otherwise, shelf-wear could fray the tailband and compromise the entire
sewing.

SEWING PROCEDURE

1a-1e. Start on the inside of the first section to be sewn. Exit station 2,
towards the head, leaving two inches of thread on the inside. Lap and
loop the core, station 1. Pack clockwise to the height of the section.

1f. Drop and slip under thread 1b to form the spine-bead.

1g. Climb to form the inside bead. See: *Two-Sided Beading,* page 139.
Proceed inside to station 2. Tie-off with the dangling thread.

2a. Proceed on the inside. Exit forward at station 3.

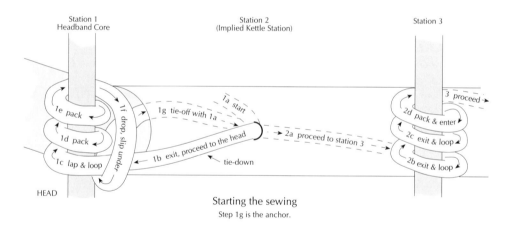

Starting the sewing
Step 1g is the anchor.

Sewing at Stations 3-7: Exit forward. Pack *clockwise* the same number of
revolutions as at the headband core, station 1. Enter on the back side of
the cord. Proceed to the next station. For all sections, stations 3 through 7
will be sewn the same as for *Raised Cords With Packing.* See page 43. Exit
station 8; proceed to the tail.

Sewing the Tailband: The tailband, station 9, is to change-over from
sewing an odd, to an even-numbered section. It is marked by reversing the
direction of the packing to *counter-clockwise* for the final station of this
odd-numbered section, and, for all stations of the following even-numbered section, except for core at station 1.

Endbands as Change-Over

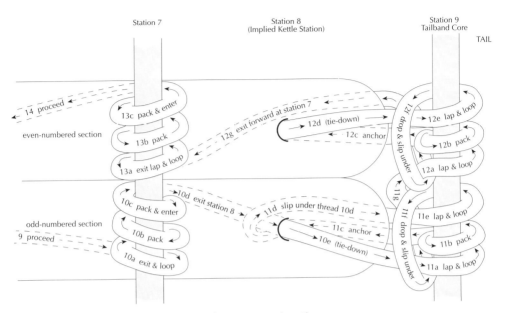

Change-over at the tail

Forming the tailband from an odd to an even-numbered section.
Step 11a marks the change in direction of packing from the odd, to the next even-numbered section.
Step 11c slips under 10d, so that the anchor will not tear out.

The diagram above, for sewing stations 7-9 of the first, and stations 9-7 of the second section serves as the example for the changeover each time at the tail:

10c, 10e Pack clockwise and enter. Exit station 8. Proceed to the tail.

11a, 11b. Lap and loop the core at the tail. Pack counter-clockwise.

11c. Enter the section. Proceed to station 8, but do not exit.

11d. Slip under the thread at station 8 (thread 10d) to lock the stitch. Proceed inside the section to the tail. This anchors the tailband and assures the stitch will not tear out.

11e. Lap the core at station 9. This should make the number of packings at the tail the same as at the head, as well as at stations 3 through 7.

11f. Drop, slip under threads 10e, 11c and 11d to form the spine-bead.

11g. Place the next section into position. Climb. Lap the tailband core.

12a. Loop the core. Make sure the thread is tangent to thread 11e.

12b. Pack counter-clockwise.

12c, 12d, 12e. Enter the section. Proceed to station 8. Exit. Proceed on the spine to the tail. Lap and loop the tailband core.

12f. Drop, slip under threads 11g, 12c and 12d to form the spine-bead.

12g. Climb. Proceed inside. Exit forward at station 7.

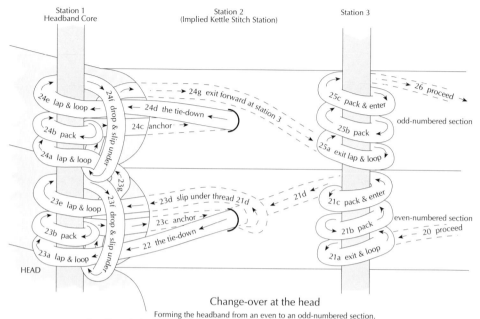

Station 1
Headband Core

Station 2
(Implied Kettle Stitch Station)

Station 3

Change-over at the head

Forming the headband from an even to an odd-numbered section.
Step 23a marks the change in direction of packing from the even, to the next odd-numbered section.
Step 23c slips under 21d, so that the anchor will not tear out.

Continue on towards the head, exiting forward at each successive station and packing counter-clockwise, the same number of times.

21a, 21b, 21c. Exit station 3, pack and enter.

21d. Exit station 2.

22. Proceed to the head.

23a. Lap and loop the core at station 1, in a *clockwise* motion, tangent to the previous packing of the headband. This marks the change-over.

23b, 23c. Pack. Enter the section, proceed to station 2, but do not exit.

23d. Slip under the thread at station 2 (thread 21d) to lock the stitch. Proceed inside the section to the head. This anchors the tailband and assures the stitch will not tear out.

23e, 23f. Lap the core at station 1. Drop and slip under threads 22, 23c and 23d. This forms the spine-bead. Place next section into position.

23g, 24a. Climb to form inside bead. Lap and loop the core. Make sure the thread is tangent to thread 23e.

24b, 24c Pack counter-clockwise. Enter the section. Proceed to station 8.

24d, 24e. Exit. Proceed on the spine to the head. Lap and loop the core.

24f. Drop, slip under threads 23g, 24c and 24d to form the spine-bead.

24g. Climb. Proceed inside. Exit forward at station 3.

Sewing the Remaining Stations:
Sew the odd-numbered sec-
tions the same as the first section. Sew the even-numbered
sections in the same manner as
the second.

After completing the final section, sew the endband for that
section. pack, drop, slip under
the threads. Enter the same section. Tie off at the following
station on the inside by hook-
ing under the stitch, then taking the needle through the
loop that is formed. Pull tightly. Hook under the stich a second time, and take the needle
though the newly formed loop
and, again, pull tightly.

The 2–Needle COPTIC SEWING II
on the right is sewn across the
spine. Three colors of thread are
used at paired stations at the head
and the tail: Sections 1, 4, 7 and
10 were sewn with the first color.
Sections 2, 5, 8 and 11 were sewn
with the second. Sections 3, 6, 9
and 12 were sewn with the third
color.

All the sections for the middle stations are sewn with a single color.
Sewing across the spine required
16 needles.

After the sewing was completed,
separate endbands were sewn,
using one of the colors in the first
sewing.

For a picture of the 2–Needle
COPTIC SEWING II sewn with
two colors, see page 241.

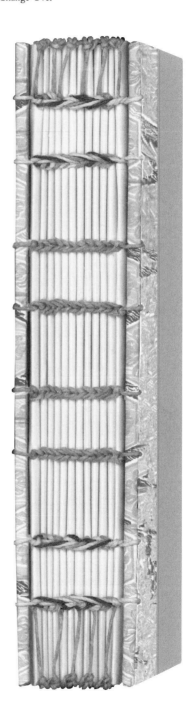

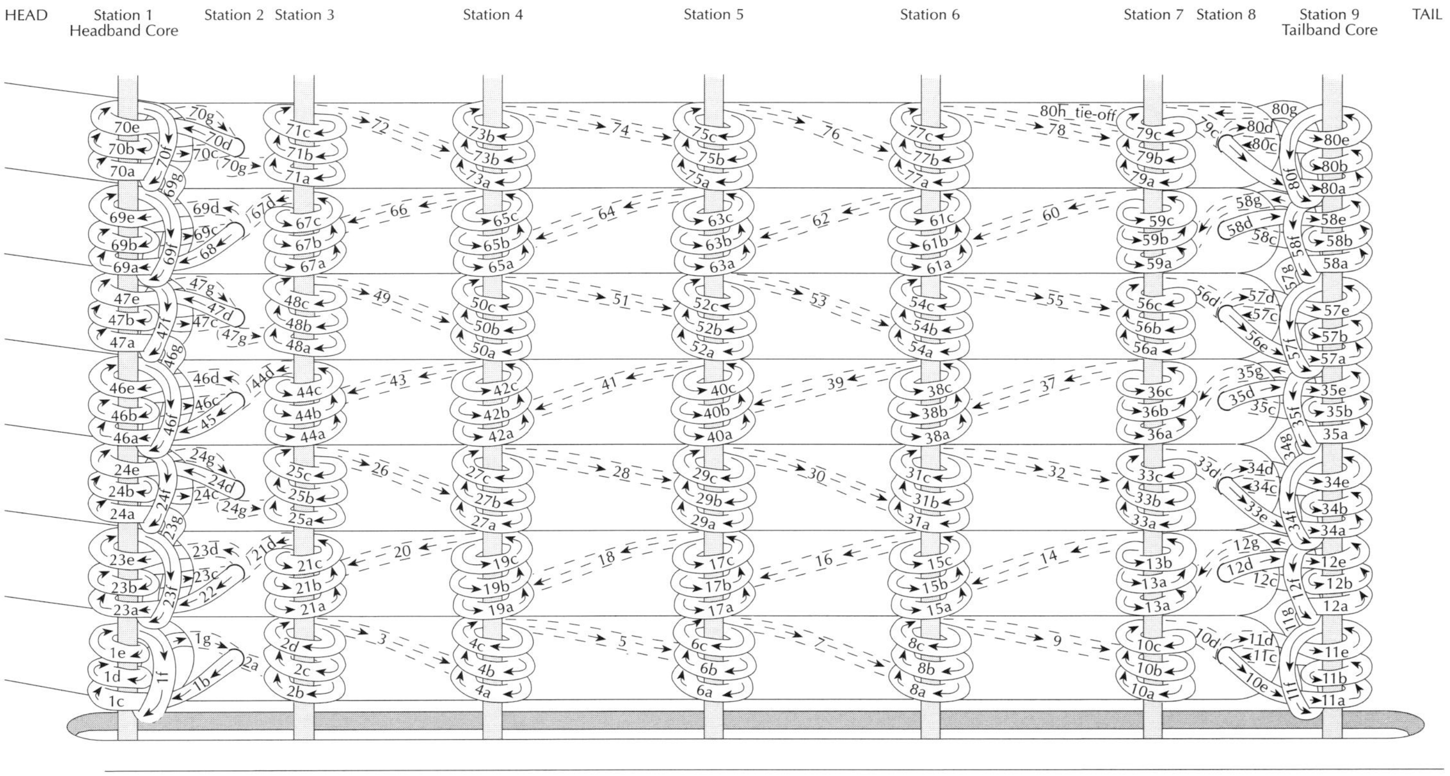
HEAD
Station 1
Headband Core
Station 2
Station 3
Station 4
Station 5
Station 6
Station 7
Station 8
Station 9
Tailband Core
TAIL
80h tie-off

PACKED CORDS *With Integrated Endbands And Ties-Down*

CORDS & CONTINUOUS SUPPORT I
Packed Cords With Integrated Endbands And Ties-Down

Spine-Cover as Support: With raised supports, tapes can contain stations, but cords are never pierced. In the digital scan to the right, the spine-cover serves as a continuous support. It is stitched, *as part of the process* to change-over.

The spine-cover is the hinge, extending onto the boards. It is pasted down. Cords may, or may not be laced through the boards. If you want the book entirely non-adhesive, holes could be drilled into the side-covers, and the spine-cover could be sewn onto the boards.

The previous sewing, Packed Cords *with Integrated Endbands and Ties-Down,* is the taking off point for this sewing. Here, the leather for the spine is slit and held in position on the sewing frame, as the sewing begins. The leather is fixed into position as the sewing proceeds. Access to sewing the raised cords is through the slits in the leather.

Packing bulges the leather; the cords protrude, giving a nice psychological feeling to the look of the spine.

Rather than re-entering at the same cord/station, entry is forward on the spine, as decorative stitches. All stations for the sections are pre-pierced. Slits in the spine-cover are made prior to sewing, but the stations for the stitches on the spine are pierced as you sew. Pierce from the section out through the leather for alignment.

The leather at the head and the tail is not pasted. It is wrapped around the endband core. The sewing which loops (or packs) the endband core holds the leather in position. It could be pasted down, as in the following two sewings described on pages 156 and 158.

The tie-down at the tail extends in from the tail two stations to link the support. See: *Tie-Down,* page 149. In the middle of the tie-down is a station used for linking. It suggests a pearl. This sewing is not diagrammed. It, and the following two sewings, suggests a direction you might wish to pursue.

CORDS & CONTINUOUS SUPPORT I *Packed Cords With Integrated Endbands And Ties-Down.* Quarter leather sewing with the spine-cover as part of the sewing 23.5 x 15.3 x 3.8 cm.

CORDS *&* CONTINUOUS SUPPORT II
Raised Cords With Integrated Endbands

Like the sewing of the book reproduced on page 155, the spine-cover is incorporated into the sewing. In effect, the spine-cover acts *as tapes*. In the following sewing, the book cloth or leather is woven onto the sewing frame. It is a Basic Raised Support Sewing. The book cloth or leather is also sewn *as a continuous support* to change-over. Unlike the sections, do not pre-pierce the leather, but only pierce when you sew, *as you exit* the section. This will insure proper alignment.

Length of the Spine Cloth: The spine-cover for the book on the previous page is slit *across* the spine. In the following, several splits in the leather are made *along* spine. Paste the leather or book cloth around the core at the head, and, at the tail. These two supports represent the endband stations, and must be precisely measured so that they extend slightly from the book block, but less than the boards. All supports, except the head and the tail, are woven through the leather, on the sewing frame prior to tying the supports in position. This results in the cords being alternately hidden beneath, and exposed on top of the leather.

Width of the Spine-Cover: The leather or cloth eventually is attached to the boards. Once the book is sewn, it is removed from the sewing frame.

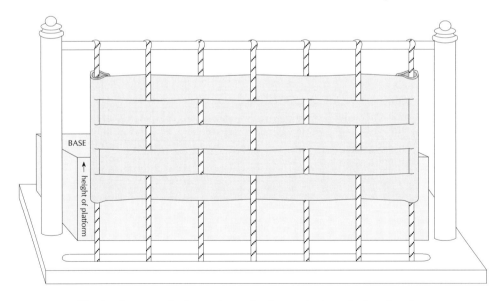

Weaving the quarter leather on the sewing frame prior to a raised cord sewing
Edges of the leather are pasted or stitched around the endband cores.

The extensions of the spine-cover are pasted onto the boards. Minimum width permits the spine-cover to be attach the boards. It might extend completely across the boards for purposes of design.

The cords are not laced through the boards. The raised cord sewing can be limited to the spine, or the sewing can extend the full width of the leather or book cloth, so that the threads continue onto the boards to attach and decorate.

Platform: Do not start the sewing of the sections at the base of the spine-cover.

Place a makeshift platform on the base of the sewing frame, tangent to the supports. Placing the first section to be sewn on the base of the platform positions the sections in the middle of the spine-cover. This keeps the area on either side of the spine free to be pasted onto the boards.

The spine-cover and supports, without sections, can be sewn from the edge up, eventually coming to the base of the plat-form. At that point, sewing of the sections begins.

CORDS & CONTINUOUS SUPPORT II
Quarter leather sewing example of BASIC RAISED CORDS WITH ENDBANDS. This sewing is a variation on the book described on page 155. Here, the leather for the spine was slit in the direction of the spine. Cords on the sewing frame were woven through the leather, prior to tying the cords in posi-tion. This results in the cords being alter-nately hidden underneath, or exposed on top of, the leather.

The raised cord sewing might continue on cords, through the leather, beyond the sec-tions. If so, the cords could not be laced into the boards. The spine-cover would be the means of attachment, and the cords would appear as if sewn through the boards. 23.5 x 15.3 x 3.8 cm.

RAISED CORDS *With Spine-Cover Units*

In this variation of the two previous sewings, the spine-cover does not hide the entire spine. The spine is partially covered with units of cloth or leather.

A strip of leather or book cloth is attached to paired supports. Wrap one edge around one of the supports and paste it down on the underneath side. The opposite edge is wrapped around the other of the paired supports and pasted. Several sets of supports with attached cloth or leather are prepared:

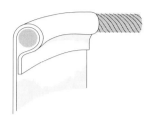

Attaching the unit
to the support

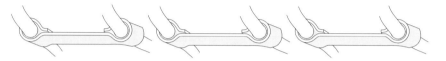

Paired supports with attached leather or book cloth are ready to be strung on a sewing frame. They are sewn as tapes. Height of the units is the depth of the spine, *plus* the overhang, which later will be used to attach the boards. See the digital scans on page 160.

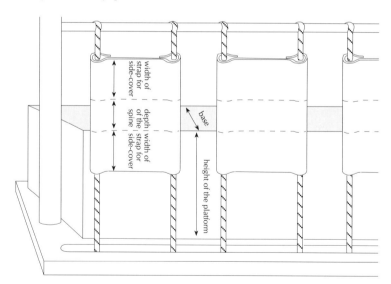

The leather or cloth attached to the supports extends beyond the width of the spine on both sides. It will later be used to attach the boards.

This means that the base of the sewing frame must be built up with a platform. The first section to be sewn is laid on the platform at the proper height on the supports, at the start of the spine.

If you wish to keep the entire process non-adhesive ,sew instead of pasting the spine-cover around the cords. You can hand stitch, or use your sewing machine.

Place a makeshift platform on the sewing frame to raise the point of sewing the sections, so they are centered on the spine-cover. See the illustration below, and at the bottom of the facing page.

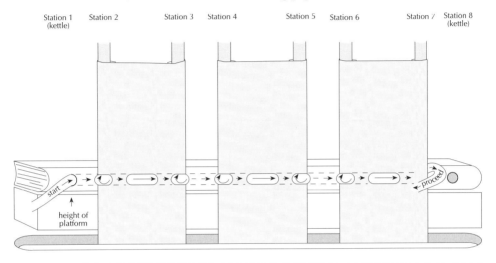

Station 1 (kettle)   Station 2   Station 3   Station 4   Station 5   Station 6   Station 7   Station 8 (kettle)

height of platform

HEAD   TAIL

RAISED CORDS *With Spine-Cover Units*
Sewing the first section

Sewing through the leather or book cloth makes the spine-cover serve as tapes. A pattern of stitches on the covering can be designed prior to sewing, in order to determine the position of the stations.

The spine-cover units are not pre-pierced, but pierced as you sew.

The spine-cover units in the diagrams on these facing pages suggests very little exposed spine. However, the area between the units could be greater. This affords options for sewing/decorating the areas of the exposed sections. There could be a row of stations for linking across the areas the exposed spine. The chain of links would also be functional, holding the sections together in these spaces. See the bottom digital scan on page 160.

In this example, a kettle stitch is used to change-over. If the spine-cover units were placed extending slightly beyond the head and tail, you could climb on the support to change-over.

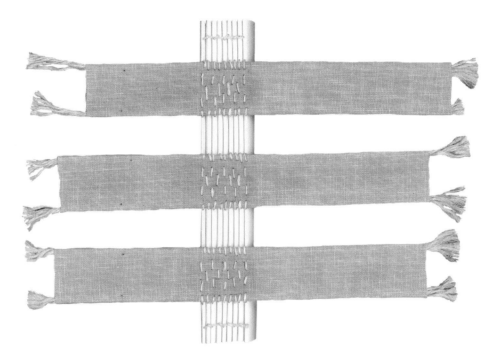

RAISED CORDS *With Spine-Cover Units,* prior to attaching the boards.

Strips of book cloth are glued around raised cord supports, which are then strung to a sewing frame. The book cloth contains sewing stations, using these spine-cover units as a tape sewing, in addition to the raised cords with kettle stitch.

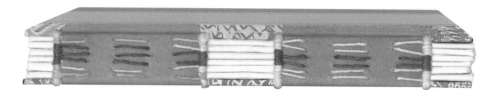

RAISED CORDS *With Spine-Cover Units.* In this example, the raised cords are not attached, but adjacent to the leather spine-cover units, sewn as tapes. Both supports—the cords and the "tapes", are attached to the boards by sewing.

The book was sewn with various scraps of color threads, resulting in a random pattern of color in the stitches and packing. This was not done just because I am frugal; it is part of my aesthetic: It introduces chance into the design, for spontaneity. And, it is a rebellion against a formal approach which does not like to see a single knot inside the book where there was a need to add thread. This book is hand–made, if not hand–crafted.

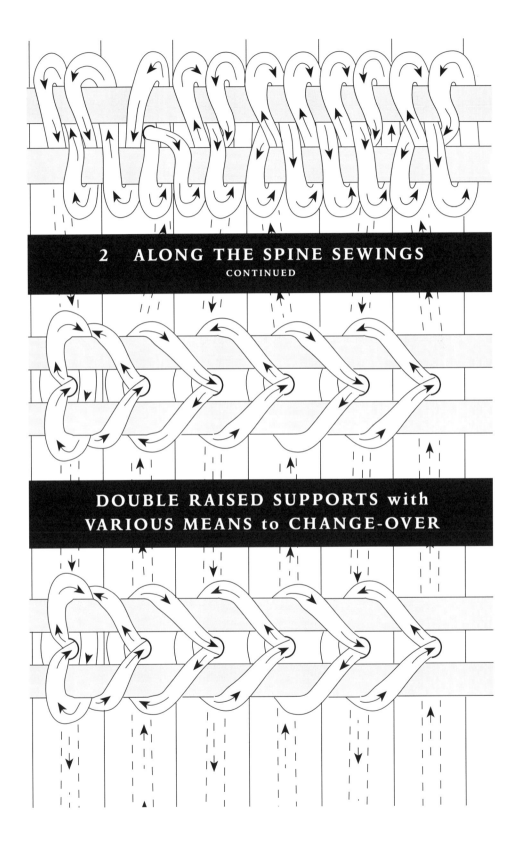

DOUBLE RAISED SUPPORTS with
VARIOUS MEANS to CHANGE-OVER

DOUBLE RAISED SUPPORTS

Volume I only touches on sewing raised cords in passing. I thought that this volume would cover the subject, but, obviously, the next few pages only introduces the possibilities.

Sewing with flat supports offer unique possibilities, impossible with cores. Flat supports can be pierced. The stitching patterns the supports. This perks my attention, and I start to wander. I know I must not venture in that direction, as it is a book in itself. A possible future Volume IV could expand into this area. Although, at this moment, I am a little weary to dream of that endeavor.

My current sewing, and thus my writing, will concentrate on double raised cords. However, most of these sewings could as easily employ flat supports. One reason I choose to begin with double cords is that they are easy to pack solidly. Cords lend themselves to endbands as change-over.

I will diagram double raised support sewings with all the previous means to change-over—kettle stitch, packed single support, the Pack & Weave, and endbands as change-over. In addition, I will diagram "English" Double Raised Cords as change-over. This can be used with any double raised support sewing, as well as with *any* sewing previously diagrammed as means to change-over. It opens a rich new approach to the climb.

It is best to use thick or medium cords when sewing double raised cords. Thread wrapped around two thin cords tends to make the thinner cords to appear as a single cord, unless you sew with very thin thread.

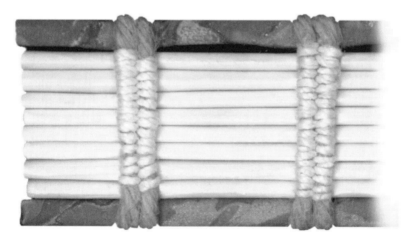

Climbing with a sold pack on double raised supports to change-over. Refer to pages 166, and 170. Compare this to climbing on a single support, page 165.

Pamela Spitzmueller, *Pleasure Studies,* 1992. Sewn on single and double raised supports, with no kettle stitch. Single raised cords are used to change-over. Side-covers are wire mesh. 19 x 12.8 x 10.2 cm.

DOUBLE RAISED SUPPORTS *With Kettle Stitch*

ENGLISH SEWING

In stringing the sewing frame, the double supports are tangent. Both supports share a single pierced station. Upon exiting, each support is looped. The thread re-enters the same station.

Forward Wrap: The route of looping can wrap the forward support first, then the back support, as illustrated on this page. Exit between the two supports. Wrap the forward most support. Bring the needle between the two supports, then wrap the support on the back side of the station. This movement forms a *B* stitch. It insures that you exit forward and enter on the back side, to lessen the stress on the paper. This prevents the tread from tearing out.

It is called the "English" manner of sewing Double Raised Supports, although the Germans and English have both sewn this version, and the so-called "German" sewing on the facing page. The *backward wrap* is preferred by the Germans.

The diagram to the right uses the kettle stitch to climb. The initial tie-off is hidden. See: *Inside Ties-Off,* page 35.

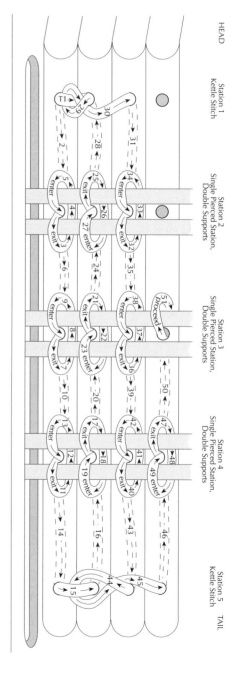

Starting to sew the *English (loop)* DOUBLE RAISED SUPPORTS *With Kettle Stitch*

Exit, loop the forward support, pass behind both, loop the backward support and enter, to form a *B* stitch. (The "German" style wraps the back support first, which also forms a *B* stitch.) The double supports will be tangent. They are illustrated with a gap in order to show the path of the thread.

HEAD

Station 1
Kettle Stitch

Station 2
Single Pierced Station,
Double Supports

Station 3
Single Pierced Station,
Double Supports

Station 4
Single Pierced Station,
Double Supports

Station 5
Kettle Stitch TAIL

DOUBLE RAISED SUPPORTS *With Packed Climb*

GERMAN SEWING

In the diagrams, the double raised supports seem to be strung far apart. They are drawn this way to show the path of the wrapping. In actuality, they will be tangent.

Backward Wrap: I prefer backward wraps. This is the "German" procedure. The exit is out *between* the two supports. By wrapping backwards is meant that instead of wrapping the support that is forward (in the direction in which you are sewing,) wrap the support which the thread has travelled beyond, prior to exiting. Then, slip behind both supports; do not enter. Wrap the forward support, then enter the same station. Just as with the "English" procedure, the thread exits forward, and enters on the back side of the support. This prevents the thread from tearing out.

The climb at the head and the tail is by means of pack cords. See: *Loop Pack With Climbing Pack,* page 75.

NOTE: The double supports are illustrated with a gap between in order to show the path of the thread. In reality, the wrapping of the threads pull the cords tightly together:

Sewing the first two sections of the *German (lap)* DOUBLE RAISED SUPPORTS *With Packed Climb* on single supports.

At stations 5 and 1, exit backward to change direction of the packing, in order to enter the new section on the back side of the support.

Exit and wrap the backward support first. (The "English" style wraps the forward support first.)

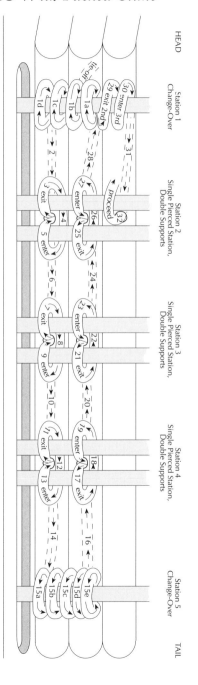

HEAD

Station 1
Change-Over

Station 2
Single Pierced Station,
Double Supports

Station 3
Single Pierced Station,
Double Supports

Station 4
Single Pierced Station,
Double Supports

Station 5
Change-Over

TAIL

SINGLE &
DOUBLE RAISED SUPPORTS

Sewing raised supports along the spine can use a combination of single and double supports. Design possibilities are increased, since double raised supports offer another means to change-over. Either the "English" loop, or the "German" lap sewing, pages 164, 165, can be used to change-over:

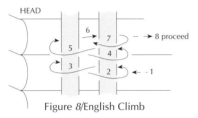

Figure *8*/English Climb

The climb, steps 2-5, is by a figure *8,* which loops the forward support.

The entry is a forward wrap of the "English" sewing, steps 5-7, of double raised supports.

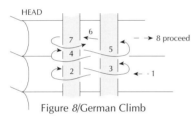

Figure *8*/German Climb

The climb, steps 2-5, is by a figure *8,* which laps the backward support.

The entry is a backward wrap of the "German" sewing, steps 5-7, of double raised supports.

Double Raised Supports to Change-Over:

1. Exit between the double supports.
2.-5.   Climb by packing with a figure *8,* except for the final pack. The "English" type starts step 2 with a loop. The "German" is a lap.
5.-7. The last pack, is not with a figure *8* pattern, but uses either the "English" loop, or the "German" lap, described on pages 164 and 165.
8. Enter the new section and proceed. An elaborate diagram of the figure *8* packing and "English" loop to climb and change-over is on page 170.

Sewing at stations 2 through 6 is PACK & WEAVE, which is on single raised (cord) supports. Climbing at the head and the tail is by means of DOUBLE RAISED SUPPORTS AS CHANGE-OVER. See page 170.

For other examples of DOUBLE RAISED SUPPORTS AS CHANGE-OVER, see pages 172, 186 and 199.

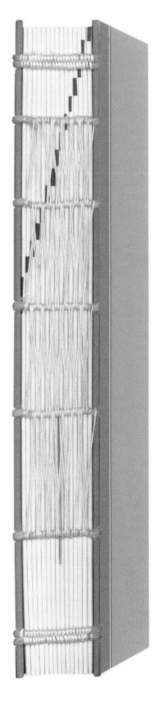

Patterning: Another variation is to play with patterning single and double raised supports on the spine. These design possibilities can enrich the look of the spine. A pair of double raised supports across the spine is such a lovely thick band.

Sometimes, using double supports can appear bulky, heavy. It takes sewing many samples to develop your own aesthetic. Bulk can be reduced by increasing the space between the supports. Another solution is to alternate with a single, solidly packed support.

BULK-UP: Bulk-up of the spine, thicker than the foredge, is caused by not only the threads inside the sections, but the linking process between sections. Bulkup can be minimized by sewing with thinner thread, and with thicker sections.

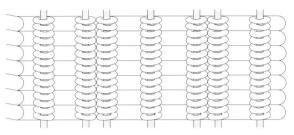

SINGLE & DOUBLE RAISED SUPPORTS
With Packed Climb
This method to change-over is described on page 75.

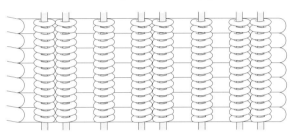

SINGLE & DOUBLE RAISED SUPPORTS
With Double Packed Climb
Double raised supports to change-over is described on page 170.

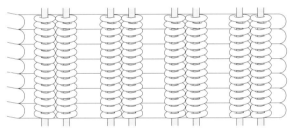

DOUBLE RAISED SUPPORTS
With Double Packed Climb
This striking sewing is described on page 170.

You can play with combining double supports with any previously shown sewing. For instance, two or more of the middle stations might be used for sewing the Pack & Weave, described on page 101. In the sewing shown on the facing page, a single thread sews along the spine with the Pack & Weave on single supports, climbing on "English" Double Raised Supports. Several other stations could be some other sewing. Change-over at the head and tail could be either via single or double raised supports, or, even—one of each.

DOUBLE RAISED SUPPORTS *With Endbands*

Double raised supports can employ endbands to change-over. The example shown here uses the "German" approach to sewing the double raised supports, as described on page 165. You could sew them "English" style, as described on page 164. To start the sewing at the endbands, refer to *Endbands As Change-Over,* beginning on page 133.

Detail of the "German"sewing of DOUBLE RAISED SUPPORTS, which uses endbands to change-over.

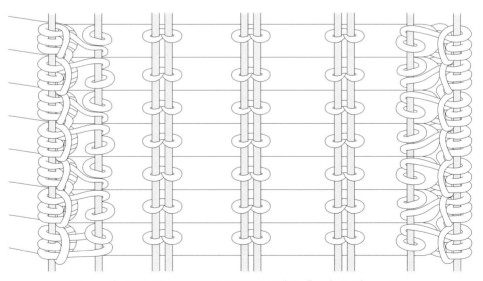

German (lap) DOUBLE RAISED SUPPORTS *With Endbands As Change-Over*

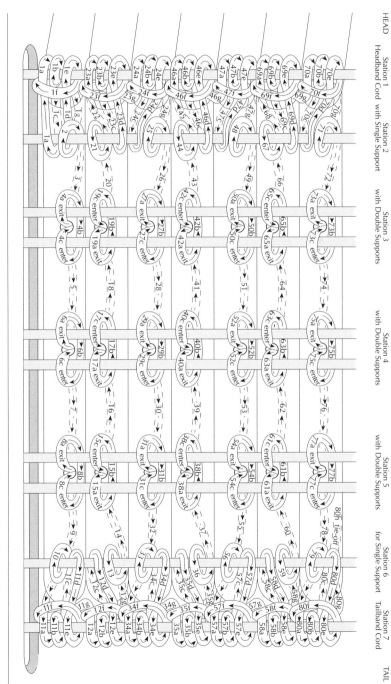

German (lap) DOUBLE RAISED SUPPORTS With Endbands As Change-Over

Exit, and wrap the back support first.
In this diagram, step f is always the bead for the endbands.

HEAD

Station 1
Headband Cord with Single Support

Station 2
with Double Supports

Station 3
with Double Supports

Station 4
with Double Supports

Station 5
with Double Supports

Station 6
for Single Support

Station 7
Tailband Cord

TAIL

DOUBLE RAISED SUPPORTS AS CHANGE-OVER
With Solid Pack Raised Supports

Another means to climb at the end of sewing a section would be to investigate double supports. The "English" sewing of Double Raised Supports, page 164, lends itself as the means to change-over (page 166). It is one of the loveliest means to change-over for an exposed spine sewing.

To start the sewing and to hide the tie-off, begin inside the second section. See illustration at top of the facing page. Step 2, only, proceeds *down* the supports. It enters the first section. Stations 2 through 4 are sewn in the regular manner as described on page 164, except that the support is solidly packed. Exit between the cords, and *wrap forward,* that is, pack the forwards support, first. See station 2 in the diagram at the top of the facing page, as well as the sewing at station 4 in the diagram at the bottom of that page. Also, see completed diagram on page 173.

Change-Over at the Tail and Head: For each change-over at the tail, refer to the diagram at the bottom of the facing page. For each change-over at the head, see the diagram on page 172, except from the second to the third section, diagrammed at the right.

At the head and tail, exit between the supports, then *wrap backwards* (wrap the back support, first).

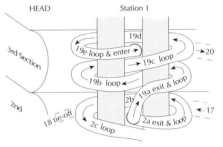

Exiting the second, entering the third section.
Step 19 exits and loops forward support, first.
Steps 19a-19c are a figure *8* for packing and climbing.
Steps 19c-19e are "English" sewing double raised supports.

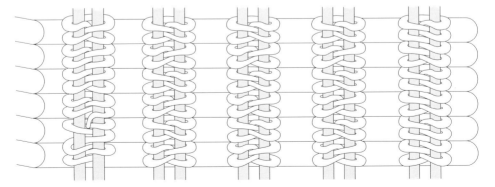

Solid pack *English* DOUBLE RAISED SUPPORTS with double raised supports at the head and the tail to change-over
At stations 2 through 4, the first pack is a figure *8*. The final pack is always the "English" (or "German") sewing.
The figure *8* climbs easily, but would not hold both supports tightly against the spine.

Double Raised Supports with Various Changes-Over

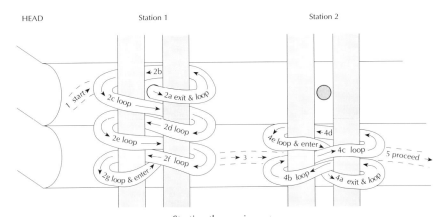

Starting the sewing
English (loop) DOUBLE RAISED SUPPORTS As Change-Over

STEP 2, ONLY: Start inside the second section, pack downward to the first. Exit forward support, first.
Steps 2a-2c start by reversing. It is a *backward wrap* (first forward wrap is step 4c- 4e). Steps 2c-2g descend in a solid pack figure *8.*

At all other supports, except the head and the tail, which exit and reverse

EXIT: Always exit *forward* support, first, except at the head and the tail.
CLIMB and PACKING: Use a figure *8,* (4a-4c) except for the final pack at each station.
FINAL PACK at EACH STATION: Use the "English" double raised support sewing for the final pack at each station (4c-4e). See page 164.

NOTE: Double supports in the diagrams are drawn with a space between in order to show the path of the thread. This is misleading. In reality, the double supports are strung on the frame tangent. They are pulled tightly together by the looping of the threads:

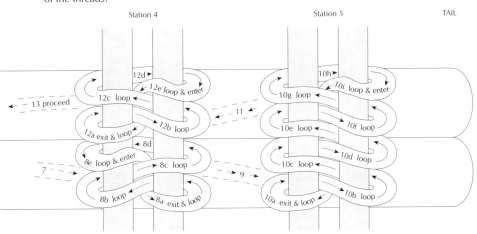

Climbing at the tail. *English (loop) DOUBLE RAISED SUPPORTS As Change-Over*

Step 8 is the same sewing pattern as step 4.
At the tail, step 10 reverses: It is a *backward wrap,* in order for step 10i to loop the back support and enter.
Steps 10a-19f are a figure *8* for packing and climbing.
Steps 10g-10i are "English" sewing double raised supports.

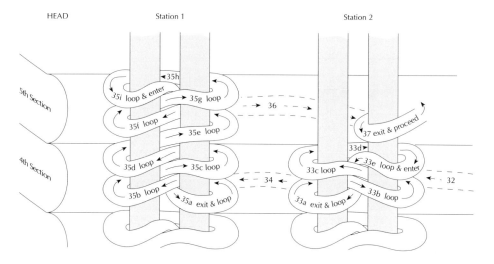

English (loop) DOUBLE RAISED SUPPORTS *As Change-Over*

All stations (step 33) *pack forward,* except the head and the tail (step 35) which *pack backward.*
Step 33 is the same sewing pattern as step 12: Steps 33a- c are a figure *8.* Steps 33c- e are "English" sewing double raised supports.

Change-Over at the head, *EXIT BACKWARD*

At the head, step 35 exits backward, between the supports. Wrap the back support, first.
Steps 35a-35f are a figure *8* for packing and climbing.
Steps 35g-35i are "English" sewing double raised supports.
Step 37 is a forward wrap, first with a figure *8,* and the final wrap with the "English" sewing.

Above: Solid pack *English (loop)* DOUBLE RAISED SUPPORTS, *With English Double Raised Supports As Change-Over.*

Below: SINGLE PACK & BEAD, *With English (loop) Double Raised Supports As Change-Over.*

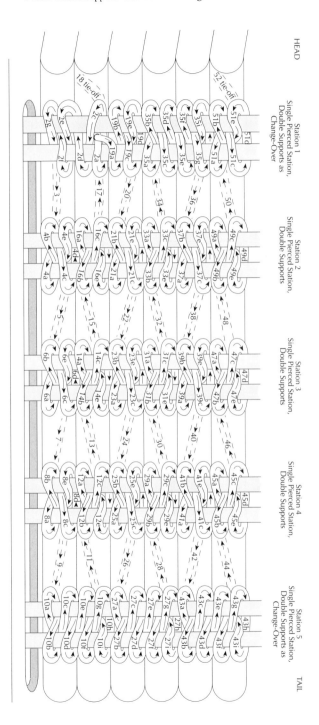

Solid Pack English *(loop)* DOUBLE RAISED SUPPORTS
With Double Raised Supports As Change-Over

ISOLATED BANDS OF PACK & WEAVE

The Pack & Weave is described on page 101. A single continuous thread solidly packs the single raised supports. At the same time, it drops and angles to pattern the spine with a cross-hatched design of threads. If this sewing continues on the inside of the section, it would permit the pattern of the Pack & Weave to alternate with blank area on the spine. See drawing at the bottom of this page. I call the result Isolated Pack & Weave.

The benefit is not only a less heavily decorated spine, but permits designing a spine which alternates the Pack & Weave with other sewings. For instance, the next sewing, described on page 178 uses the Isolated Pack & Weave to change-over. This sewing is alternated with Double Raised Supports.

The Isolated Pack & Weave could be alternated with link stitches, or with whatever sewing you might wish to add to the looks and structure of the spine.

SEWING PROCEDURE

The sewing begins identically to the Pack & Weave, described on page 101. The variation begins in the third section with step 26. See detail on page 175, and completed diagram on page 176. A scan is on page 177.

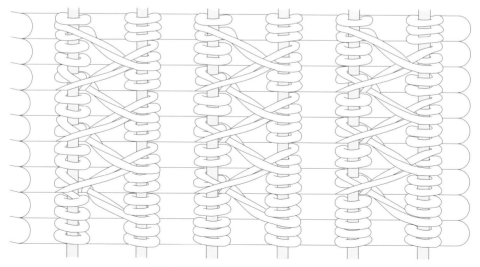

ISOLATED BANDS OF PACK & WEAVE

Double Raised Supports with Various Changes-Over

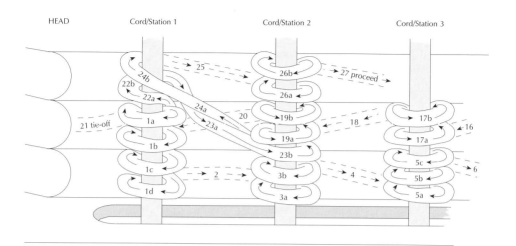

Starting the ISOLATED BANDS OF PACK & WEAVE

Start inside the second section. Pack solidly down to the first section, and enter
the first section. At all other stations, pack upwards.

Step 26 packs the support, enters on the back side. It continues on the
inside, exiting the next station to form another separate band of Pack &
Weave between the next two supports. Compare this with step 26 of the
continuous sewing of Pack & Weave in the diagram on page 107.

In this manner, the Isolated Pack & Weave forms a band between the first
and second supports, the third and forth, and another between the fifth
and sixth supports.

Number of packs in a solid pack depends upon the thickness of the section, and the thread. More important than the tightness of the pack is uniform number of packs. Maintain the same number of packings at each support along a particular section. Alternate sections may have one fewer, or
more number of packs at each station, but every station for that section
must have the same number of packs, in order not to warp that section. If
the sections require 2½ packs to reach the height of the sections, use three
packs for the first, and two for the second. Alternating will equal out to
2½ packs.

NOTE: In the above drawing, the first section has three packs at station 3
with step 5. Station 2 has only two packs. However, in sewing the third
section, step 23 drops at an angle and loops the support. The end result is
that all supports along the first section will have the same number of
packs.

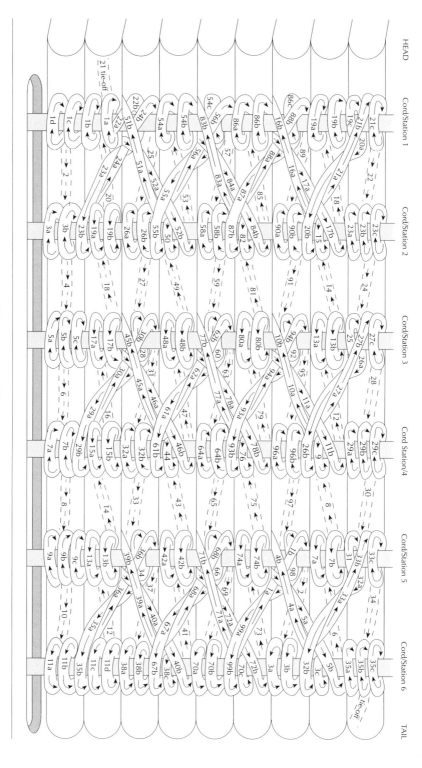

ISOLATED BANDS OF PACK & WEAVE

After step 99, numbering returns to single digits.

Left: ISOLATED BANDS OF PACK & WEAVE, which is described on page 174. The supports are four threads of two colors which are plied and strung on the sewing frame. After the sewing is completed, each thread is individually sewn through the boards with *TYPE 1* Attachment.

Right: In a single sewing with a single needle, Bands of the ISOLATED PACK & WEAVE are employed as the means to change-over at the head and tail.

As the sewing proceeds along the spine, the middle stations, 3 through 8, are sewn "German" style, DOUBLE RAISED (thread) SUPPORTS. This combination is described on page 180.

The double thread supports for the middle stations are two colors, one very dark, the other very light. A dotting of the supports is visible across the spine, between the sewing.

The supports at the head and the tail are four threads, plied.

Edward Hutchins, *Editions.* Six edi-
tioned books produced without
using a printing press.

Top: *Extended Family,* 1990.
Edition of 20 copies. 4.5 x 4.5 cm.

Middle: *World Peace,* 1991.
Edition of 30 copies. 9 cm. diameter.

Bottom: *Juke Box Quilts,* 1990.
Edition of 10 copies. 12.6 x 8.7 cm.

Edward Hutchins, *Editions.*

Top: *Dulce Rey,* 1991.
Edition of 30 copies. 3.8 x 2.5 cm.

Middle: *Grandma's Closet,* 1991.
Edition of 30 copies. 20.9 x 13.3 cm.

Bottom: *The Rabbit Report,* 1989.
Edition of 20 copies. 15.2 x 12.7 cm.

DOUBLE RAISED SUPPORTS
With Isolated PACK & WEAVE As Change-Over

A single needle and thread is used to sew along the spine. The stations for the climb employ single raised supports, while the middle stations are double raised supports.

In this sewing, the Isolated Bands of Pack & Weave, described on page 174 is used to change-over at the head and the tail. This requires stations 1 and 2 at the head, and stations 5 and 6 at the tail, on single supports.

In the middle of the spine, stations 3 and 4 are sewn with the "German" type of Double Raised Supports, described on page 165. The middle stations use a backward wrap.

If you wish, the double supports could be solidly packed. Stations 3 and 4 would be sewn as described on page 170.

A digital scan of this sewing is on page 177.

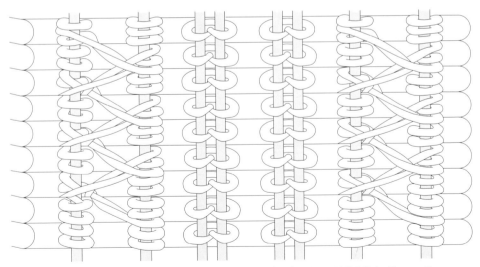

German (lap) DOUBLE RAISED SUPPORTS *With Isolated PACK & WEAVE As Change-Over*

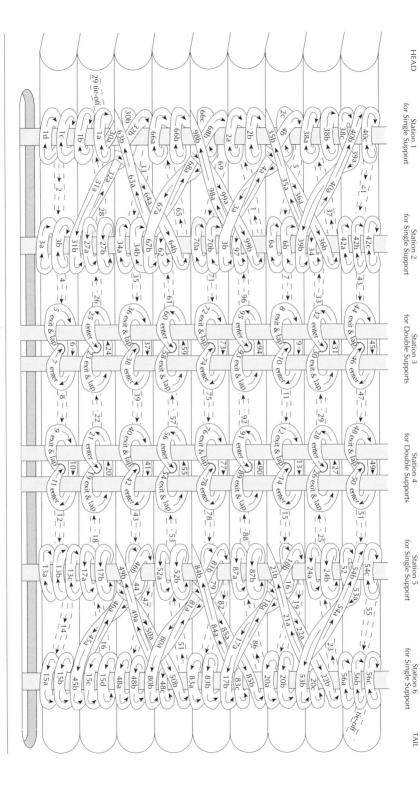

German (lap) DOUBLE RAISED SUPPORTS *With Isolated PACK & WEAVE As Change-Over*

After step 99, numbering returns to single digits.

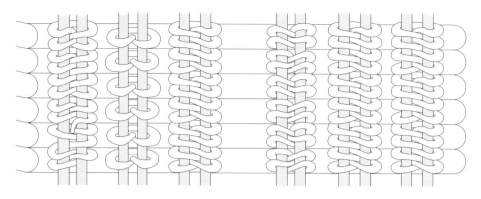

German (lap) With Solid Pack *English (loop)* Double Raised Supports As Change-Over

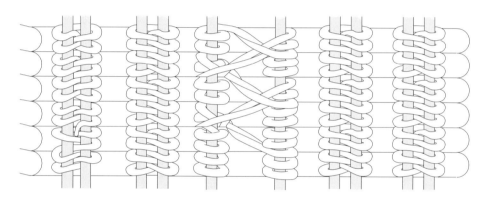

PACK *&* WEAVE With *English (loop)* Double Raised Supports As Change-Over

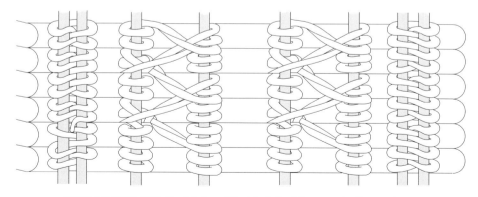

PACK *&* WEAVE With *English (loop)* Double Raised Supports As Change-Over

HERRINGBONE *With Solid Pack Double Raised Supports As Change-Over*

With single supports, the Pack & Weave makes use of angling and linking. In a similar manner, double raised supports can angle and link under. This creates a herringbone pattern: Exit, drop forward at an angle, lapping the forward support. Link under both supports. Climb at an angle, lapping the back support. Re-enter.

1-15. The first section is sewn in the "German" manner of a backward wrap, described on page 165. It is more related to the Herringbone than the path of the "English" wrap. To start, choose your change-over. I have illustrated double raised supports as described on page 184 and 185. For more detailed information, see: *Double Raised Supports As Change-Over*, page 170.

Detail: The HERRINGBONE. This sewing makes a rewarding pattern of double raised cords on an exposed spine. See photograph on page 186, on the left.

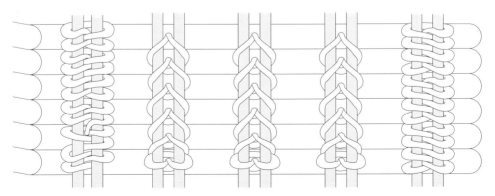

Middle stations: HERRINGBONE
Change-Over at head and tail: *English (loop)* solid pack DOUBLE RAISED SUPPORTS

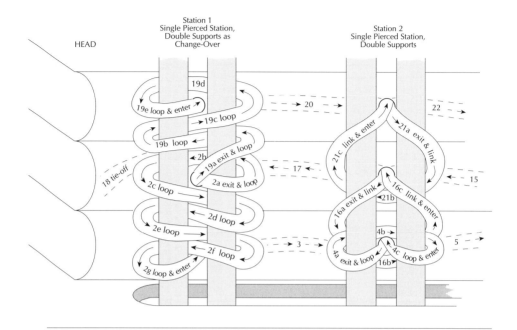

Starting the HERRINGBONE
with solid pack *English (loop)* DOUBLE RAISED SUPPORTS *As Change-Over*

The reason the first section is not sewn with the Herringbone is because the linking process cannot begin until the second section. Otherwise, it would link under between the book block and the side-cover; it would not be secure.

Forming the Herringbone:

16a. Exit between the supports. Drop forward at an angle.

16b. Link under both supports at the last two connected sections.

16c. Climb at an angle, lapping the back support. Re-enter between the supports.

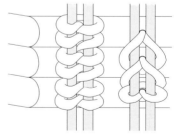

Sewing from the diagram at the top of the page will appear more like this.

Odd-Numbered sections are sewn with the *same* written instructions.

You will be headed in the opposite direction, thus the terms *forward* and *backward,* rather than to the *right* or *left.*

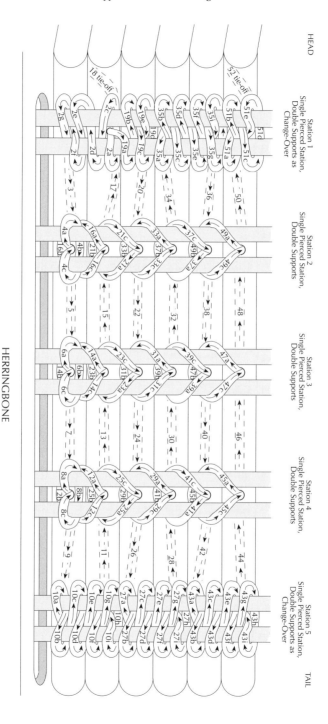

HEAD

Station 1
Single Pierced Station,
Double Supports as
Change-Over

Station 2
Single Pierced Station,
Double Supports

Station 3
Single Pierced Station,
Double Supports

Station 4
Single Pierced Station,
Double Supports

Station 5
Single Pierced Station,
Double Supports as
Change-Over

TAIL

HERRINGBONE
with solid pack *English (loop)* DOUBLE RAISED SUPPORTS *as Change-Over*

Stations 2, 3 and 4 of the first section are sewn with a backward wrap (*German style*).
The same could be done with the final section, after forming the herringbone. See digital scan on page 183.

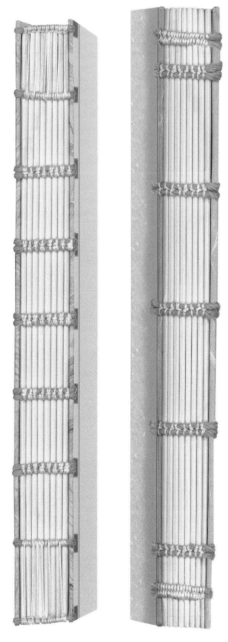

Left: The HERRINGBONE described on page 183. In the middle is the PEARL, shown on page 187. On the right is the SEED PEARL described on page 190.

PEARL *With Endbands As Change-Over*

When Betsy Palmer Eldridge showed this sewing to me, I was ecstatic. It is such an elegant sewing. The bas-relief effect of the ""pearl"" is striking. It is a joy to sew, watching it form.

Rather than sew with "pearl"s at each double support, I prefer to see the "pearl" in combination with other sewings at some of the stations on the spine.

Use whatever change-over you wish. I have shown endbands as change-over in the diagram on page 189. Refer to page 141 for detailed text and diagramming of the change-over.

Forming the Pearl for Odd-Numbered Sections: When exiting, the back support is always wrapped first.

1a. Exit and loop the back support. Proceed forward, between the supports and the section.
1b. Loop the front support.
1c. Lap both supports; proceed behind the back support.
1d. Come out between the supports. Loop thread 1c.
1e. Re-enter the station. Apply tension as you enter to form the "pearl".

Proceed to the next station. Exit, and repeat step 1a-1e. Continue in this manner to the tail, where the change-over will be executed to climb to the next section.

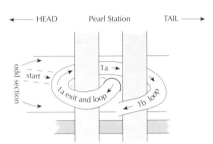

Starting the PEARL
for an odd-numbered section

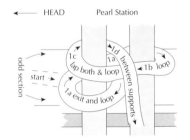

Forming the PEARL
for an odd-numbered section
Step d is the "pearl".

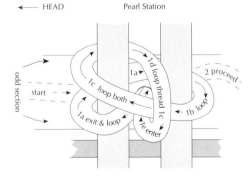

Completing the PEARL
for an odd-numbered section

Forming the Pearl for Even-Numbered Sections: Proceed in the same manner:

1a. Exit and loop the back support. Proceed forward, between the supports and the section.

1b. Loop the front support.

1c. Lap both supports; proceed behind the back support.

1d. Come out between the supports. Loop thread 1c.

1e. Re-enter the station. Adjust the tension as you enter to form the "pearl".

Proceed to the next station.

Exit, and repeat step 1a-1e. Continue in this manner to the head, where the change-over will be executed to climb to the next section.

In the case of endbands as change-over, there are two stations each, at the head and the tail, devoted to forming the endband.

At stations 3-5, the back cord is double packed; the forward cord is packed once. This gives an alternating pattern across the spine.

Forming the PEARL
for an even-numbered section
Step *d* is the "pearl".

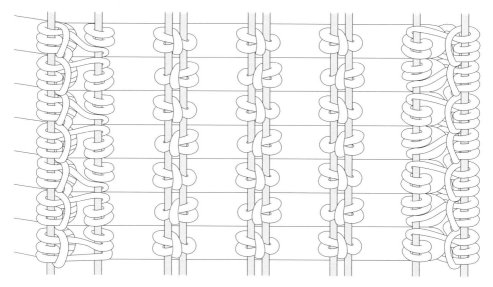

Middle stations, 3-5: PEARL *With Endbands As Change-Over* at head and tail

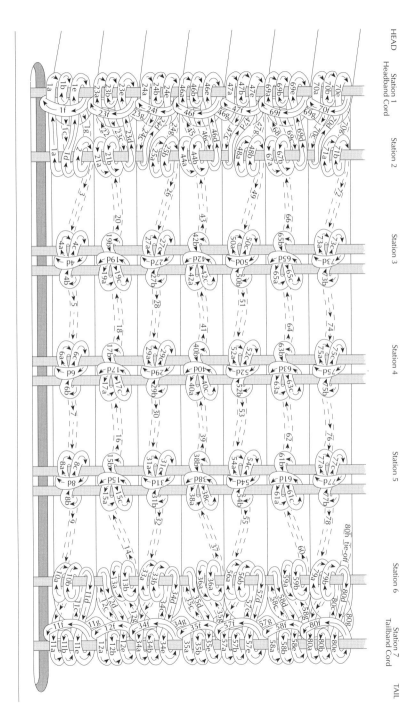

PEARL *With Endbands As Change-Over*

Step d for all sections, stations 3 through 5, is the "pearl".

The "pearl" is similar to the bead, step f, at the head and the tail. The "pearl" with the bead makes an attractive exposed spine.

SEED PEARL *With Solid Pack Double Raised Supports As Change-Over*

There is a pleasant syncopation in the previously described "pearl" sewing: The back support has two packings, and the forward has only a single pack. This forms a triangle, pointing in the direction of the sewing for that section. The rows of pointing triangles alternate direction.

This is a variation, which Betsy Palmer Eldridge refers to as the Seed Pearl. There is only a single pack on both the double cords. It lacks the dynamics of alternating pattern of the previous sewing. This is more formal in its symmetry. But it has the elegance of a bow tie worn with a tuxedo.

The "pearl" reminds me of the bead in an endband. That is why I used endbands as change-over in the previous sewing. With this sewing, the symmetry of packed double supports as change-over seem appropriate.

Examining the path of the exit, loop and beading, this sewing is a German double raised support sewing, with the addition of the bead prior to entering.

Start at station 1 in the second section. Pack the double supports solidly to the first section. Refer to Double Raised Supports As Change-Over, page 170.

Forming the Pearl: Exit the first "pearl" station.

1a. Wrap the back support. Proceed forward, between the supports and the section.
1b. Loop the forward support.
1c. Link under thread 1a.
1d. Lap thread 1c.

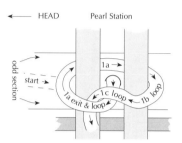

Starting the SEED PEARL
for an odd-numbered section

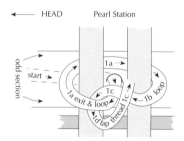

Forming the SEED PEARL
for an odd-numbered section

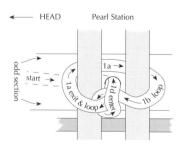

Completing the SEED PEARL
for an odd-numbered section
Step d is the pearl.

1e. Re-enter the station.
Carefully adjust the tension to form the "pearl".

At the end of the odd-numbered section, form the change-over at the station at the tail.

For the next even-numbered section, form the seed "pearl" in the same manner as for the odd-numbered sections:

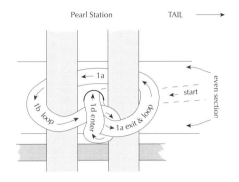

The SEED PEARL
for an even-numbered section
Step d is the "pearl".

1a. Wrap the back support. Proceed forward, between the supports and the section.
1b. Loop the forward support.
1c. Link under thread 1a.
1d. Lap thread 1c.
1e. Re-enter the station. Carefully adjust the tension to form the "pearl".

At the head, form the change-over. Continue with the next odd-numbered section.

Digital scans of this sewing are shown on pages 186 and 199.

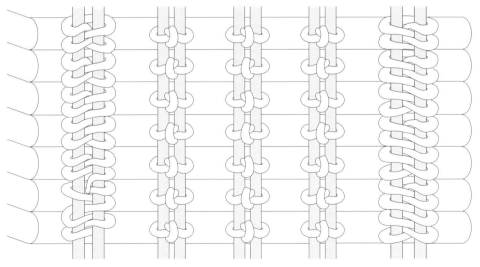

SEED PEARL *With Solid Pack Double Raised Supports As Change-Over*

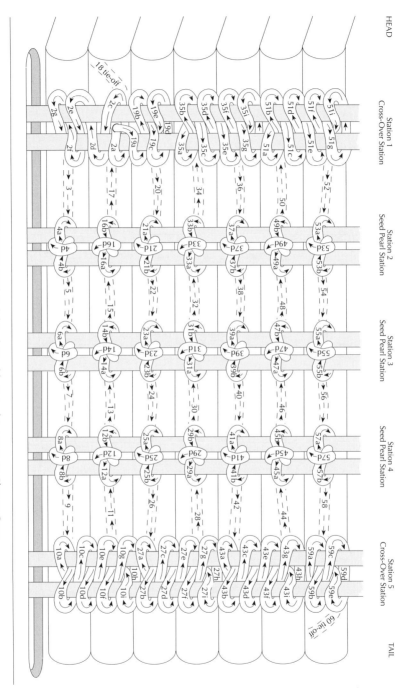

SEED PEARL With Solid Pack Double Raised Supports As Change-Over

Step d for stations 2 through 4 is the "pearl".

ATTACHING SUPPORTS TO BOARDS

PREPARING THE BOARDS

Thickness of the board varies with the size of the book. Pressed paper book board generally comes in three thicknesses. The thinnest should be used on small books. Books about the size of this volume would require the middle weight board. Thick book board is rarely used, except for oversize books.

FLATBACK: It is good to *sand the outside* of the board at the foredge. This gives a tapered look and *feel* in handling the book:

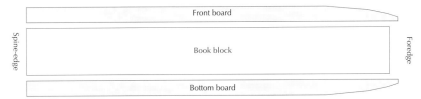

Sanding the foredge of the boards for a flatback book block

Tapering the foredge is recommended for all bindings, unless some kind of latch is attached to the depth of the board on the foredge. For a flatback, the boards are now ready to be covered.

I generally pierce the stations on the board after they are covered. You might consider drilling the holes prior. See page 201. Any bulge on the surface, a ring of board around the pierced hole, should be sliced off. In traditional lacing in, this bulge is left. After the supports are laced in, the bulge is hammered back into the hole and pasted. However, if you are only threading the supports through to be tied, you will not be hammering the board, and you will want a clean hole and smooth board.

ROUNDED BOOK BLOCK: You may wish to round and back the book block. See page 45. If so, it is good to *sand the inside* of the boards at the spine-edge, to accommodate the shoulder of the rounded spine:

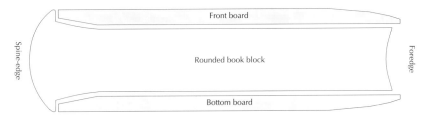

Sanding the spine-edge of the boards for a rounded book block.
This could be a natural round, or rounded and backed. See pages 47 and 70.

LACING CORDS THROUGH BOARD

The raised support sewings previously described all use cords. in a future volume, I might explore sewing onto tapes and split thongs. For now, the discussion is limited to attaching raised cords to boards, after the book block has been sewn. The separate side-covers may be book board made of pressed paper, or wooden boards.

In Part 3, *Across the Spine Sewings,* the thread, itself, is used to attach the boards. Various types of board attachment using thread supports are described beginning on page 212.

Attachment of thread or cord supports proceeds over the board, entering from the outside to the inside of the board. See diagram above.

NOTCHING the BOARD: For a more flush appearance, and less wear of the supports on the corners, notches can be cut to inlay the supports where cornering the board. See diagram and explanation at the right:

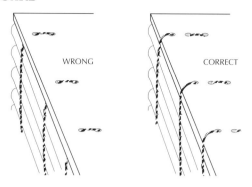

The supports are brought across the outside of the board, entering from the outside to the inside, as diagrammed on the right. Otherwise, the board would be forced back, away from the spine when inserting the book onto a shelf.

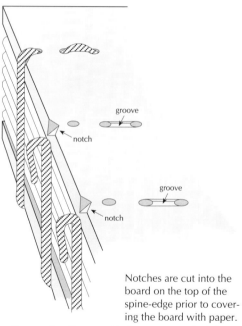

Notches are cut into the board on the top of the spine-edge prior to covering the board with paper.

The notches line up with the supports, which fit into the notch as they are brought across the outside of the board. This is similar to similar to traditional lacing–in the boards.

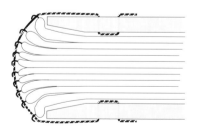

Lacing the cords on a rounded, and backed book, over the notched boards.

Grooves can be cut and layers of board peeled away to inlay the cord between the holes.

The IDEAL HINGE: On the previous page the supports enter down through the surface of the board. Examples are shown on the following pages. However, supports can enter *through the depth* of the board, producing ideal hinging action. Generally, cord is too thick, and the board too thin to accommodate such an entry. With thread supports, hinging through the depth of the board is relatively easy. See: page 216, *TYPE 3* BOARD ATTACHMENT.

LACING–IN CORDS: If the ends of the cord are separated after the sewing is completed, they can be threaded onto a needle and laced through the board. See diagram to the right, and digital scan below.

Some fray the cords. The tip is moistened and twisted. Stray threads are trimmed at an angle. Otherwise it will come untwisted when you try to thread the point through the hole in the board. Hold the trimmed cord closed to the tip. Push it through the hole with a slight rotation in the direction of the twist. This will help keep a tight point on the tip. Grab the protruding cord on the other side and pull the cord through.

1. cut   2. frayed   3. moistened & twisted   4. trimmed

Fraying the cord to lace through the board.
This is frowned upon by some. See page 196.

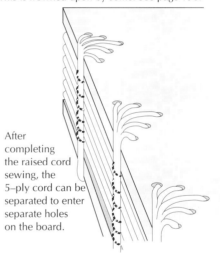

After completing the raised cord sewing, the 5–ply cord can be separated to enter separate holes on the board.

Cords can be sewn to the board.

ATTACHING SUPPORTS WITHOUT PASTE

Growing out of 19th century commercial concerns, often cords laced through to the inside are *frayed* and pasted to the boards, prior to covering. Fraying weakens the twist at the most critical point, according to Betsy Palmer Eldridge.

Moreover, I would like to suggest you explore attaching boards without the use of paste. This is *not* because I think the bindings should be devoid of any paste or glue—I invariably paste decorative papers, and sometimes a leather edge onto my boards. Rather, it will force you to explore non-traditional methods of attaching the boards.

Why? Allowing the attachment process to show, the functional act will create decoration: Supports can be sewn to the boards. Across the board, supports can be packed and beaded as they are sewn through the board, reflecting the sewing on the spine. Supports can be laced and knotted. Cord endings can be frayed, as in the upper left picture. Frayed endings can be used on the inside or outside of the board as decoration.

Cord can be untwisted, and sewn to boards as shown on the previous page.

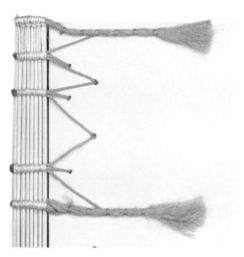

Detail: Solid pack supports of cord and thread give variation on the spine, while opening possibilities of decorative attachment on the boards.

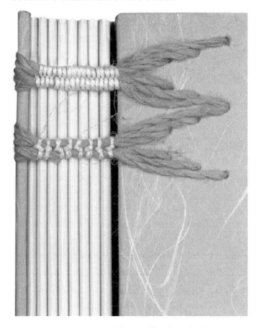

Detail: Decorative and less bulky than feeding both double raised cords through a single hole on the board, each 6–ply cord was unravelled and re-twisted as three 2–ply cords. Each segment was threaded on a needle and laced separately through the board. See page 199 for a picture of this binding.

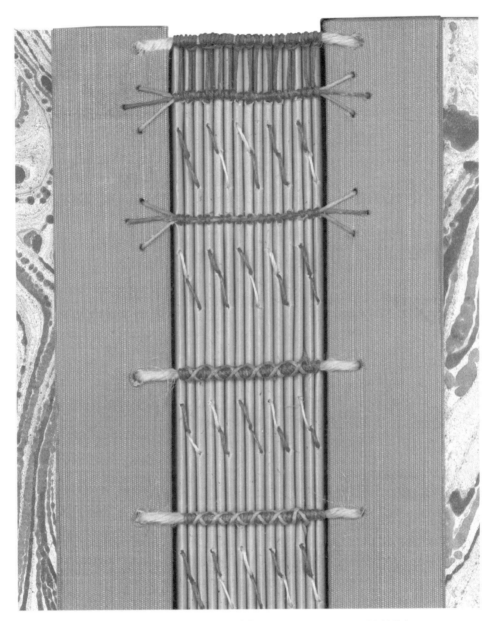

Detail: The raised supports for this solid PACK CORDS WITH ENDBANDS are
6–ply cord and 3–plied thread. Three colors of thread are attached on the key at
the base of the sewing frame. Each set of three threads is twisted before attached
to a hook at the crossbar. After the sewing is completed, the 3–ply thread supports are untwisted to attach each thread at a separate location on the board.

SANDWICHING BOARDS

Each side-cover can be comprised of two thin boards which are glued together as a single unit. The supports are attached by sandwiching in between. For each cover, prepare two boards the same dimensions, but half the required thickness, since they will be glued together.

Set the bottom half of the front cover on top of the book block. Mark the position of the supports on the spine-edge on the top of this bottom board. Cut channels and peel off the areas of the boards which have been traced.and cut, so the supports later can be glued flush with this board. With the supports inlaid, they will not cause a bulge when gluing the top board to this board.

Covering the Boards: Cut the papers which will cover the boards. Cut wax paper to place between the boards, to prevent moisture from blistering the book block.

For the top side-cover, the bottom board is covered on one side, which rests against the top of the book block. The top board is covered only on the top side. These must be pasted simultaneously, so that the two boards can be glued together quickly. Otherwise, the boards will warp, since they have been pasted on one side, only.

Apply PVA glue to the tapes or frayed cords, and position them into the cut out channels of the board. Press the supports flush with the board with a bone folder.

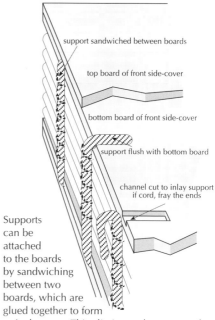

support sandwiched between boards

top board of front side-cover

bottom board of front side-cover

support flush with bottom board

channel cut to inlay support if cord, fray the ends

Supports can be attached to the boards by sandwiching between two boards, which are glued together to form a single cover. This eliminates the supports from being seen either on top, or on the inside of the cover. Hinging is ideal through the depth of the board.

Cords sandwiched in the boards are visible only on the spine. Detail of THE SPIRAL BINDING. See page 86.

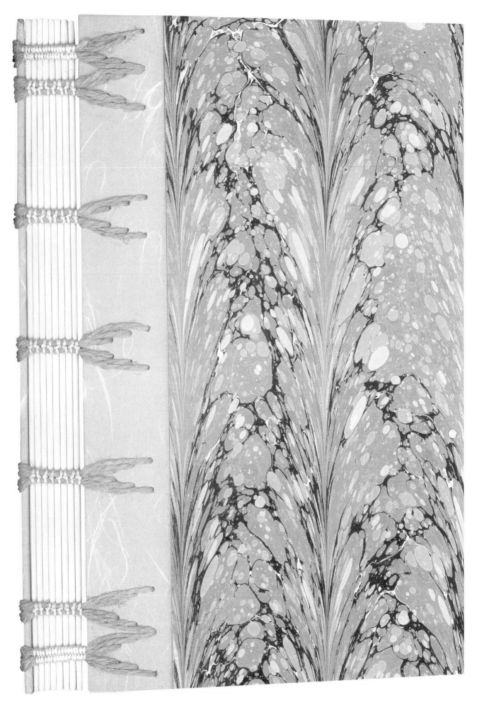

SEED PEARL is described on page 190. Another digital scan of a SEED PEARL sewing is on page 186. The double raised supports are 6–ply cords. After the sewing was completed, each cord was untwisted to three 2–ply cords, and threaded into the boards with a needle.

LOOP PACK WITH CLIMBING PACK. This sewing is described on page 75. The variable size raised supports are 5–ply cord and #18 thread. The supports are sewn into the boards for function, as well as for decoration.

ATTACHING WOODEN BOARDS

Wooden boards are quite attractive in an exposed spine sewing. Supports of cord or leather thongs add to the variety of materials. Attachment of the supports can be exaggerated as elements of decoration. Gary Frost is unparalleled in this area. See Volume I and pages 70, 71 in this volume.

SUPPLY: It is difficult to find a binder's supply which keeps wooden planks on hand. I have found it easier and cheaper to go to a fine cabinet maker who sells exotic hardwoods. You can choose a grain you like, and have it planed to probably 3/16", depending on the dimensions of the board.

QUARTER-CUT VS GRAIN: Fred Jordan's lesson on buying wood: Boards can be cut with the grain, or quarter-cut. Hardwood floors are a good example of with the grain—Flowing grain pattern is evident. Quarter-cut appears dotted, as it has been cut against, or perpendicular to the grain.

The advantage of with the grain is the beauty, but it tends to warp far easier than quarter-cut.

The advantage of quarter-cut is that it tends not to warp, but is extremely apt to crack and break in two, since the stress in hinging is parallel with the grain—movement is on the fault line, so to speak, of the grain.

DRILLING the HOLES

The easiest method of drilling in wood is to use a Dremel® Moto-Tool. It is a handy tool for delicate needs of grinding, sanding, drilling polishing and buffing.

The hole created through the board as a sewing station can be sized to fit your needle. You can curve the pathway.

Recessing the support in the board is easy. The shank diamond wheel points come in a variety of sizes and shapes. Shaping a groove or beveling an edge of the board is like waving a wand over a block of butter. You can even cut out the depth of your paper or leather, so that when it is applied, it is flush with the wooden board.

Stress on Wooded Boards: Board is brittle. The stress on the wood is markedly at the spine-edge of the board, in the area closest to the book block. (Inside of the board.) It is diagrammed below in a darkened color.

Hinging action of the board places stress at this point:

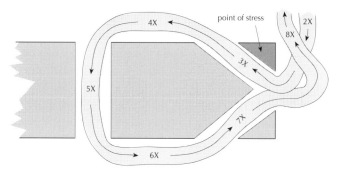

Critical point of stress on a wooden board is the inside, at the spine-edge. Cross section of *TYPE 3* BOARD ATTACHMENT, described on page 216.

To lessen the stress, the support that goes through the depth, (3X) to the inside of the board should be slightly slack, as suggested below.

Step 7X, enters the board from the outside and exits on the depth of the spine-edge. With step 7X, the thread should be slightly more taut, in order to carry the stress:

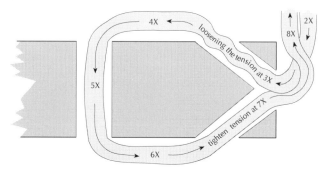

Transferring the stress to the outside of the board.

All of this is an attempt to put more of the hinging action of the exiting support (8X) and less on the entering support (2X).

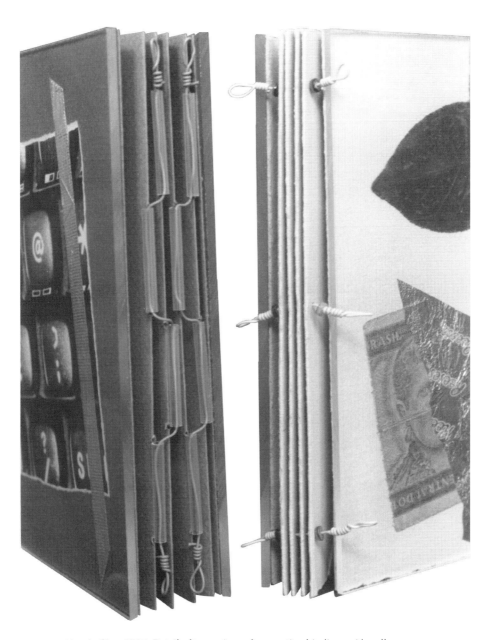

Marcia Ciro, 1995. Detail of two spines of concertina bindings with collage under Plexiglas covers, supported by telephone wire. One-of-a-kind, each is approximately 17.7 x 14 x 2 cm.

SEWN BOARDS

A brilliant "attachment" to boards was devised by Gary Frost. It is not an attachment per se: The book board is folded in half; it is sewn as if it were a folio, as *part* of the sewing, rather than later attached.

"There are three characteristics of the sewn board... (1) the book is sewn with chains of stitches, with thread alone, (2) the covers are sewn to the book as if they were the outermost sections, and (3) the finished book is squareless." —excerpt from a letter from Gary Frost, 10 October 1995.

A thin board, 2– to 4–ply is used, since it is folded prior to sewing, and glued and covered afterwards.

The covers have good hinging action, since the thread extends from the depth of the board to the section, similar to *TYPES 3 and 4* BOARD ATTACHMENT, pages 216 and 217. Gary says his approach is best suited to books of two to eight sections.

The process will not be elaborated here. Complete information on Frost's *Sewn Boards* is described in his book titled *Three Bookbindings.* It is available from Gary Frost, Post Office Box 86, Utopia, TX 78884.

THREAD AS HINGES

We might assume cords or tapes laced into boards is the proper means of attaching boards. The very idea of using thread to attach boards seems flimsy. This is not necessarily so. Number of thread hinges, and number and dimensions of the sections are critical. Obviously, heavy boards should not be attached to a large book with a couple pairs of thread.

If one examines any book sewn across the spine, it is always hinged by thread. The ancient Coptic sewings are a prime example.

Sewing across the spine sews the boards, *as* the sections are sewn. This process no doubt inspired Frost's Sewn Boards. Since thread attachment is a necessary part of sewing across the spine, I have explored the possibilities in Part 3 of this volume. Seven types of board attachment with thread are described from page 212 through 219:

- *Types 1-4* Board Attachment with thread offer means of sewing all the across the spine sewings, except for the Caterpillar, which has its own unique thread board attachment.

- The Caterpillar packs a core of many threads, so that the thread itself becomes a support. It is literally a raised support sewing.

- *Types 5 and 6* Board Attachment with thread were devised for sewing double raised thread supports.

- *Type 7* Board Attachment, as well as *TYPES 5* and *6*, are used for double raised (thread) support sewings in the process of the *Book As Sewing
  Frame*. See pages 273 through 293.

Type 3 Board Attachment lends itself for single raised thread support
sewings. Refer to the *Book As Sewing Frame*. See page 273.

Traditionally, double raised support sewings are along the spine. However,
it is possible to sew double packed supports across the spine, and, I have
devised a sewing referred to as the Centipede. See page 282.

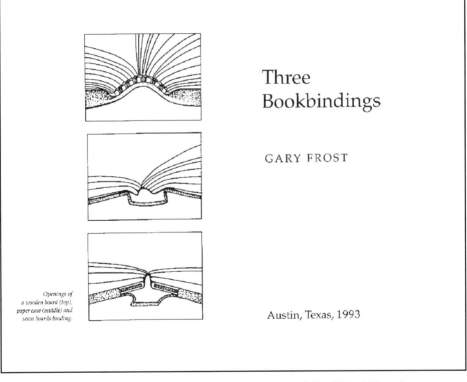

Three
Bookbindings

GARY FROST

Openings of
a wooden board (top),
paper case (middle) and
sewn boards binding.

Austin, Texas, 1993

Gary Frost, *Three Bookbindings,* Austin, Texas, 1993. Self published. The edition was hand bound using Frost's method, under the direction of Priscilla
Spitler. Above is a two page spread. 21.5 x 14 x 1 cm.

Hedi Kyle, Scroll book, 1993. A western codex that emanates from a scroll-like spine.

Scott McCarney, *Survey of Grant Funding,* altered found book, 1990. Two meters x 120 cm. diameter.

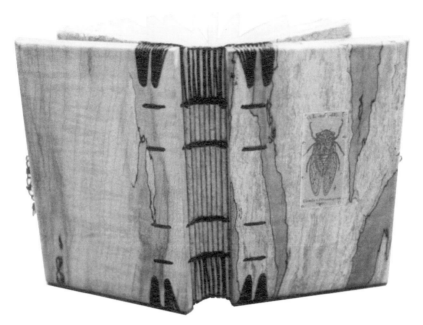

Above: Daniel Essig, Untitled 2–Needle COPTIC SEWING II with linked endbands of Greek origin, 1995. Spalted maple boards with cicada dictionary illustration inlaid behind mica window. 12.7 x 8.8 x 3.2 cm.

Below: Margo Klass, *Bark Book,* 1995. U. I. C. B. flax paper case, with stones, shells and driftwood, with bark pages. 2–Needle COPTIC SEWING II, 11.4 x 11.4 x 4.4 cm.

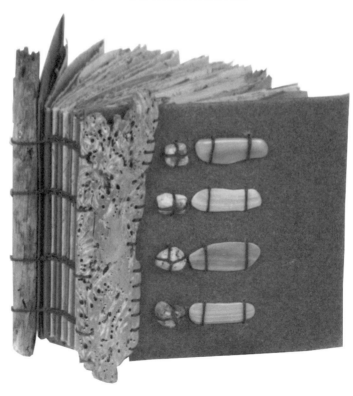

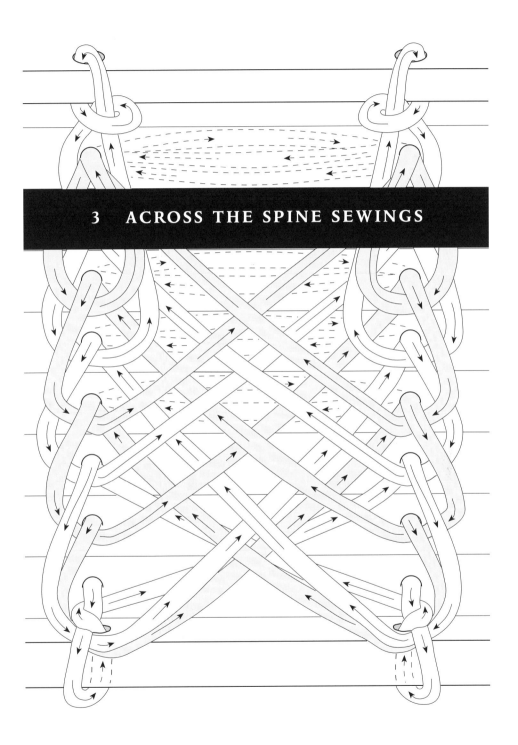

3 ACROSS THE SPINE SEWINGS

ADVANTAGES OF ACROSS THE SPINE SEWING

ALL ALONG: All the previous sewings in this book are sewn *all along* the spine. As one section is sewn along the fold, the needle climbs at the head or the tail to the next section. This is referred to as the change-over. The new section is sewn along the fold to the other end. Again, the needle climbs. In this sense, the sewing is across the spine, as it eventually sews level by level. However, the single thread moves *along* each section, then climbs.

Periodically, the change-over proceeds, *across* the spine. Traditionally this climb is by means of a kettle stitch at the head and the tail. Since I am partial to exposed spine sewings, I have investigated other means as the change-over in Part 3 of this Volume.

In "all along" sewing, traditionally the spine is meant to be covered. With an exposed spine, effort has to be made to make the sewing presentable. I prefer hiding the ties-off inside the sections. I find any means other than the kettle as my change-over. As a plus, along the spine sewings make use of supports. These are a rich resource, easily made to be decorative, while remaining structurally sound. The cords, thongs or tapes make it a "supported" sewing.

ALL ACROSS: A very different approach to sewing is not to travel along the section before climbing, but to sew directly *across the spine.* Several needles are used. The threads are always linking down and climbing. Sometimes this is at an angle, as with the sewing called the Celtic Weave. It might use a span. This type of sewing is referred to as unsupported sewing. It relies solely on the sewing threads, or an aggregate of sewing threads. This sounds like a flimsy, fragile approach. It is not.

Across the spine sewing is strong, and excellent for any book which is to be a non-adhesive binding:

- If the Coptic Stitch sewn along the spine frays a thread, the entire sewing is jeopardized, since it is sewn with a single continuous thread.

  In common to all sewings across the spine, each alternately exits paired stations, perhaps links, climbs and enters. Each needle then exits the paired station. On the right, the CELTIC WEAVE is sewn at the head and tail. The three middle sections have been pierced and braided for design, not function.

The various link sewings all move across the spine with paired stations. Each sewing across the spine, limited within the paired stations, is independent. If a thread is broken, only that portion of the spine is weakened.

- Many of the link sewings, like the 4–Down, as well as the Caterpillar, build up an accumulation of sewing thread which acts like a support, strengthening the connection.

- Separate sewings suggest using several colors of thread. See page 228.

- The thread, itself attaches the boards. The thread hinge is quick and easy.

- If it is a 2–needle sewing, there is no tie-off to start the sewing. See diagrams on pages 214 and 215.

- Any unsupported sewing opens well. It is flexible without supports. The structure allows perfect action in turning pages. The book opens flat to any two facing pages. Individual pages never spring out of control in self-turning defiance of the reader.

- Exposed spine sewing along the spine can be lovely, especially when effort is made to eliminate the kettle stitches and hide the ties-off. These are not problematic in sewing across the spine. Every move of the thread is part of the act of change-over—and, quite lovely.

Every exit is a decorative climb, because each across the spine sewing is conceived as an exposed spine sewing. Each flaunts the sewing as structure and as decoration.

Disadvantages are few. Since several threads are travelling simultaneously across the spine, several needles are employed. This is generally a process of 2 needles for each set of paired stations. The needles and threads tend to become tangled. To alleviate this, always start from one end and work to the other. Perform a single task, or a limited number of steps, or even a single step with each successive needle until all the needles for that section have been worked. It is generally an identical, or alternating instructions for each needle at that level in the sewing. This tends to help keep track of what you have done, more than to keep the threads untangled in the compound, but not complicated procedure. You might sew the paired stations at the head and tail to hold the book together. Then sew the middle stations. This avoids confusion of keeping track of many needles.

It is a flexible spine, ideal in use, but a problem in storage. It loses its round without paste. It is recommended that you eliminate the square of the book, at least at the tail, so that the sections rest on the shelf, rather than eventually sagging to rest. Otherwise, if the book is stored standing, on a shelf, sections will sag to rest upon the shelf. This will occur, even if the books are stored standing snugly, side by side.

ATTACHING THE BOARDS WITH THREAD

1–NEEDLE ATTACHMENT: All sewings across the spine utilize paired stations, requiring an even number. A few across the spine sewings use a single needle, but the sewing paths utilize paired stations. These are the various 1–Needle Coptic Sewings. *TYPES 1-4* Board Attachment are simply modified for 1–needle Coptics, or any sewing across, or along the spine. *TYPE 5* Board Attachment, page 217, is for 1–needle sewing, only.

2–NEEDLE ATTACHMENT: Most of the described across the spine sewings not only use paired stations, but a needle on each end of the thread to sew the sections and to attach the boards. The first four types of attaching separate side-covers are described for paired stations, for 2–needle sewing across the spine.

TYPE 1 BOARD ATTACHMENT

Preparing the Boards: Side-covers are attached to the sections with the threads, *as* the book is sewn. The thread becomes the hinge.

Sewing the First Section and the Board: Draw a line on the cover, in about 1/8" from the spine-edge. Draw lines on the board at each station, to intersect perpendicular with the first line. This marks where to pierce. Place the book board slightly off the edge of a table, so the table will support the board. Use a bradawl, whose shaft does *not* increase in diameter, as with a common awl. This insures the hole will not expand as you pierce. *If the hole is too near the edge, it will rip out.*

Of seven methods, the first to be described will be referred to as *Type 1:*

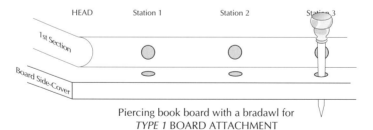

Piercing book board with a bradawl for
TYPE 1 BOARD ATTACHMENT

Pierce close to the spine-edge of the board, about 3/8" in, without ripping through.
Remember, the needle may enlarge the hole even farther.

The book block has the same number of sewing stations as the sections. The board is hinged to the book block through a single hole in the board at each sewing station.

Types 2, 3 and *4* are described on pages 215, 216 and 217. For stringing double raised thread supports, see *TYPES 6* and *7,* pages 218 and 219.

STARTING the SEWING: All 2–needle sewings across the spine start inside the first section. After the first section is sewn, the board is attached.

Start on the inside of the first section to be sewn. Exit with one needle at one station, and the second needle at the remaining station of that pair. Pull the thread to the outside, Evenly distribute the thread from each needle. Start separate threads for each pair of stations. You will need two needles for each thread:

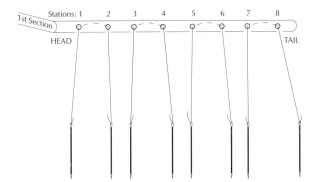

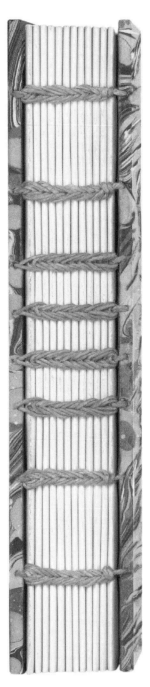

There is no tie-off at the beginning of the sewing, only at the end. This is because the thread loops through the paired stations, requiring no knot. Consequently, the board that is sewn to the first section requires no knots. Only the ending of the paired stations are tied. The final section is sewn, and the board is attached. The needles re-enter the final section for the tie-off.

The 4–DOWN LINK SEWING is sewn *across* the spine at the head and the tail. All stations were pre-pierced. Paired stations at the head and tail were sewn. The book was then turned upside down, and the two sets of paired stations in the middle of the spine were sewn in the other direction. This is why the links on the ends point up, while the middle rows point down.

ADDING the BOARD to the FIRST SECTION: For any sewing across the spine, start with the needle closest to the head in the first section. Proceed around the side-cover, entering the board from the *outside*. Exit the board on the inner side of that set of paired stations.

The term *inner* will be used, rather than "inside" which refers to the valley side of the section. The *inner* side will mean that for each of the two needles in that pair, the needle closest to the head will veer to the right, and the needle closest to the tail will veer to the left. This will keep the threads confined within the boundaries of the sewing for that pair of stations.

Continue on the first section towards the tail, taking each thread to the outside of the board, entering the board from the outside. Exit the board on the inner side of that particular pair of stations:

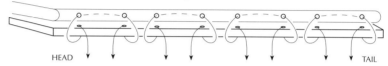

HEAD   TAIL
TYPE 1 BOARD ATTACHMENT, after exiting the first section
This diagram shows 8 needles for 4 threads at 4 paired stations.

Line up the section with the spine-edge of the board. Tighten the threads so the section is tight to the board. The board must be pierced close to the spine-edge. *Be careful the needle does not enlarge the cover holes, ripping out.*

LOCKING the BOARD: The board is locked in place by looping the thread around the *outer* side of the vertical thread which spans between the section and the board, ending on the inner side The term *outer* should not be confused with the term *outside*. The lock forms a horizontal stitch.

The needles dangle on the inner side of the boundaries of the sewing stations for each pair, until you are ready to sew the next section for any Coptic Sewing, or, any other sewing which proceeds across the spine:

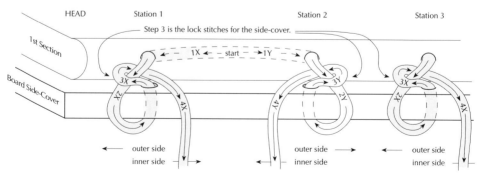

TYPE 1 BOARD ATTACHMENT for 2–needle sewings across the spine

Locking the first section to the board. Locking ends on the inner side of the paired stations. Use 1 thread with 2 needles for sewing at each of the paired stations. Thread for *X* needle is coded gray. Steps 2 and 3 can be repeated for double stitches and locks on the board.

TYPE 2 BOARD ATTACHMENT

This is sewn the same as *TYPE 1,* except for extra hole in the board at each station.

Sewing the First Section and the Board: Start inside of the first section.

1X, 1Y. Exit with one needle at one station, and the second needle at the remaining station for that pair. Pull the thread to the outside. Evenly distribute the thread from each needle. Start separate threads for each pair.

2X. Proceed around the side-cover, entering the board station closest to the spine-edge from the *outside* to the inside.

HEAD   Station 1   Station 2   Station 3

TYPE 2 BOARD ATTACHMENT for 2–needle sewings across the spine

Variation of *Type 1,* with 2 holes in the board, it is sewn on the bench.
This view is from under the table.
Step 4 is a stitch on the inside of the side-cover.
Step 6 is on the outside of the board.
Step 8 is the lock stitch.

3X. Exit the board, only, to the inside of the board.

4X. Enter the second hole on the board at station 1.

5X Exit to the outside.

6X. Enter the board, only, at the first hole on the board.

7X. Exit the board.

8X Lock board by looping thread 2X.

9X. Climb and enter the next section at the same numbered station.

10X. Exit the paired station.

2Y-10Y. Proceed in the same manner as with the X needle. Repeat the procedure at each paired station.

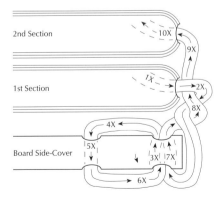

Cross section view of
TYPE 2 BOARD ATTACHMENT

Step 9X enters either first or second section,
depending upon which sewing.

TYPE 3 BOARD ATTACHMENT

This attachment was sent to me by Bert Borch, who learned it from Larry Yerkes at the University of Iowa. It is superior in hinging action, since it attaches at the thickness of the board.

Start inside of the first section. 1X, 1Y. Exit with one needle at one station, and the second needle at the remaining station of that pair. Pull the thread to the outside, Evenly distribute the thread from each needle. Start separate threads for each pair.

2X. Exit one station. Enter the depth of the board.

3X. Exit the board, only, to the inside of the board.

TYPE 3 BOARD ATTACHMENT for 2–needle sewings across the spine

Attaching through the depth of the board for a better hinge. Sewn on the bench, this view is from under the table. Step 4 is a stitch on the outside of the side-cover. Step 6 is on the inside of the board. Step 8 is the lock stitch.
OPTIONAL: Steps 3-7 can be repeated prior to step 8. This will give 2 threads seen on both sides of the boards, and tends to stabilize the board attachment. *TYPE 3* Board Attachment can be modified for 1–needle sewings across or along the spine.

4X. Enter the second hole on the board at station 1.

5X. Exit to the outside.

6X, 7X. Enter the board at the first hole. Exit the board at the depth.

8X. Lock the board by looping thread 2X.

9X. Climb and enter the next section at the same numbered station.

10X. Exit the paired station.

2Y-10Y. Proceed in the same manner as with the X needle. Repeat the procedure at each paired station.

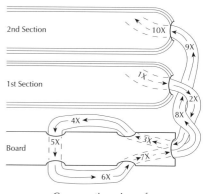

Cross section view of
TYPE 3 BOARD ATTACHMENT

Hinge is through the thickness of the board. It is superior to *Types 1* and *2*. CAUTION: *Type 3* can only be used on thick binders board or wooden boards. It can tear out on thinner matt board. Do not use cheap binders board, as it will spit and flake when pierced through the depth.

TYPE 4 BOARD ATTACHMENT

This attachment is for paired stations, and *only* for sewing across the spine. It is almost identical to *TYPE* 3. There is an extra station pierced in, and perpendicular to, the board. This is to allow step 7X to go from the outside to the inside of the board.

This attachment was sent to me by Marcia Ciro, who learned it from Rebekah Gardiner at the North Bennet Street School in Boston. In appearance, it is nice with the double stitches on the boards. Marcia says it is "elegant, strong... and limits the amount of play the book is prone to." Like *TYPES 1-3*, *TYPE 4* can be used at paired stations, or modified for 1–needle Coptics, sewn across, or along the spine.

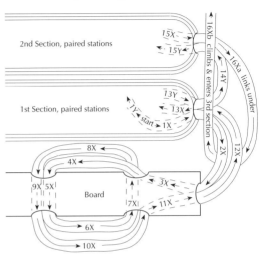

Cross section view of
TYPE 4 BOARD ATTACHMENT

Hinge is through the depth of the board. CAUTION: Use only on thick binders board or wooden boards. It can tear out on thinner matt board. Step 13X enters either first or second section, depending upon which sewing.

TYPE 5 BOARD ATTACHMENT *Lark Spur*

This attachment. has the two stitches showing on the inside and outside of the board, similar to *TYPE 4*.

It is beautiful in that it has the convenience of the easy piercing of the board of *TYPE 1*, as opposed to the difficult piercing of *TYPE 3*. It is *only* for sewing 1–needle across or along the spine.

TYPE 5 is cinched on the depth of the board, where the two threads go through the loop. This slip knot is called a *lark spur*. The advantage of this is that the hinging action is ideal, as it located on the depth of the board, just as with *TYPES 3* or *4*, but without the painstaking effort of piercing *TYPES 3* or *4*.

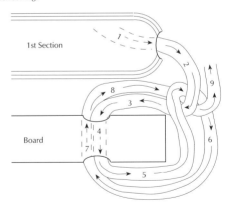

Cross section view of *the Lark Spur,*
TYPE 5 BOARD ATTACHMENT

Piercing the board is the easy, the same as *TYPE 1*. Hinging action is ideal, the same as *TYPES 3* and *4*.

This attachment is meant only for 1–needle sewings across, or along the spine.

TYPE 6 BOARD ATTACHMENT

TYPE 6 is also the Lark Spur. Here, it is used to string double raised thread supports, *not* for sewing the sections. See: *Stringing Double Raised Thread Supports,* page 278.

The bottom board is threaded. The needle by-passes the sections, and attaches the top board.

Type 6 is ideal for stringing double raised thread supports, using the *Book as Sewing Frame.* See: *Stringing Double Raised Thread Supports,* page 278.

The difference between *TYPE 5* and this, is the navigation through the board is necessarily different, and, happens to be easier. A loop is formed at the depth of the bottom board. With a needle on each end of the thread, take both needles through the board from the outside to the inside, leaving a small loop at the depth. Take both needles through the loop and tighten tension to form the lock at the depth of the board. Proceed to the top board.

TYPES 1-5 can be used for stringing double raised thread supports. If two needles are used at paired stations, start inside the first section then attach the bottom board. Proceed to, and enter final section. Then attach top board. This gives a thread hinge from the final section to the top board, permitting a lock. Re-enter final section to tie-off the supports. A scan of the resulting procedure is on page 277.

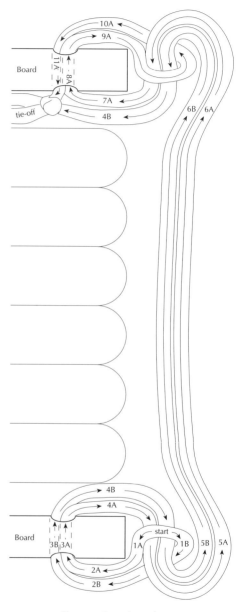

Cross section view of
TYPE 6 BOARD ATTACHMENT
This use of the Lark Spur is not for sewing. It is for stringing double raised thread supports. See page 278.

TYPE 7 **BOARD ATTACHMENT**

This attachment of boards does *not* attach the boards to the sections, as it is not the sewing, but merely the stringing of double raised thread supports, when using the *Book As Sewing Frame.* See page 273

Type 7 attaches one board to the other, by-passing the sections. It is specifically designed to string double raised thread supports

Type 7 Board Attachment cannot be used for the primary sewing of a book. First, the book is sewn at the head and tail with an across the spine sewing. The remaining stations are then used for a second sewing, using the first sewing to fix the sections to the boards, and set the distance between the boards.

The boards, strung with *Type 7* Board Attachment becomes a sewing frame for any traditional double raised support sewing, on thread supports along the spine. In addition, the Centipede, page 282, is sewn across the spine using double raised supports.

Type 7 attachment, sewn with two needles at paired stations, could begin within the first section. It would then attach the bottom board, and proceed to the final section. Enter the final section and exit. Attach the top board, re-enter final section and tie-off. If so, then it would be the same as *Type 3.*

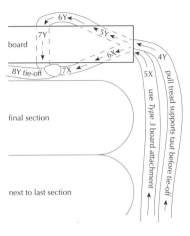

Cross section view
Adjusting the tension and tying-off

TYPE 7 BOARD ATTACHMENT creates double raised thread supports.

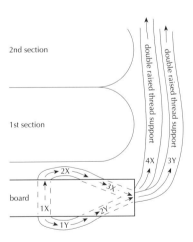

TYPE 7 BOARD ATTACHMENT is not part of a sewing, but merely the stringing of double raised thread supports from one board to the other. It is limited to the secondary sewing. when using the Book As Sewing Frame. See page 273.

THE BUTTERFLY   *Yamato Toji*

DOUBLE SPAN-SPAN SPAN-SPAN

According to Rigby Graham, the original name of this sewing, developed in the 11th-12th century, is Yamato Toji. Some refer to it as the Japanese 4–Needle Sewing. I prefer not use that term, so it is not confused with the Japanese 4–Hole Sewing, Yatsume Toji. The 4–Hole sewing is a stab binding, described in *Non-Adhesive Binding,* Volume I, page 75.

Betsy Palmer Eldridge refers to this sewing as the Butterfly, and that is the name I will use. She calls the movement of this sewing, *double span-span, span-span.* In addition to learning the sewing from Betsy, I wish to thank Lloyd Trainor, River Bend Books, for his correspondence, description and information about this sewing.

Since it is one of the most basic examples of sewing across the spine, it is a good first sewing to describe. With four sewing stations, height of the spine is limited. However, you could expand it to a 6-needle sewing with the addition of two more sewing stations. This would require a third, independent sewing at the fifth and sixth stations.

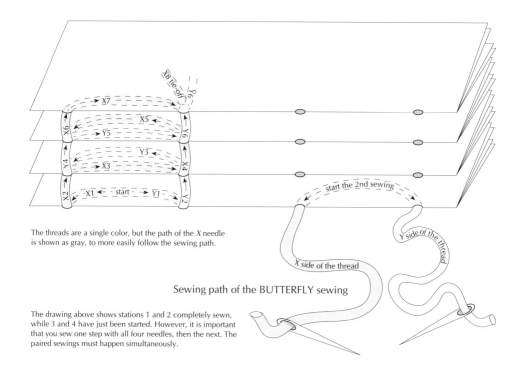

The threads are a single color, but the path of the *X* needle is shown as gray, to more easily follow the sewing path.

Sewing path of the BUTTERFLY sewing

The drawing above shows stations 1 and 2 completely sewn, while 3 and 4 have just been started. However, it is important that you sew one step with all four needles, then the next. The paired sewings must happen simultaneously.

The Butterfly is suitable for sewing small booklets, and generally has a paper cover, rather than sewn boards. Any of the six types of board attachment could be used. See pages 212 through 219. If a paper cover is desired, three covers for the Butterfly are described on page 224. These are courtesy of Lloyd Trainor.

SPAN: To span is to climb directly to a station above, without linking to the previous sewing below. Thus, the Butterfly pivots on the threads. It is a tight sewing. The connection does not loosen up when it opens, as with the link sewings.

SEWING PROCEDURE

This sewing must be sewn on the bench. Do not try to sew it hand-held. Keep the sewing tight as you go, and there will be no gaps when opened.

Simple Diagram: The sewing path in a basic diagram is shown on the facing page: Exit the section with both needles. Span with each needle and enter. The needle that exits station 1, enters station 1 of the next section. The needle that exits station 2, enters station 2. On the inside of the section, each needle exits the opposite station. Whichever needle exits station 1 spans and enters station 1 of the next section. The sewing continues in that manner.

To better show the path of the two needles, the half of the thread coded X has been shaded gray. If the diagram on page 220 does not seem clear, an elaborate description with many drawings follows on the next three pages. Understanding this simple sewing across the spine is critical, as it is the concept for all the more intricate sewings in the remainder of Volume III.

Elaborate Diagramming: The elaborate drawings require coding of a letter, as well as a number. The two separate sewings are identical, and, must be sewn simultaneously. One thread with two needles (*A* and *B*) sews stations 1 and 2. The other two needles (*X* and *Y*) sew stations 3 and 4.

LABELING THE STEPS:

- The number, as always, is the step in the procedure of sewing.
- The step number is followed by a letter, *A, B, X* or *Y*. The letter refers to the needle. *Left* and *right* are irrelevant terms, since each needle alternates sewing *both* of the paired stations.

Example of the Japanese BUTTERFLY Sewing. It is also referred to as the Japanese 4–Needle Sewing.

The sewing will be described without side-covers. Attaching covers will be described at the end of the sewing. You might want to read that first.

1X and 1Y. Start inside with one of the threads. Needle *X* exits station 1, and *Y* exits station 2. On the outside, adjust the threads to equal lengths. There is no need for a tie-off at the beginning of sewing paired stations.

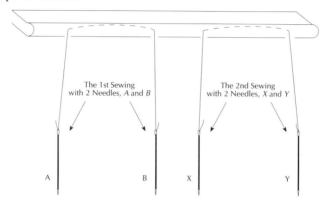

The 1st Sewing
with 2 Needles, *A* and *B*

The 2nd Sewing
with 2 Needles, *X* and *Y*

A   B   X   Y

Sewing the first section

Sewing the Second Section: Set on the second section to be sewn.

2X and 3X. The *X* thread spans and enters station 1 of the second section. Exit station 2.

4X and 2Y. Allow thread *X* to pause, hanging on the outside. Thread *Y*, which extends from station 2, spans and enters station 2 of the second section. Pull thread 4X to the left as you enter, so that you do not pierce it.

3Y. Exit station 1. Pull the threads which extend from stations 1 and 2 to tighten the threads inside. Be sure to pull in the direction of the sewing, to not rip the paper.

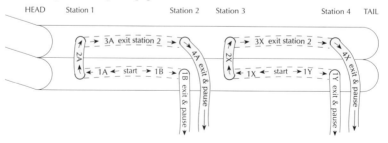

Stations 1, 2, 3 and 4: Sewing the second section with the *X* needle
All four stations must be sewn at once.
The *X* needle originates on the left of the paired stations, the *Y* needle on the right.
Complete the sewing at stations 1 and 2, before beginning the sewing at the other paired stations.

Sewing the Third Section: 4Y and 5Y. Span and enter station 1 of the third section. Exit station 2.

4X, 5X and 6X. Span, enter third section at station 2. Exit station 1. Set on next section. Span and enter at station 1.

Continue in this manner. When finished, tie-off on the inside at station 2. Sew stations 3 and 4 with the other thread. Tie-off inside the final section.

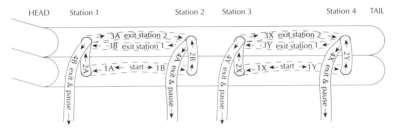

Stations 1, 2, 3 and 4: Sewing the second section with the *Y* needle

Push thread 4X to the left, so that the *Y* needle does not pierce it, when step 2Y enters the second section.

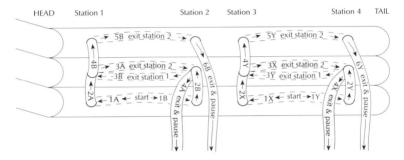

Stations 1, 2, 3 and 4: Sewing the third section with the *Y* needle

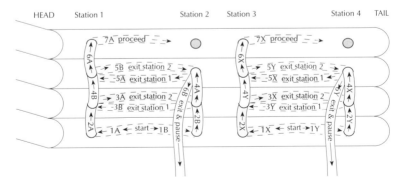

Stations 1, 2, 3 and 4: Sewing the third section with the *X* needle

Push thread 6Y to the left, so that 4X can enter the third section without piercing the thread.

Traditional ties-off: The ties-off would be on the outside. For the first sewing, the thread at station 1 spans and enters the final section, then exits station 2. The other thread does not enter the final section. It spans to station 2, where the knot is made on the outside.

The sewing at stations 3 and 4 ties-off on the outside at station 3. The four threads extending from the two knots at stations 2 and 3 are then tied together.

Cover Variations: Example 1, below, is two separate paper side-covers with an exposed spine. The paper covers are sewn along with the sections. There is a foredge turn-in.

Cover 2 is a single piece paper cover with spine, and a foredge turn-in. Sewing the final section and cover is tricky, but can be done.

Cover 3 is constructed separately to fit the text block. The front foredge turn-in slips onto the first two pages of the book. The foredge turn-in for the back cover slips over the final two pages of the text block. The areas of the cover denoted as gray on the turn-ins at the head and the tail may have to be cut away. This helps prevent binding (crow's feet) at the folds.

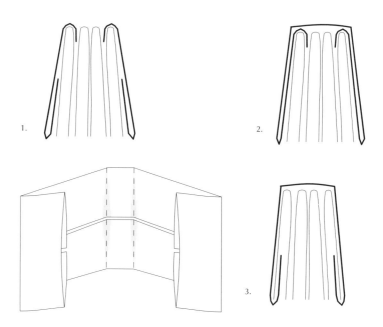

1.

2.

3.

Three covers for the BUTTERFLY sewing

VARIOUS "COPTIC" SEWINGS

ALONG THE SPINE VS ACROSS THE SPINE COPTIC

Coptic Sewing Along the Spine: The Coptic described on page 174, Volume I, is a *loop/link stitch* sewing. See page 28, Volume III. Since the sewing is done *along* the spine, there is a kettle stitch at the head and the tail:

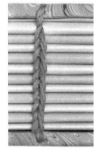

Detail 1–Needle Coptic sewn along the spine

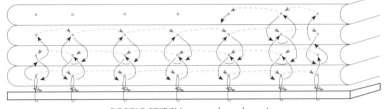

1–Needle Coptic Stitch sewn along the spine, in the photograph above and diagram below, is described in Volume I. Rows of link stitches on the spine combine with kettle stitches at the head and tail as the change-over.

COPTIC STITCH sewn *along* the spine
as described in Volume I on page 174

In the Coptic Sewing, the kettle stitch seems to me to interrupt the pattern of the chains on the spine, since the kettle looks like an imperfect chain.

"Coptic" Terminology: "The term *Coptic Sewing* is a semantical mess," Betsy Palmer Eldridge. The various single and double needle link sewings presented in this chapter will be referred to as "Coptic" sewings. Each is an unsupported sewing, along, or, across, the spine. Each employs link stitches. They could just as easily be called *Single-Needle Link Sewings,* and *Double–Needle Link Sewings,* rather than "Coptics".

Sewn at paired stations across the spine, there is no need for a kettle to climb at the head and tail: *Every* link at *every* station climbs. *Each* acts to change-over. The link stitches form a pattern of chains. Five differently sewn 2–Needle "Coptic" Sewings and three 1–Needle "Coptic" Sewings, (or *Link Sewings*) all across the spine, are described on the following pages. They were taught to me by Betsy Palmer Eldridge. Many thanks.

Detail left to right: The 2–Needle COPTIC SEWING I, page 235; 2–Needle COPTIC SEWING II, page 239; and 2–Needle COPTIC SEWING III, page 240. This sewing uses two colors of thread tied together. One color comes out each paired station to alternate colors of the links and the spans.

The 2–Needle COPTIC SEWING IV is shown on page 242, and the 2–Needle COPTIC SEWING V, on page 244.

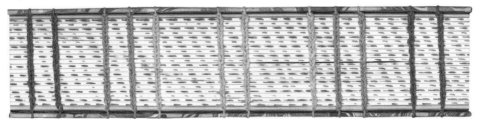

Contending with swelling

Above: A view of the spine of a 2–Needle COPTIC SEWING It is attractive.

Left: However, to the left is a cross-section view, seen from the head, standing on the foredge. Compare the thickness of the spine to the foredge. This is undesirable, because shape of the spine will distort on the shelf, as pressure is applied to the side-covers.

All Coptic Sewings have an excessive amount of linking, since linking occurs between every section. Bulk of the thread *swells* the spine thicker than the foredge.

•   *To utilize* this massive spine-edge, round and back the book. See illustration at the bottom of page 47.

•   *To prevent* or reduce swelling (increasing the thickness of the spine), sew with a thinner thread. If possible, construct sections of more, rather than fewer pages.

1– AND 2–NEEDLE COPTICS SEWN ACROSS THE SPINE

STRUCTURAL INTEGRITY: Sewing a Coptic Stitch along the spine creates a continuous thread inside. Whereas the sewing pattern on the inside the various 1–Needle, and 2–Needle Coptic Sewings leaves an interrupted path of double threads.

Fred Jordan examined one of my link stitch sewings. He informs me it is a weak sewing, because I have utilized only 28% of the length of the spine for the stitches:

Valley view of a weak sewing of a
1-Needle or 2–Needle COPTIC SEWING

He suggests either increasing the number of stations, or doubling the width between paired stations to structurally improve the sewing. Here, the stitches are about 57% of the length of the spine:

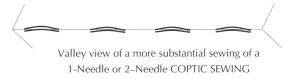

Valley view of a more substantial sewing of a
1-Needle or 2–Needle COPTIC SEWING

Sewing strength must be kept in mind, not only true for the 1–Needle, and 2–Needle Coptic Sewings, but for all sewings across the spine.

Tension Tension varies with each sewer. It varies even if one person stops for a break. It is best to start and sew the entire book at once. The operative word is *snug.* Tension should not be loose, but neither should it be tight. In sewing a coptic binding, or any sewing with chaining, many people have a tendency to use too much tension. Pay attention to the forming of the chain on the spine. The links should not be pulled to a straight line, but curved in a teardrop shape. Just as importantly, apply uniform pressure so that each link in the chain is uniform in size and shape.

Planning the Colors: Since there are several separate sewings across the spine, the opportunity for more than one color thread is possible. Two colors of threads can be tied together. Exiting the first section, two separate colors appear on paired stations. The resulting linking will be in two colors. If this is not desirable, each set of paired stations can have a different color. See illustration at top of the following page. Alternating colors can be pleasing, or, may result in a monotonous spine design.

Even Spacing of Paired Sewing Stations: Below is evenly paired stations:

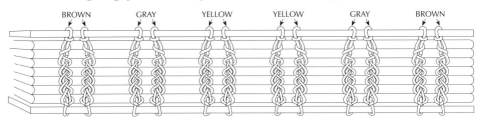

Positioning of paired stations, evenly spaced, sewn across the spine

2–NEEDLE COPTIC SEWING I, sewn across the spine, is shown here with 12 stations as 6 paired stations. The six threads have a needle at each end. It is sewn with 12 needles. This sewing is described on page 235.

Uneven Spacing of Paired Sewing Stations: To camouflage the pattern of obviously paired stations, play with their placement on the spine:

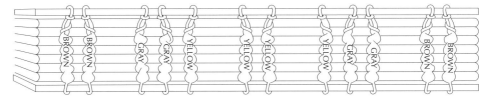

Uneven space between paired stations camouflages that they are paired

Uneven spacing of stations broadens the possibilities of design. The yellow thread of the linking at station 5, above, appears to be grouped with the sewing at stations 3 and 4. Actually, it is paired with station 6. This design was employed in the sample sewing which appears in a digital scan in the middle of, and, at the bottom of, page 226.

Planning the Stations: In planning a sewing, draw on a rectangular sheet of paper, the height and width of the spine. Lightly with pencil, and without a ruler, quickly draw lines that might be pleasing for the stations, perpendicular to the hinge-fold. The spontaneity is critical to bring new approaches to design.

Keep erasing and lightly drawing other possibilities until you find something you like. Remember, there must be an even number of stations. Once you are satisfied, then comes the time for calculated measurement of the stations to clean up your sketch. Transfer the measurement to the spine of your book block, and you are ready to pre-pierce the stations and to sew any 1– or 2–needle Coptic.

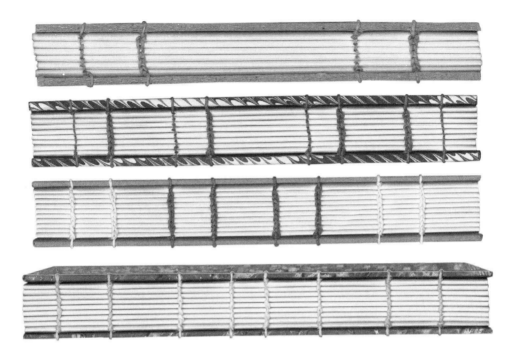

Top to bottom: The 1–NEEDLE COPTIC SEWING I, page 230, spans at the left paired station and enters. It exits the right paired station, drops on the inner side, links, climbs and re-enters. The second scan is the same, but every other paired station has been sewn symmetrically. The third scan, the 1–NEEDLE COPTIC SEWING II, page 232, drops to the outer side, links, but *does not lock,* climbs and enters. It is a false kettle. However, it is an acceptable variation, giving a different, more open look to the sewing on the spine. The bottom scan, the 1–NEEDLE COPTIC SEWING III, page 233, forms a true kettle, entering the same station with one needle. It forms a second kettle, entering the next section with the other needle.

Detail, left to right: The 1–NEEDLE COPTIC SEWING I, page 230; 1–NEEDLE COPTIC SEWING II, page 232; and the 1–NEEDLE COPTIC SEWING III, page 233.

1–NEEDLE COPTIC SEWING I

SINGLE SPAN-LINK

PREPARATION

Prepare two separate side-covers. There must be an even number of stations, as they are paired for individual sewings. One paired station should be within 1/2" of the head, and one, equally as close to the tail. This will support the extremes of the sections. Pierce as many pairs of stations on the spine as needed. *TYPE 3* Board Attachment, page 216, is modified to be sewn with a single needle, as diagrammed on the facing page.

1. Start inside the first section. Exit the paired station on the left.
2-7. Attach the board, hinged through the depth of the board.
8, 9. Span and re-enter the first section. Exit the paired station.
10-15. Attach the board, hinged through the depth of the board.
16-18. Span and re-enter the first section. Tie-off. Exit the paired station.
19. Set on the next section. Span and enter at the same numbered station.
20. Exit the paired station.
21a. Drop backward, link under the last two connected sections (between the board and the first section.)
21b. Climb on the outer side. Re-enter the same section.
22. Exit the paired station.

For Each Additional Section: Repeat steps 19 through 22.

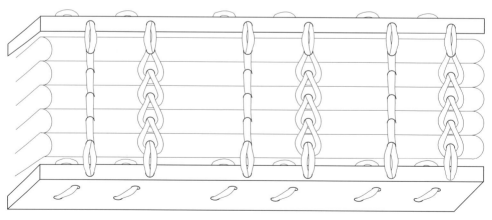

1–NEEDLE COPTIC SEWING I

This is sewn across the spine at paired stations. *TYPE 3* BOARD ATTACHMENT is modified for a 1–needle sewing. Refer to the text above and diagram on page 231. A digital scan of this sewing is on page 229.

Sewing the Final Section and Attaching the Board: Span and enter the final section. Exit the paired station and link. Re-enter. Exit the left station. Span and enter the board through the depth. Attach the board in the procedure of *TYPE 3*, exiting through the depth. Span and re-enter the final section. Exit the paired station. Span and enter the board through the depth. Attach the board using *TYPE 3* pathway, exiting through the depth. Span and re-enter the final section. Tie-off on the inside with a half hitch. See top two digital scans on page 229.

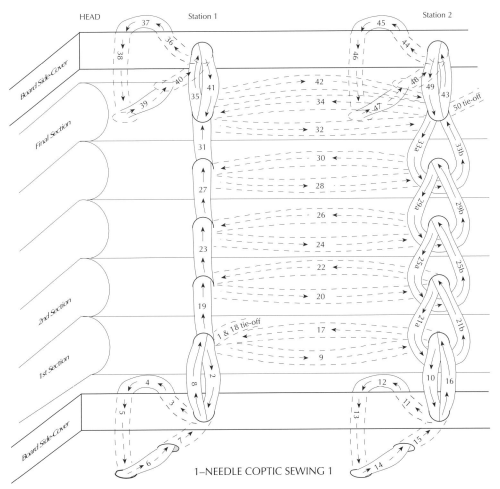

1–NEEDLE COPTIC SEWING 1

The 1–needle Coptic Sewings use a modification of the *TYPE 3* Board Attachment. The board is attached at the left station. Span and re-enter the first section. Exit the paired station and attach the board. Span and re-enter the first section.

1–NEEDLE COPTIC SEWING II

SINGLE KETTLE-LINK

Steps 1 through 18, a modification of *TYPE 3* Board Attachment, sews the first section to the board. The procedure is identical to the previous sewing on page 230, and the diagram on page 231.

The remainder of this sewing uses the same steps as the previous, except for steps number 19, 23, 27 and 31. Instead of spanning at the left paired station, a true kettle is used as cross-over:

- Drop to the inner side, link between the last two connected sections,
- slip under the *a* thread to lock, and
- climb and enter the next section.

Enter the final section, exit the right station, link and re-enter. Exit the left station. Form a kettle, climb and attach the board. Span, re-enter the final section. Exit the right station and attach the other board. Re-enter the final section and tie-off.

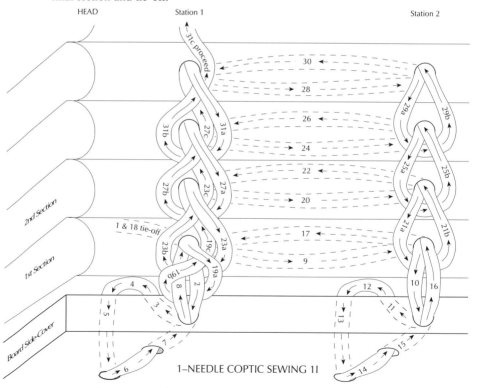

1–NEEDLE COPTIC SEWING 1I

Steps 1-18 are a modification of the *TYPE 3* Board Attachment, described on page 216. Exit the right station and link. Re-enter. Exit the paired station on the left. A true kettle is formed: drop to the inside, link, slip under to lock, climb and enter the next section. A digital scan of this sewing is the third from the top on page 229.

1–NEEDLE COPTIC SEWING III

SINGLE KETTLE–KETTLE *inside*

Steps 1 through 18, a modification of *TYPE 3* Board Attachment, sews the first section to the board. The procedure is identical to the sewing on page 230, and the diagram on page 231.

The remainder of this sewing uses a true kettle stitch at both of the of the paired stations:

- Drop to the inner side, link between the last two connected sections,
- slip under the *a* thread to lock, and
- climb and enter the next section.

After sewing the final section, exit. Form a kettle. Climb and attach the board. Span, re-enter the final section. Exit the paired station. Span and enter the depth of the board. Attach the board. Span and re-enter final section and tie-off.

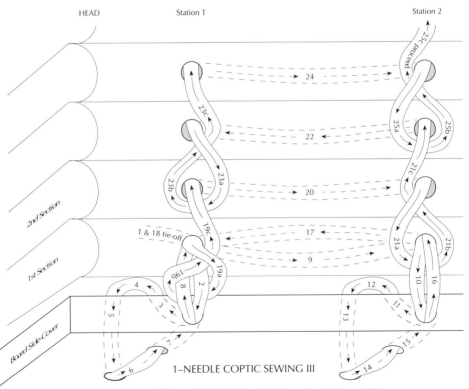

1–NEEDLE COPTIC SEWING III

Steps 1-18 are a modification of the *TYPE 3* Board Attachment, described on page 216
With step 19, each exit at both paired stations is a kettle stitch that drops to the inside, links, slips under to lock, climbs and enters the next section.
A digital scan of this sewing is at the bottom of page 229.

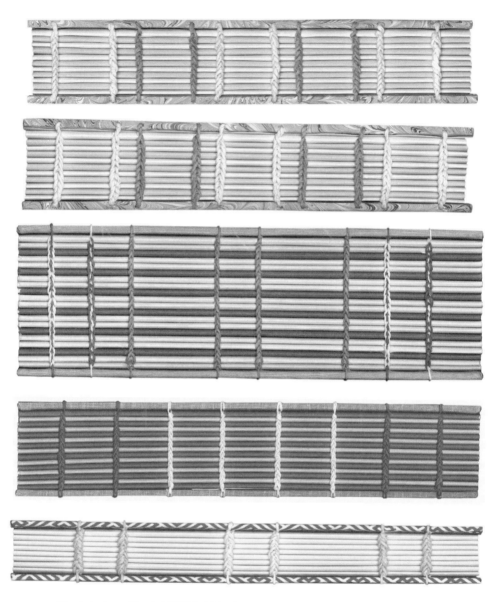

Top to bottom: The 2–NEEDLE COPTIC SEWING I, page 235, drops to the outer side of the paired stations, links, *slips under to lock,* climbs and enters. It is a true kettle stitch. 2–NEEDLE COPTIC SEWING II, page 239, drops to the outer side, links, but *does not lock,* climbs and enters. It is a false kettle. However, it is an acceptable variation, giving a different, more open look to the sewing on the spine. 2–NEEDLE COPTIC SEWING III, page 240, spans with one needle, links with the other at each paired station. 2–NEEDLE COPTIC SEWING IV, page 242, links at each station, then forms a kettle stitch at the same station, climbing to the next section. 2–NEEDLE COPTIC SEWING V, page 244, forms a true kettle, entering the same station with one needle. Forms a second kettle, entering the next section with the other needle.

2–NEEDLE COPTIC SEWING I

PREPARATION

Prepare two separate side-covers. There must be an even number of stations, as they are paired for individual sewings. One paired station should be within 1/2" of the head, and one, equally as close to the tail. This will support the extremes of the sections. Pierce as many pairs of stations on spine as needed. Choose type of board attachment. See pages 212- 219.

1-3. Sew the first section and board as described on those pages.

Sewing the Second Section: Set on the second section. Start at the same end with each section. The descriptions will start at the head.

4-5X. Pick up the needle closest to the head. Span, enter second section directly above (station 1). Proceed to the paired station (2) and exit.

4-5Y. Pick up the remaining needle for this pair. Push thread 6X to the inner side so it is not pierced. Span, enter the second section in the station directly above (2). Proceed inside to the paired station (1). Exit:

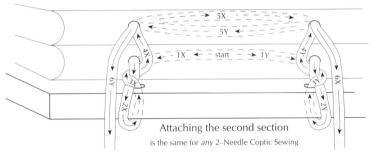

Attaching the second section
is the same for *any* 2–Needle Coptic Sewing

Continue along the spine repeating steps 4 and 5 for each of the paired stations. Return to the head to begin the linking process for all stations of the second section.

6Y-9Y. Pick up the needle closest to the head. Drop to the outer side. Link under the last two connected sections. (For the second section, linking takes place between the side-cover and the first section.) Climb. Slip under to lock. (Compare locking to not, page 238 to 239.) Enter the new section (third) at the station directly above (1). Exit the paired station (2).

6X-9X. Pick up the remaining needle of this paired station. Drop to the outer side, link under the last two connected sections. Climb. Slip under to lock. Enter the new section directly above (station 2). Exit the other paired station (1). See illustration at the top of the following page.

Sewing the Remaining Sections: Set on the next section. Start at the head. Repeat steps 6 through 9. Drop to the outer side, link under the last two connected sections.

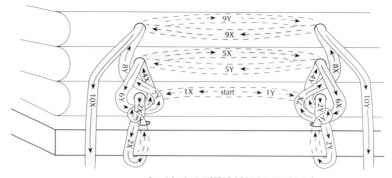

Step 6 for the 2–NEEDLE COPTIC SEWING I, *only*

Forming the link

Step 7 slips under to lock. It is optional. See page 238 and 239.

Climb at at angle. Slip under to lock. Enter the new section at the same numbered station. Exit the paired station.

For the fourth section, this will be steps 10 through 13, as diagrammed below. After this has been done at all paired stations for this section, set on the next section, and continue. I have given 3 step numbers to each linking process: *to link, to lock* and *to climb,* in order to more easily track the path in the congestion of threads in the diagrams for this sewing. You can omit the locking, if you wish. Compare this Coptic Sewing (I) to the next variation, (II) on page 239.

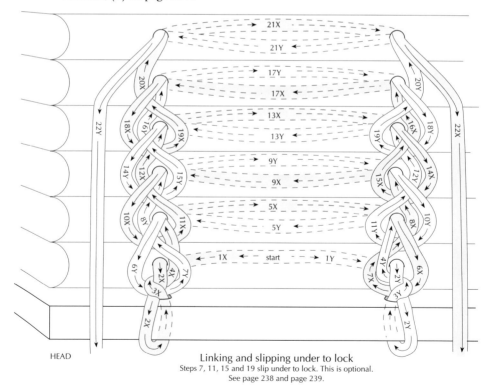

HEAD

Linking and slipping under to lock

Steps 7, 11, 15 and 19 slip under to lock. This is optional.

See page 238 and page 239.

Sewing the Final Section: 21X and Y. Exit the next to last section.

22X and Y. Drop to the outer side.

23-24X and Y. Link, slip under to lock. Climb and enter the final section.

25X and Y. Exit the paired station of the final section. Do not link. The board will be attached before linking. Set on the board.

Attaching the Board: These steps are numbered for the diagrams on page 237 and 238, but not 239. On page 239, it is the same procedure to attach the boards to the 2–Needle Coptic Sewing II. However, the steps are numbered differently, since the earlier link stitches were not locked.

26X and Y. Climb *above* the board and enter from the outside of the board. Exit the board, only, on the *outer* side of the paired stations.

27X and Y. Lap and loop from the outer to inner side, between cover and the final section.

28X and Y. Drop to the outer side. Link under between the next to last, and second to last sections.

29X and Y. Slip under the thread marked step 28 to lock the link.

30X and Y. Enter the final section.

31X and Y. Tie-off the X and Y threads on the inside at either of the paired stations.

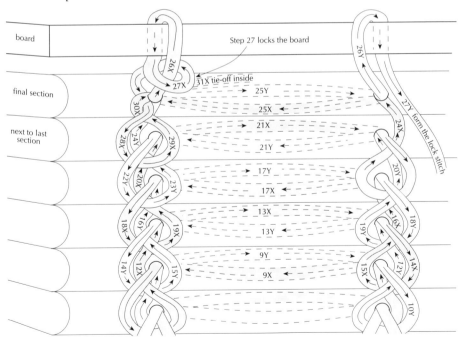

Step 26 Attaching the board
Enter the board, only, from the outside to the inside of the board.
Step 27 Locking the board

Slipping Under to Lock: As diagrammed on pages 235-238, in the 2–Needle Coptic Sewing I, the link stitch is locked: Exiting the paired stations, each needle drops symmetrically to the outside and forms a true kettle stitch. This builds a rope-like pattern on the spine. See the digital scan on page 234, and the diagram below. This link and lock 2–Needle Coptic Sewing I always:

- drops to the outer side and links
- slips under to lock
- climbs and enters.

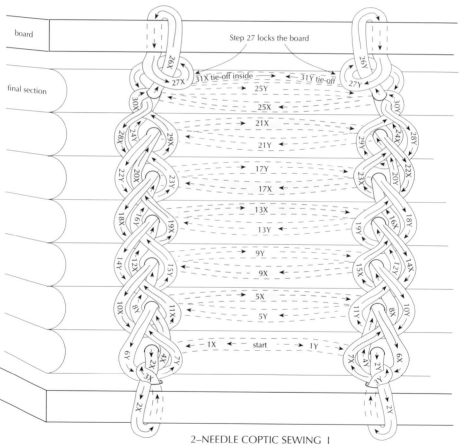

2–NEEDLE COPTIC SEWING I
Linking, slipping under to lock before climbing
A digital scan of this sewing is at the top of page 234.
Compare to the diagram of the 2–Needle Coptic Sewing II on the facing page.

2–NEEDLE COPTIC SEWING II

Sewing Pattern without Slipping Under to Lock: The digital scan on page 235, and the diagram below, show a variation of the previous sewing, referred to as the 2–Needle Coptic Sewing I. Sewing II eliminates the lock for a more open pattern of sewing, maintaining the teardrop shape of the links on the spine:

- drops to the outer side and links
- does *not* slip under , therefore, does not lock
- climbs and enters.

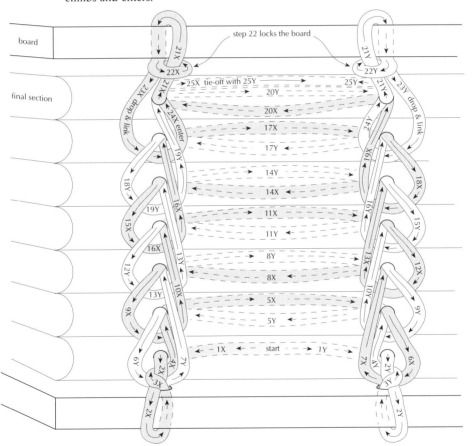

2–NEEDLE COPTIC SEWING II
Linking, but not slipping under, not locking before climbing

A digital scan of this sewing is on page 234.
Compare to the 2–Needle Coptic Sewing I, diagrammed on the facing page.

2–NEEDLE COPTIC SEWING III

DOUBLE SPAN–LINK LINK–SPAN

This variation gives a vertical thread (span) in the middle of the link stitches, forming a thicker, and quite pleasant sewing. Pierce, do not saw the stations; so the spans will not recess. Don't pull the span tight, or the spans will disappear. Link exits are critical, on one or the other side of the span, so as not to cross and hide the span.

Steps 1-5 for this 2–Needle Coptic Sewing are the same as Sewing I. See pages 235. With step 6, the thread spans one section and enters, exiting the paired station. Drop to the outer side, link, climb, but do not lock. Re-enter the same station. Exit the paired station and span. This places four threads inside all but the first section.

ATTACHING the BOARD: Step 16 spans, enters the final section, exits the paired station (17). Enter the board from the out to the inside (18). Step 19 locks the board. Step 20 drops and link under the next to last section, then climbs and enters the final section. Step 21 ties-off on the inside.

See pages 241 and 293 for a different color span from that of the link.

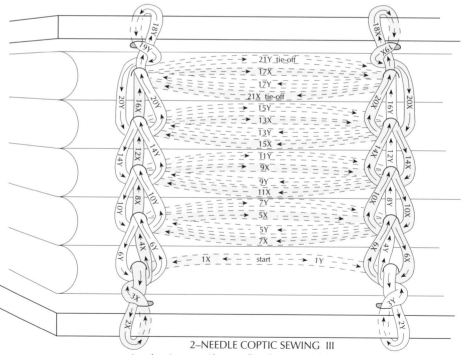

2–NEEDLE COPTIC SEWING III

At each station, span with one needle and enter. Exit with the other and link.
A digital scan of this sewing is on page 234.

2–NEEDLE COPTIC SEWING III. Two colors of thread were tied together, with one color exiting one of the paired stations, and the second color exiting the other. This gives a different color to the span from the link.

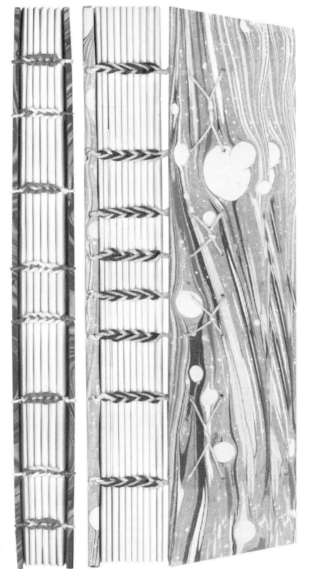

Left: 2–NEEDLE COPTIC SEWING III.

Middle: 2–NEEDLE COPTIC SEWING II. Each of the paired stations were sewn with two threads and four needles: The odd-numbered sections were sewn with white thread, even-numbered sections with brown. A total sixteen needles were required.

Right: 2–NEEDLE COPTIC SEWING IV.

2–NEEDLE COPTIC SEWING IV

DOUBLE KETTLE–LINK LINK–KETTLE

This variation of the Coptic Sewing is similar to the previous. The difference is that instead of spanning to enter the next section, this sewing climbs with a kettle stitch.

The previous sewing, on page 240, climbs by spanning. The first span is step 8, which climbs from the second to the third section.

With step 12, the span is from the third to the fourth section. See diagram to the right, as well as on page 240.

The 2–Needle Coptic Sewing IV is diagrammed on the facing page, as well as the detail at the bottom of this page.

Steps 1 through 7 are sewn the same as the previous sewing.

In fact, all the steps are identical to the last sewing, except for steps 8, 12 and 16. These are the climbs. In this sewing, the climb is by means of a true kettle stitch: Step 8Xa drops to the inside and links. 8Xb slips under 8Xa to lock. 8Xc climbs and enters the new section. Step 8Ya, b and c proceeds in the same at the paired station. Steps 12 and 16 are sewn the same as step 8.

This sewing builds up a thickness of threads in the spine, creating its own supports. I suggest you sew versions I, II and II before attempting this logical progression.

See the digital scan on page 234.

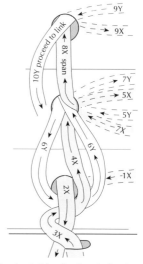

Step 8 for the 2–Needle Coptic Sewing III
spans from the second to the third section

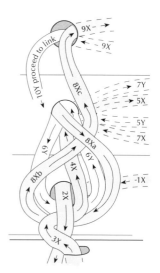

Step 8 for the 2–Needle Coptic Sewing IV

Step 8a drops to the inner side and links, 8b slips under to lock and 8c climbs and enters the third section.

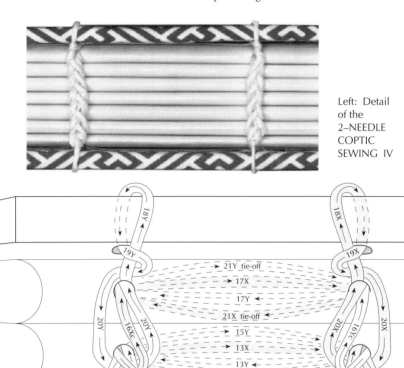

Left: Detail
of the
2–NEEDLE
COPTIC
SEWING IV

2–NEEDLE COPTIC SEWING IV

Linking with one needle and re-entering the same station, then forming a kettle at the
same station with the other needle, climbing and entering the next section.
A digital scan of this sewing is on the left on page 234.

2–NEEDLE COPTIC SEWING V

DOUBLE KETTLE–KETTLE KETTLE–KETTLE

This variation of the Coptic Sewing is similar to the previous. The difference is that instead of linking with step 6, a kettle links, locks and re-enters the second section, rather than climbing to the next. See diagram below and page 245.

Steps 8, 12 and 16 are the same as on the previous sewing. The kettle links, locks, climbs and enters the *next* section.

In fact, all the steps are identical to the last sewing, except for the linking steps 6, 10, 14 and 20. Each is replaced by a kettle stitch which links, locks and re-enters the *same* section.

This sewing builds up a thickness of threads in the spine, creating its own supports. I suggest you first sew the earlier versions of the 2–Needle Coptic Sewings. The progression makes the more elaborate sewings easier to understand.

See the digital scan on page 234.

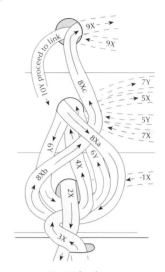

Step 8 for the
2–NEEDLE COPTIC SEWING IV

Step 8a drops to the inner side and links, 8b slips under to lock and 8c climbs and enters the third section.

Detail of the 2–NEEDLE COPTIC SEWING V
See the digital scan on page 234.

The double kettle
2–NEEDLE COPTIC SEWING V

Step 6 drops, links, locks and re-enters the same (2nd) section. Step 8 drops, links, slips under to lock and climbs and enters the next (3rd) section. All drops are to the inner side.

Steps 18-20. In sewing the final section, exit and attach the cover. Then drop to the inner side, link under the next to last section, slip under to lock and re-enter the final section. 21 X and Y can tie-off with each other.

In beginning the sewing, step 4 can re-enter the first section, rather than spanning to the second, if you wish. Step 5 would then form a kettle, linking under between the board and first section, slip under to lock, climb and enter the second section. In this manner, you would start to build the rope effect of the linking right from the board, rather than from the first section.

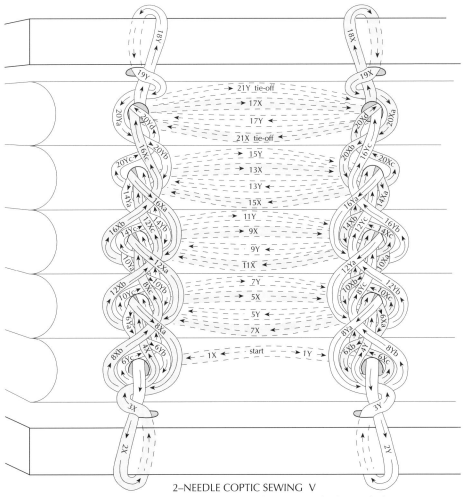

2–NEEDLE COPTIC SEWING V

Forming a kettle with one needle and re-entering the same station, then forming a kettle at the same station with the other needle, climbing and entering the next section. The drop is always to the inner side. A digital scan of this sewing is on the left on page 234.

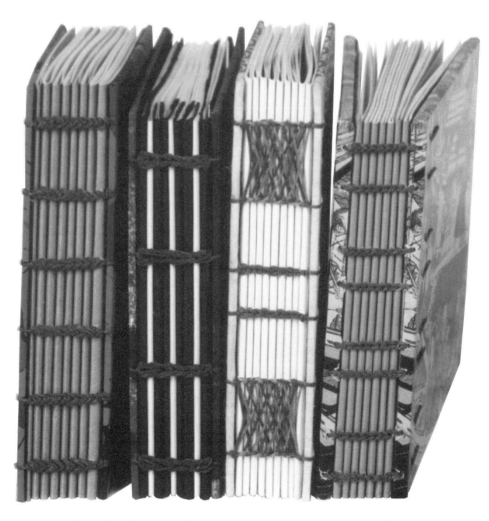

Margo Klass, Some examples of across the spine sewings from Session 2, Penland, 1995. Left to right: 2–Needle COPTIC SEWING II, followed by the 4–DOWN LINK SEWING. The third sewing has the CELTIC WEAVE sewn at the head and the tail, with the 2–Needle COPTIC SEWING II in the center of the spine. On the far right is an example of the 2–Needle COPTIC SEWING I. The first three sewings have *TYPE 1* Board Attachment. The book on the right has *TYPE 3*. Each of the four books is approximately 15 x 10 x 2.5 cm.

CELTIC WEAVE

The pattern of the 2–Needle Coptic Sewing I, page 235, alternates exits of paired stations. It then drops, links, slips under to lock and climbs.

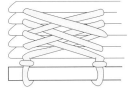

Prototype 1 of the
CELTIC WEAVE
This is an inferior sewing; it can rip out, because it does not link to anchor, prior to climbing.

I played with the concept. My first prototype of what I refer to as the Celtic Weave suggests a figure 8 pattern. To exaggerate this I eliminated the link stitch. Instead, I angled diagonally across the spine, creating a band of interwoven *X's*:

Although I was pleased with the appearance, the pattern is functionally a disaster; stations are vulnerable to stress with a diagonal climb.

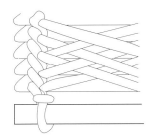

The final solution
to designing the
CELTIC WEAVE

To salvage the lovely shoestring lacing effect of the *X's* at paired stations, it was necessary to support the stations by linking, prior to angling, to avoid the thread tearing out. Unlike the kettle, you do not slip under to lock, but anchor two down. If two colors of thread alternate, you are anchoring on the same color.

PREPARATION

Fold as many sections as desired. An even number of sections results in both side-covers being attached with the same color thread. This is because the cover is attached with the next to last section. An odd number of sections has the top board attached with the second color of thread. Cut and cover the boards with pasted cloth or decorative papers.

Sewing Stations: Determine how many paired stations of the Celtic Weave you wish to have across the spine. Paired stations should be approximately 5⁄8 to 3⁄4" apart.

Since the overlaid *X* stitches of the Celtic Weave are rather dense, you may desire this sewing only at the head and the tail. The spine would appear heavy with several. Each of the paired stations is a separate sewing, but sewn simultaneously across the spine. To strengthen the middle of the spine, you might use a lighter treatment of linking or a running stitch.

Sewing at each of the paired stations requires two threads, preferably of a different color, to exaggerate the pattern. Needles are threaded at each end. It is easier to sew on the bench, beginning all the sewings at once, rather than to completely sew one, then begin the next.

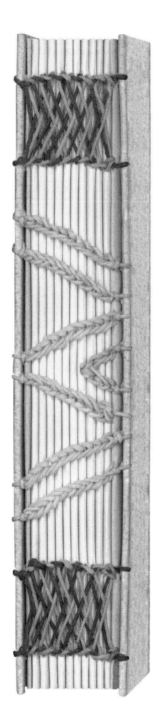

In sewing the Celtic Weave, the drop is on the *outer* side to link under. The angled climb proceeds on the inner side. The angling from the paired stations forms the *X* threads on the spine. The drop to the outer side gives a rope-like border.

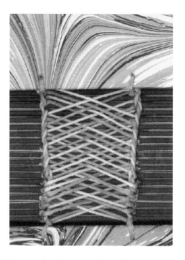

In the digital scan on the right, the first few drops were incorrectly on the inner side of the paired stations. Notice how the rope border is lacking for the first few sections.

Piercing the Stations for the Boards: See: *Attaching the Boards with Thread,* page 212-219 for seven methods. *Type 1* BOARD ATTACHMENT is used in the diagrams of the Celtic Weave. Appearance and hinging action of *Types 3, 4* and *Sewn Boards* are preferable to *Types 1* and *2*, as they allow the book block to sit right on the spine-edge of the boards.

This is the first prototype for the CELTIC WEAVE, sewn at the head and the tail. June 1993. 16 x 3 x 17 cm. The middle of the spine was sewn in the shape of an *M*, for McCarney, with diagonal bands of the 2–Needle COPTIC SEWING II, described on page 239.

NOTE: Directions of the diagonal link stitches equalize the tension. If the book were sewn with the link stitches all angled in the same direction the spine would be distorted to a parallelogram. Even if the linking were done with loose tension, the spine would warp. The book block then could be physically re-adjusted to square, but turning the pages, the block would return askew. Diagonal sewing always creates tension. It must be counterbalanced by sewing diagonally in the opposite direction. See scan at the top of page 101.

SEWING PROCEDURE

Sewing the First Section: 1XY-3XY. Exit the first section with all needles at
the paired stations with threads of one color. I will refer to the color of
the thread for the odd-numbered sections as orange. Steps for the
orange thread will be numbered, and coded "X" and "Y" for the two
needles at paired stations. Attach and lock the board. See page 214.

Line up the section with the spine-edge of the board. Tighten the threads
between the section and the board. The needles dangle on the inner side
of the boundaries of the paired sewing stations. *Inner* and *outer,* as opposed
to *inside* and *outside,* are defined on page 214, as well as in the Glossary.

Sewing the Second Section:

1AB-3AB. Take the second color of thread (green) and exit the second
section with one needle through one station, and the second through
the paired station. Do this for all paired stations. Set on the second
section with its needles dangling on the spine, on the outer side of the
orange threads at each of the paired stations.

Start at the head. Take the left needle, with green thread, and drop to the
outer side. Link under the stitch directly below which connects the board
to the first section. Exit on the inner side. Dangle the green thread on the
outer side of the orange thread.

Take the right needle coming from the second section and drop to the
outer side. Link under the stitch connecting the board to the first section.
Exit to the inner side. Allow this green thread to also dangle on the outer
side of the adjacent orange thread. Link all the paired stations to connect
the second section to the first and to the board:

Sewing the Third Section, Forming the X Stitch:

4XY-5XY. Set on the third section. Climb with the left orange thread
diagonally to the right station of the third section. Enter the right station and exit the left. Allow the thread to dangle on the outer side of
the paired stations.

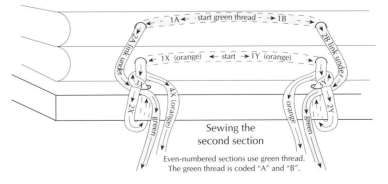

Sewing the
second section

Even-numbered sections use green thread.
The green thread is coded "A" and "B".

Pick up the remaining orange thread at the first section. Angle left to the paired station of the third section. Enter, being careful not to pierce the exiting thread. Exit the paired station. Allow thread to dangle on the outer side of the paired stations, ready to link. It is more efficient in forming the *X* stitch to enter and exit with one thread before angling with the second thread to form the other arm of the *X*. Do this for all paired stations.

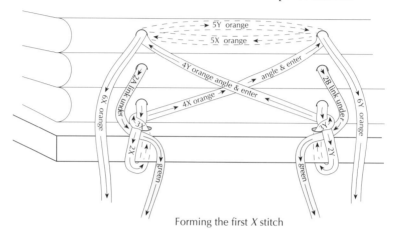

Forming the first *X* stitch

TIGHTENING: After making the *X* stitch, tighten by pulling both threads at the same time, the left thread to the left, the right thread to the right, parallel to the spine:

The *X*'s on the spine should always be consistent in how they are layered. Always angle with the left thread first (or the right, if you prefer) to maintain a uniform pattern:

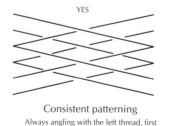

Consistent patterning
Always angling with the left thread, first

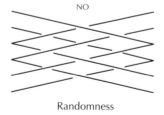

Randomness

6X. *LINKING the* X *STITCH:* The orange thread drops to the outer side,
links under the last two connected sections (between the board and the
first section). Keep the green thread on the inner side of the orange,
ready to angle, without getting caught up with the other color thread.

6Y. The right orange thread drops to the outer side of the station and links
under the last two connected sections (between the board and the first
section). Keep the green thread on the inner side of the orange:

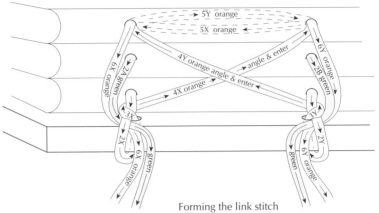

Forming the link stitch
Link under the last two connected (board and first section).

CONSISTENT PROCEDURE: Since you are sewing with two needles on
each thread, it is important to maintain a consistency in procedure: With
each change of color, first, angle with the left thread, enter and exit. Angle
with the other thread, enter and exit. Do this at all paired stations. Then
link under from the outer to the inner side will this color at all stations
prior to changing colors to sew the next section.

ADJUSTING the TENSION: Minor tightening is done after linking,
because only a small amount of pressure can be applied after linking without distorting the shape of the chain. The major tightening of a new section to those already sewn, is done after sewing the *X* stitch, as illustrated
in the middle drawing on the previous page. This also tightens the threads
in the *X* stitch.

After linking, adjust the tension of the links by grasping all four dangling
threads of the paired stations and gently pull downward, but not so much
as to distort the links. Take the threads which were just used in linking
and place them to the outer side of the other two threads so they will not
be caught up as you form the next *X* stitch with the new color thread.

It is critical when finishing linking and adjusting the tension to remember
to position the current thread on the outer side.

LOCATING the LEVEL DESIRED: This binding is sewn on the bench. As with any binding with linking, I use two bookmarks to readily find my positions. One is placed in the valley, in the center of the section now being sewn. The other, between the last two connected sections. This speeds up the sewing. See: *Tabbing the Positions,* page 32.

THE CLIMB: To avoid entanglement, the thread exiting a station is placed on the outer side of the other color of thread. Again, when you drop to the outer side and link under at each station, the thread is hung to rest on the outer side of the color of thread which is not being used.

This is so when you set on the next section, and climb at an angle with the other color, you will not hook the previous thread. This would result in a distorted *X* shape to your newly angled thread. If your threads become tangled, simply pick up the thread with which you will angle. Pull it to the inner side of the other thread, then proceed to angle.

Sewing the Fourth Section:

7AB-8AB. Set on the fourth section. Angle with the left green thread (7A) to the right station of the fourth section. Enter the right station and exit the left. Allow the thread to dangle on the outer side of the orange thread. Angle with the right green thread, enter the left station, exiting the right. Position the thread to the outer side.

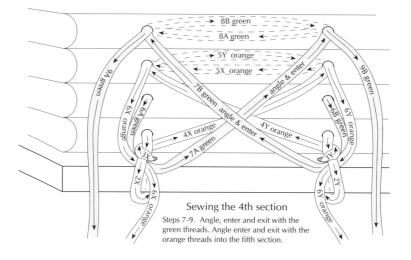

Sewing the 4th section
Steps 7-9. Angle, enter and exit with the
green threads. Angle enter and exit with the
orange threads into the fifth section.

Repeat this procedure at all the paired stations for that section to form the angled *X* stitches. Enter and exit. Then link under at each station, from the outer to the inner side. Link under *only* the outer-most thread; do *not* link under any arm of an *X* of any angled thread. Set the next section in position. Adjust the two bookmarks upwards one section.

Continue in this manner sewing the sections with the alternating colors of thread until all but the final two sections have been sewn.

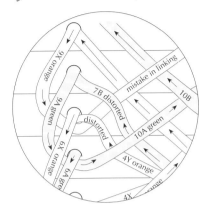

An improper linking

Step 9X. Orange should only link thread 6X. It has mistakenly additionally caught and distorted the angled threads 4Y orange and 7B green.

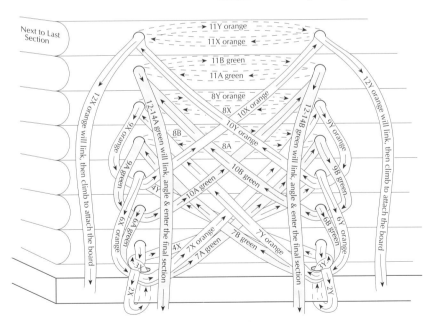

Sewing the next to last section

Steps 6-8. Link under, angle, enter and exit with the green threads. Repeat steps 6-8 for the orange threads.

Steps 9-11. Link under, angle, enter and exit with the green threads. Repeat steps 9-11 for the orange threads.

Sewing the Next to Last Section:

9X-11X. Set the next to last section into position. Drop to the outer side. Link under 6X with left thread. Angle and enter the right station of the next to last section. Exit the left.

9Y-11Y. Drop to the outer side. Link under 6Y. Angle and enter the left station of the next to last section. Exit the right.

12X, 12Y. Drop to the outside. Link under 9X and 9Y.

13X, 13Y. (orange) Climb and enter the next to last section.

14X, 14Y. (orange) Tie-off inside the next to last section.

Sewing the Final Section: Set on the final section. Pick up the dangling green thread on the left at the paired station. (If the total number of sections in your book is an odd number, the top side-cover will be attached with orange thread, the same as the bottom board.)

12A, 12B. Drop to the outer side. Link under 9A and 9B, respectively.

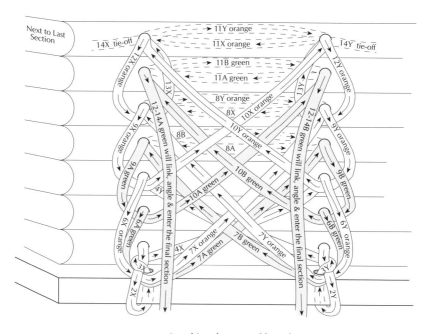

Attaching the second board
The final section has not yet been sewn. It is in place to position the board.

13A-14A. Angle and enter the final section at the right paired station. Exit the left station.

13B-14B. Angle and enter the final section at the left paired station. Exit the right station.

15A, 15B. Span and enter the board from the out to the inside.

16A, 16B. Lock the board.

17A, 17B. Drop to the inner side. Link under 12 A and 12 B, respectively.

18A, 18B. Enter the final section on the outer side of the paired stations.

19A, 19B. Tie-off on the inside.

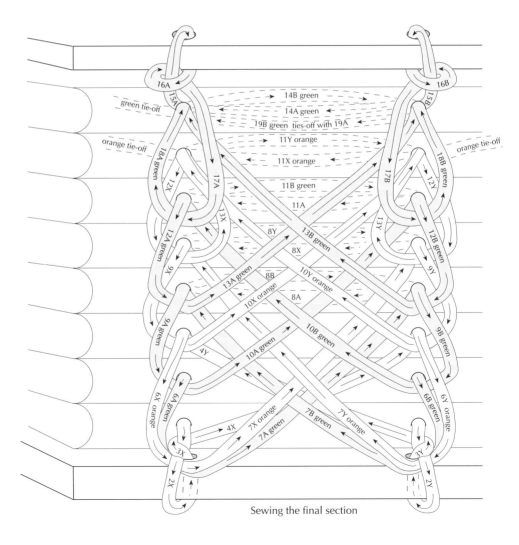

Sewing the final section

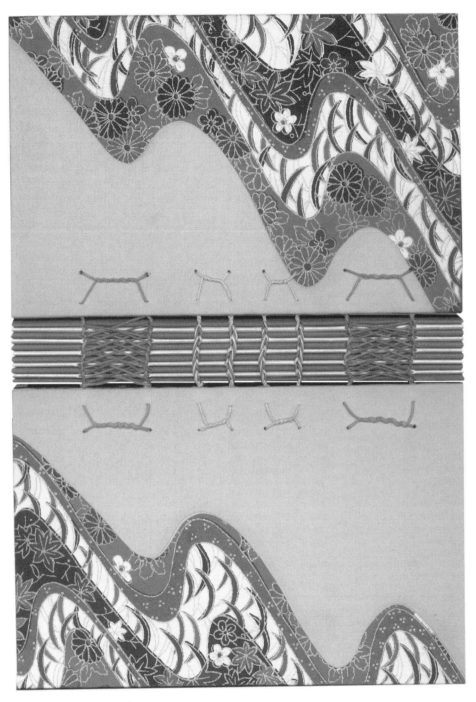

CELTIC WEAVE, sewn at the head and the tail. The middle of the spine was sewn with the 2–Needle COPTIC SEWING II, described on page 239. Two threads and four needles at each paired stations. For explanation, see page 241. Both sewings use *TYPE 3* Board Attachment.

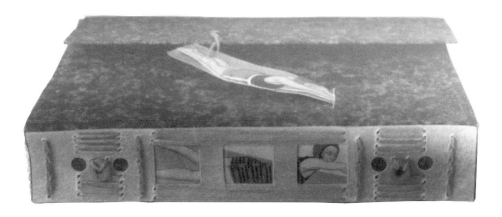

Above, Barbara Tetenbaum, *Untitled*, LONG STITCH/LINK STITCH sewing, vellum, cigarette cards, cronoids, paste papers. 1984. 12.6 x 9 cm.

Below, Barbara Tetenbaum, *Specimen No. 34*, GREEK SEWING, 1984. 9 x 6.5 cm.

GREEK SEWING

Pamela Spitzmueller describes this sewing in her 1985 Oxbow Diary notes, derived from examining "a single fragment, said to be Greek." She continues that it interests her "because it forms a very substantial chain, almost like a cord, from the use of the sewing thread alone."

Her "interpretation of the fragment is a two step construction. One half of the text is sewn to one board and the other half to the remaining board. The two halves are joined in the middle using a figure *8* type stitch."

PREPARATION

The following description paraphrases her instructions to fit my illustrations: The book block must contain a minimum of 20 sections. The book described has four sewing stations. Stations are paired, so there will be two separate sewings. Each sewing uses a single thread with a needle at each end. Prepare the boards. See: *Type 1 Board Attachment,* page 212.

SEWING PROCEDURE

Start with one side-cover and half the sections. The first sewing will be confined to stations 1 and 2. This is sewn on the bench.

1X, 1Y. Start inside the first section. Exit station 1 with one needle, which I will refer to as *X*. Exit station 2 with the other, needle *Y*. Adjust the dangling threads to equal lengths.

2X, 2Y. Attach the boards, but do *not* lock as with *Type 1 Board Attachment,*. Linking will lock the cover to the sections.

3X, 3Y. Re-enter the first section with each needle.

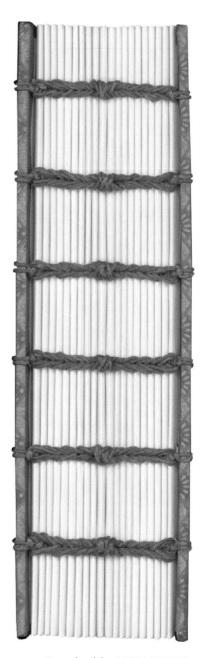

Example of the GREEK SEWING.

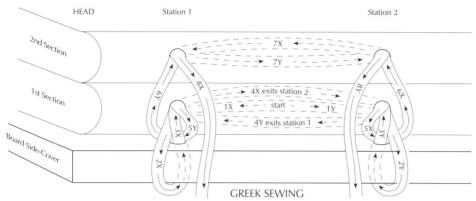

GREEK SEWING

The board is attached without locking. Linking with steps 5, 8 and 11 will secure the board.

4X, 4Y. Exit the other paired station. This makes 3 lengths of thread inside the first section. All remaining sections will have 2 lengths.

5Y, 6Y, 7Y. Set on the second section. Drop to the *inner* side. Link under between the board and the first section, but do not slip under to lock. This is not a kettle stitch. Climb on the outer side and enter the second section at station 1. Exit station 2.

5X, 6X, 7X. Drop to the inner side. Link under between the board and first section. Climb. Enter second section at station 2. Exit station 1.

8Y -10Y. Set on the third section. Drop on the inner side. Link under between board and first section. Climb on the outer side. Enter the third section at station 1. Exit station 2.

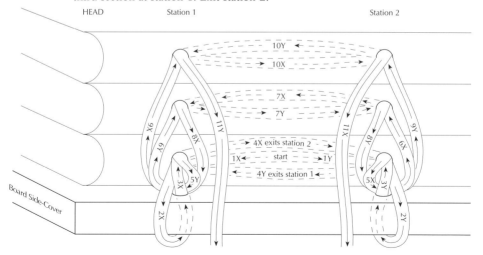

Continuing the GREEK SEWING

After exiting section 1, drop on the inner side, link under between the board and first section, but do not lock. (It is not a kettle stitch.) Climb and enter the second section. After exiting section 2, drop on the inner side, link under between the board and first section. Climb and enter the third section.

8X -10X. Drop on the inner side. Link under between board and first section. Climb on the outer side, but do not lock. Enter the third section at station 1. Exit station 2.

8Y-10Y. Drop on the inner side. Link under between board and first section. Climb on the outer side, but do not lock. Enter the third section at station 2. Exit station 1.

11Y-13Y. Drop on the inner side. Link under between board and first section. Climb and enter the fourth section at station 1. Exit station 2.

11X-13X. Drop on the inner side. Link under between board and first section. Climb and enter the fourth section at station 2. Exit station 1.

14-16. Repeat steps 11-13, linking under between the board and first section. Climb and enter the fifth section.

Sewing the Remaining Sections of this Half of the Book: With the fifth section, drop three sections, on the inner side, link under between the first and second sections. Climb and enter the next section. From then on, with each new section, drop three sections, link under, climb on the outer side and enter the next section. Continue this procedure until the first half of the book is sewn.

Sewing the Second Half of the Book: Sew the second half of the book in the same manner. Start from the other side-cover and last section. Sew each additional section towards the middle of the book.

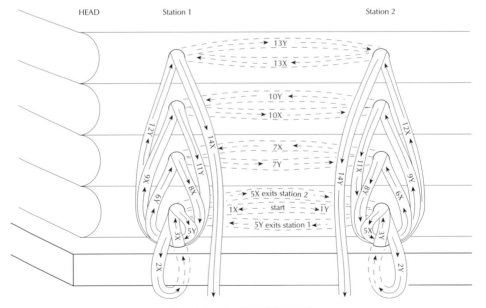

Continuing the GREEK SEWING

Exiting sections 1 through 4: Each time, drop on the inner side, link under between the board and the first section to build up the thickness of the chain.

NOTE: The Greek Sewing exits and drops on the *inner* side of the paired stations to link under. The climb is then on the outer side. This is unlike the 2-Needle Coptic Sewing I, page 235, and the Celtic Weave, page 247, both of which drop on the outer side to link under.

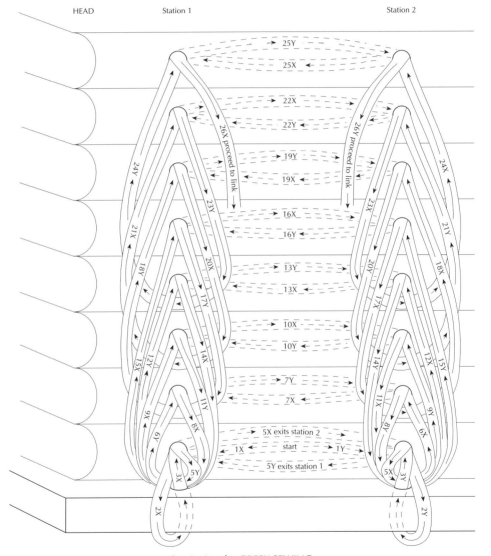

Continuing the GREEK SEWING

Exiting at sections 1 through 4, drop on the inner side, link under between the board and the first section to build up the thickness of the chain. With section 5, exit, drop three sections, and link under between the first and second sections. Thereafter, exit each section, drop 3 sections to link under.

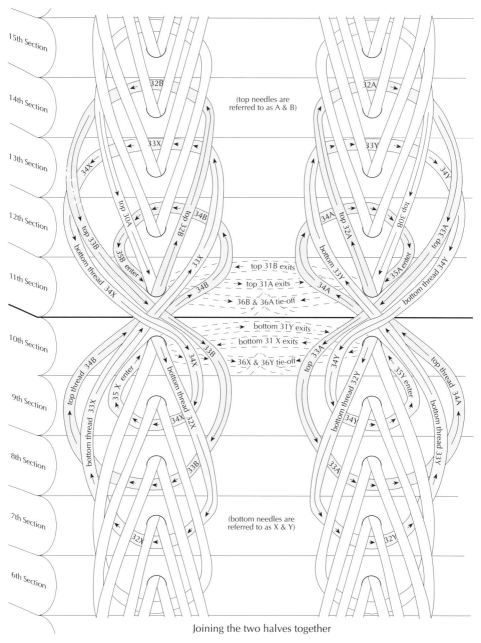

Joining the two halves together

Top and bottom threads are alternately linked: Sit the two halves together. Work at each paired station separately. First alternate linking the *B* and *X* threads. The path is a figure *8*. Linking is always from the inner to the outer side of the paired stations.

After the linking path of the *B* and *X* threads is completed, take the threads to the inside. Then alternate linking at the other paired station with the *A* and *Y* threads. Take the threads to the inside of the sections. The *A* and *B* threads tie-off inside section 11. Tie-off the *X* and *Y* threads inside section 10.

4–DOWN LINK SEWING

The Greek Sewing, page 258, is unusual in how the two halves are sewn separately, then joined. It is lovely, somewhat formal in its symmetry. The drawback is that it requires a minimum of twenty sections. For me, it is a little awkward to tie-off. The following is a *single sewing*, from board to board, but lacks the characteristic symmetry of the Greek Sewing:

SEWING PROCEDURE
Fold an even or odd number, and a minimum of twelve sections. Prepare two side-covers. Sew all but the final section in a single sewing, identically as with the Greek Sewing.

Sewing the Final Section: Set on the final section. Exit the next to last section at each paired station. Drop three sections on the inner side, link under. Climb on the outer side. Enter final section. Exit other paired station, *but do not link.*

It is critical when exiting the final section to immediately attach the cover, prior to linking. The thread going from the section to the cover is not only the hinge, but will serve as an *anchor* for the completion of the linking process.

Attaching the Cover:
PROCEDURE IF USING TYPE 1 BOARD ATTACHMENT:
Set on the board. Climb and enter the board from the top. Exit the board, only, on the inner side of the paired stations. Loop the anchor 360° starting and ending on the inner side of the paired stations to form the lock. (The anchor is the thread that exits the final section and enters the board.)

Detail
4–DOWN LINK
SEWING

4–DOWN LINK SEWING with *Type 1* BOARD ATTACHMENT
The herringbone pattern of the sewing is identical to the Greek Sewing. However, the Greek Sewing, by definition, is sewn in two parts, for a mirror image of the herringbone pattern.
Other digital scans of the 4–Down Link Sewing can be seen on pages 213, 263, 264, 279 and 290.

PROCEDURE IF USING TYPE 3 BOARD ATTACHMENT: Set on the board. Climb and enter the board from the station on the depth of the board, exiting to the top (outside) of the board. Enter the board, only, to the inside. Exit through the depth of the board. Lock the board. See page 216. You can sew the board and lock a second time, before proceeding.

Valentine book for Judy Natal, 1995. 4–DOWN LINK SEWING with *Type 3* BOARD ATTACHMENT.

Completing the Sewing: Drop on the inner side, down three sections, and link under.

Climb on the outer side. Link between the top board and the final section around the anchor. The importance of the anchor, described on the previous page, was less for purposes of locking the board, than providing an anchor for the links: If you had not formed the anchor this link would ride down the spine.

Drop on the inner side, down two sections, and link under. Climb on the outer side. Link between the board and the final section. Drop on the inner side, down one section, and link under.

Climb on the outer side. Enter the final section at each station. Tie-off the paired threads on the inside of the final section.

The procedure of this variant sewing will loop the anchor between the top board and the final section, the same number of times as was done earlier between the first section and the bottom board. This builds up the thickness of the chain at the end of the sewing.

Likewise, the final section will have three threads inside, the same as the first section. All other sections will have two threads in the valleys.

4–DOWN LINK SEWING with *Type 3* BOARD ATTACHMENT. All eight stations were initially pierced. Stations 1 and 2, as well as 7 and 8, were sewn from the tail to the head. The book was turned over. Two paired sewings were done with the middle stations, from the head to the tail. A different color thread was used sewing in this direction. Direction of the *V's* in the linking are reversed, relating to the look of the Greek Sewing, on page 258.

CATERPILLAR

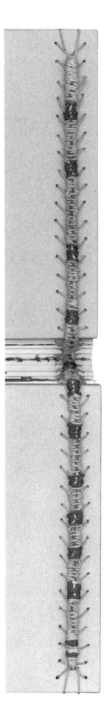

Paired sewing stations for the sections and the boards

The Caterpillar was learned from Betsy Palmer Eldridge.

The Caterpillar, is a *single station* sewing using paired holes. The "station" is between the holes. Paired holes are pierced on the folds of each of the sections, as well as extend onto the boards.

Paired stations on the boards are pierced the same width as for the spine. Distance between is at least the same as for the sections: Pierce at least five levels of stations on the boards, beginning close to the spine-edge, proceeding towards the foredge.

Pierce the stations for the sections and the boards. Sewing begins on the board, at row of stations closest to the foredge. Sew at paired stations; proceed across the board, into the first section to be sewn, thus, attaching the board to the section. Sewing continues across the book block at paired stations, onto the remaining board. It then proceeds across the board at paired stations, towards the foredge, to the final row of stations.

Detail: This version of the CATERPILLAR was sewn with two colors of thread. The darker color is usually hidden within the core of the lighter. Periodically, the darker thread is used to pack, producing cylindrical stripes. It is also woven in and out along the top ridge, dotting the animal.

The sewing starts on the edge of the front board, proceeds to, and across the spine, sewing the sections. It then sews the back board, extending to the edge of the board. See diagrams on page 267.

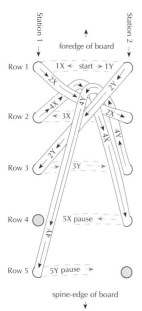

Starting the
CATERPILLAR
Sew 1-4X, then sew 1-4Y.

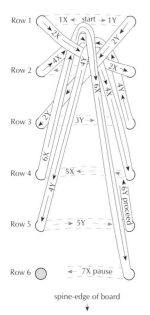

SEWING PROCEDURE

Starting the Sewing in the Middle of the Board: This is a 2–needle sewing. Begin on the inside of the board at Row 1, the stations closest to the foredge. I suggest you sew two sets of paired stations, one at the head (stations 1 and 2), and the last two stations at the tail. After they are completely sewn, the book block and boards are held together. Then begin again. Sew all the remaining sets of paired stations. There will be fewer needles with which to contend.

1X. Exit row 1, station 1.

2X. Angle and enter row 2, station 2.

3X. Span and exit station 1.

4X. Slip under thread 2X, lap 2X, enter row 4, station 2. Pull taut to bring center of thread 2X half way between rows 1 and 2. Now sew with Y needle.

1Y. Exit row 1, station 2.

2Y. Angle and enter row 3, station 1.

3Y. Span and exit station 2.

4Y. Slip under thread 2X, lap 2X, enter row 5, station 1. Now sew with the X needle.

5X. Span and exit row 4 station 1.

6X. Climb at an angle. Lap all threads except 2X. Slip under thread 2X. Lap all thread and enter row 6, station 2.

5Y. Span and exit row 5 station 2.

6Y. Climb at an angle. Lap all threads except 2X. Slip under thread 2X. If it is easier, you can slip under any other adjacent threads, as well. Pull thread 6Y towards station 2 prior to packing.

6Ya, b, c. Pack solidly in a clockwise motion slipping under all threads. Pack from near station 2, towards station 1, using as many packs as necessary. This is the only coil packed perpendicular to the spine. It will look like the drawing on the bottom left of page 267.

If you have more than 6 rows of stations on the board, continue sewing all the rows. Once all the rows on the board are sewn, the next drop at an angle will enter the top section. Then span to the paired station in the section. Exit and climb back to the proper row on the board.

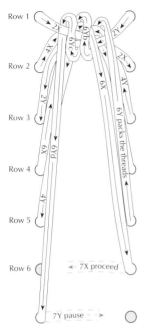

Row 1
Row 2
Row 3
Row 4
Row 5
Row 6

← 7X proceed

7Y pause →

6Y packs the threads

Step 6Y packing for rows
starting in the middle of the
board

Pack solidly from station 2 to station 1.

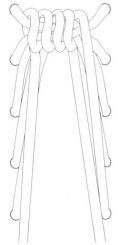

Step 6Y will look like this if the
sewing starts in middle of the
board.

On the left is step 6Y for starting the rows *in the middle* of the board. See the digital scan on page 271.

Starting the Sewing on the Foredge of the Board: The sewing is the same as on the previous page, except for the first two steps. Start on the outside of the board. Go through to the inside, and come around the foredge. This extends the "antennae" of the caterpillar over the edge of the board.

On the right is designing the sewing to extend *over the foredge* of the front side-cover. Rows begin close to the foredge. See the digital scan on page 265.

Sewing procedure continues on the following page with step 7.

NOTE: Starting with step 7, the pattern of sewing is the same for starting in the middle, or on the foredge of the board. With step 7, there is a repetition of the same procedure, with no variations, until ending the sewing on the other board.

If there are only five rows of stations pierced on the board, "row 6" will actually be the stations in the first section to be sewn. "Row 7" would then be the second section.

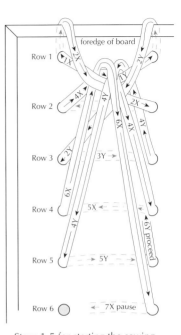

foredge of board

Row 1
Row 2
Row 3   3Y →
Row 4   5X ←
Row 5   → 5Y →
Row 6   ← 7X pause

6Y proceed

Steps 1-5 for starting the sewing
at, and extending over, the
foredge of the board

Step 1 starts on the outside of the board.

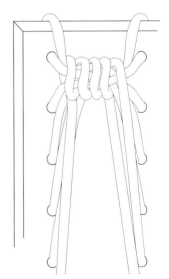

Step 6Y will look like this, if the
sewing extends over the foredge.

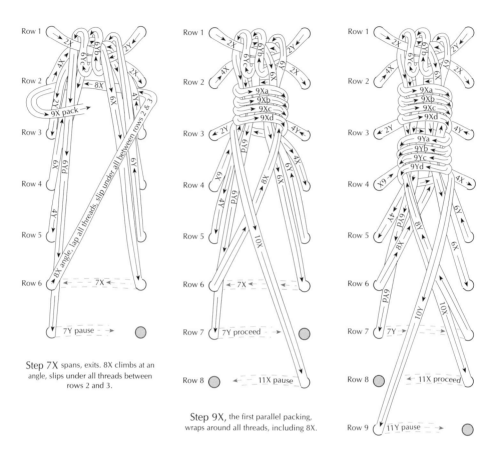

Step 7X spans, exits. 8X climbs at an angle, slips under all threads between rows 2 and 3.

Step 9X, the first parallel packing, wraps around all threads, including 8X.

7X. Span and exit station 1 of row 6.

8X. Climb at an angle. Slip under all threads between rows 2 and 3, close to the stations of row 2. Take the needle from the outer side of station 2 towards, and past station 1. See diagram in the upper left of this page. The climb of 8X will not be seen, since it is also inside the packing.

9X. Pack solidly in a clockwise motion as many times as necessary until you come to the stations of row 3. All the angled threads are bundled within the packing, forming a core. The packing, in effect, will create its own cord. This is a "raised cord sewing", created by the sewing threads.

(The packing need not be solid. See the example on the left in the digital scan on the next page.)

10X. After the final pack, lap all the threads, drop at an angle and enter station 2 of row 8. See middle diagram above.

Step 9Y packs solidly between the next rows, whether the stations are on the board, or, by now, are the sections.

7Y. Span and exit station 2 of row 8.

8Y. Climb at an angle. Slip under all threads between rows 3 and 4. Take the needle from the outer side of station 1 towards, and past station 2. See diagram on the right on the facing page.

9Y. Pack solidly in a counter-clockwise motion as many times as necessary until you come to the stations of row 4 of the board, or the station of the section, if you have completed all the stations of the board.

10Y. After the final pack, lap all the threads, drop at an angle and enter station 2 of row 8. See the right diagram on the facing page.

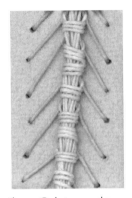

Above: Only two packs leave the angled threads (legs) showing. They are squeezed perpendicular to the packing.

Below: Length of the caterpillar body is solid packed, which hides all the angled threads, except for the legs of the caterpillar.

Greek Sewing, 3 Down to Link: This sewing is somewhat related to the Greek Sewing, page 258. In the latter, exiting the paired stations, the drop is on the inner side, and links under between the board and the first section. Exiting each of the first four sections, linking always takes place between the board and first section. This is to build up the thickness of the chain.

Then, sewing the fifth section, the position of the link starts to advance: Exiting the fifth section, the linking under is between the first and the second section—*three sections down.* With each successive exit from a section, the link is three sections down: Exiting the sixth section, drop on the inner side, link under between the second and the third section. The climb is again on the outer side, entering the next section (7).

After the initial build-up of the chain, exiting the fifth section onward, the drop is three sections to link under. This creates a massive chain. Compare it to the 2-Needle Coptic Sewing I, page 235. Here, no matter what section you are exiting, the drop, on the outer side this time, is always down one section to the last two connected sections. Since the drop is only one section, the chain cannot build up in a thick overlay.

Caterpillar, 3 Up to Pack: The Caterpillar angles three sections up to pack. Like the Greek Sewing, the first several steps builds up a thickness of threads. In this instance, it is not a chain that is being built up, but a core of threads, *V* shaped, between the paired stations. They are a *core,* because they will be packed as a unit. This forms a raised support, a cord comprised of the sewn threads.

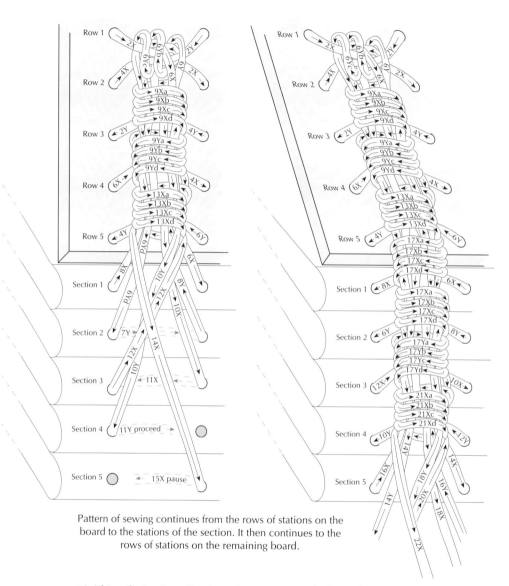

Pattern of sewing continues from the rows of stations on the board to the stations of the section. It then continues to the rows of stations on the remaining board.

Finishing the Sewing: Continue the pattern: With the *X* thread, exit, climb at an angle, slip under the threads. Pack, then angle back to the other paired station, two rows below that exit.

Alternate with the *Y* thread. To end the sewing on the other board, simply enter and tie-off. See digital scan on the facing page. Or, continue packing to the end of the stations, to eliminate the "tail".

Keith Smith, CATERPILLAR sewing of *Books without Paste or Glue,* 1994. Sewing begins on the front board, with the antennae and the head of the animal. Sewing continues on the spine, attaching the book block. It proceeds to, and ends on, the back board. Each "caterpillar" is sewn separately.

Betsy Palmer Eldridge devised the Caterpillar, "While exploring traditional and historical sewings, it was a discovery or invention made that proves sewing techniques are not a dull dry subject."

Denise Carbone, Flexible Book, 1993. Text is Bartram green paper, cover, binders board, painted with acrylic. Sewing is "3up to pack".
6.4 x 3.1 x 7.6 cm.

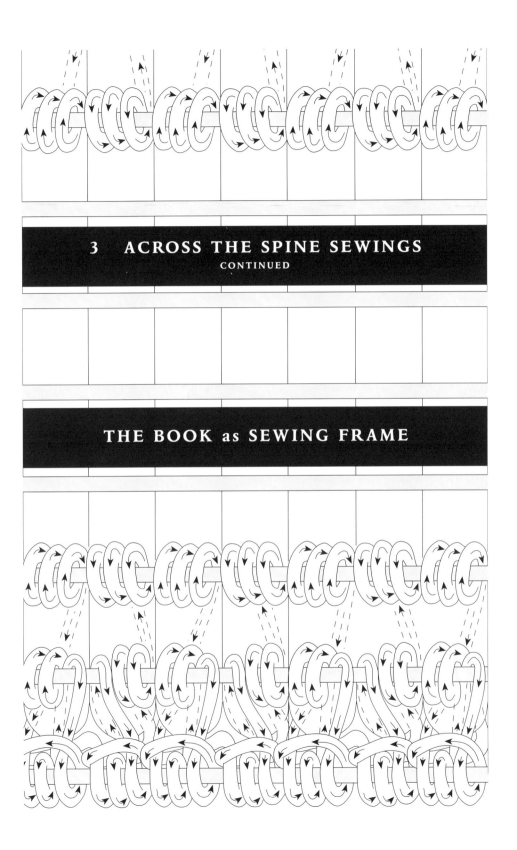

3 ACROSS THE SPINE SEWINGS
CONTINUED

THE BOOK as SEWING FRAME

CONTINUAL ADJUSTMENT SEWING FRAME

The *book itself* can be used as a sewing frame. Two approaches to using the book as its own sewing frame are *continual adjustment,* and *pre-set tension.*

Continual adjustment of tension of the supports allows the boards and supports to function as a sewing frame.

FOR SEWINGS ALONG THE SPINE, ONLY: TYPE 3 Board Attachment, page 216, is required as supports. Cover and pierce the boards. Paired stations *form the raised supports* of thread. The supports attach the first section to the bottom board, then directly attach, but not lock the top board: It must be continually adjusted as each section is sewn.

1. Exit the first section at paired stations, with a needle on each end of the thread. There will be one thread for each of the paired stations. Refer to the illustration on page 213.
2. Attach bottom board with *TYPE 3* Board Attachment. See page 216.
3. Partially attach the top board: Each needle enters the hole on the depth of the board, exiting to the outside.

The book as sewing frame, using continual adjustment of tension

Paired stations are pierced for stringing the raised thread supports, in preparation for a sewing along the spine. If you do not climb on the supports, pierce additional kettle stations at the head and tail of the sections.

String the raised thread supports: Exit the first section and attach the bottom board with *TYPE 3* Board Attachment. Immediately take the needles through the top board, but do not lock or tie-off. Tension has to be adjusted as each section is sewn.

The example to the right is a Basic RAISED SUPPORT SEWING *with Packed Supports as Change-Over.* The first four sections have been sewn, and the top board raised to place on the next section to be sewn. The supports will be made taut prior to sewing the fifth section.

Enter the station on the top of the board, exiting on the inside of the board. Do not complete the *TYPE 3* attachment at this time. This permits adjustment of the board as each section is added.

4. Set on the second section. Adjust the tension of the raised thread supports which extend vertically from one board to the other.

5. Determine which raised support sewing you wish to do, *along,* not across, the spine. A new needle must be threaded, as the sewing thus far is only the raised thread supports. If you do not climb by using the support as change-over, you must add kettle stations at the head and the tail.

6. Start the raised support sewing with the new thread, in the first section. Proceed as usual, exiting around the raised thread supports, sewing along the spine.

Tension of the raised supports must be loosened to set on each new section. Then the tension must be adjusted so that the supports are taut from board to board. After the sewing is completed, finish attaching the board by exiting from the inside of the board through the depth of the board. Each support thread then enters the final section and is tied-off.

It is a single sewing.

The book as sewing frame, using continual adjustment of tension

After all sections are sewn, tie-off the sewing inside the final section. Lock on the cover. Enter the final section with each raised thread support, and tie-off the supports inside.

PRE-SET TENSION SEWING FRAME

The second approach to the book as sewing frame is my favorite. It requires two separate sewings, the first being across the spine. The second sewing can be across, or along the spine.

Prior to the first sewing, all stations in the sections and boards are pierced. In all instances, *TYPE 3* Board Attachment, page 216, is used.

FIRST SEWING: The first sewing uses paired stations at the head and tail, or, in the middle of the spine.

Stations 1   2   3   4   5   6   7   8

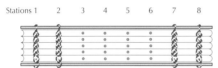

First sewing at the head and tail

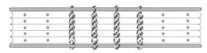

First sewing using the middle stations

The first sewing

- hinges the boards,
- fixes the book block to the boards, and, more importantly,
- sets the height of the spine.

SECOND SEWING: After the first sewing is completed, the thread supports are strung at all remaining stations for the second sewing.

The book as sewing frame, using pre-set tension on the raised supports

Completing the first sewing across the spine, using 4 of the 8 pre-pierced sewing stations. Now the raised thread supports will be strung from board to board at stations 3 through 6. A digital scan of the finished book is on page 292.

Preparing for the Second Sewing: The second sewing is at the remaining stations, not yet been sewn. In this instance, stations 3-6. They will have single raised thread supports strung from one board to the other:

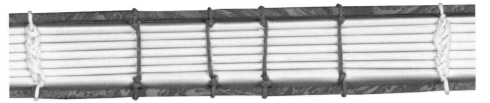

The book as sewing frame, using pre-set tension on the raised thread supports

Detail of stations 2 through 7: All stations are pre-pierced. The first sewing at stations 1 and 2, and 7 and 8 is across the spine with white thread. Paired stations 3 and 4, 5 and-6 are strung as single raised thread supports with gray thread. The book is now its own sewing frame. The second sewing can be along, or across the spine, using stations 3-6. Finished book is on page 290. The first sewing is on the facing page.

STRINGING SINGLE RAISED THREAD SUPPORTS: Unlike the Continually Adjusted Supports described on page 274, these supports can only be attached *after* the first sewing is completed. Paired stations are required to string single raised thread supports. The sewing on the raised supports can be either across or along the spine. If the second sewing is along the spine, I suggest at least four raised thread support stations in succession. If this second sewing is along the spine, the supported station closest to the head (3) will facilitate the climb. The last strung station (6), closest to the tail, will be used as the change-over. This is because stations 1 and 2, as well as the final two stations at the tail, already have been sewn as the first sewing.

Attach the thread supports at those stations which were not used for the first sewing:

1. Start inside the first section and attach the board. Use *TYPE 1, 2, 3 or 4* Board Attachment. Refer to pages 212 through 217. Do the same for each of the paired stations.

2. Span to the top board. Do not enter any other sections. Attach the top board, exiting on the inner side of the paired stations. Do the same for the remaining stations.

3. Adjust the tension of these raised thread supports, so that it is not slack. Do not tighten so as to warp the boards.

4. Lock the boards. Loop the raised thread support 360° starting and ending on the inner side of the paired stations.

5. Enter the final section at each station and tie-off the paired threads. An example of single raised thread supports, see stations 3 through 6 in the digital scan detail above. That same book is shown sewn with Solid Pack Raised Supports as the second sewing on page 292.

STRINGING DOUBLE RAISED THREAD SUPPORTS:

For the second sewing, using the book as sewing frame, there are two approaches to stringing double raised thread supports. *TYPES* 6 and 7 Board Attachment are used. Neither is part of a sewing path, but merely the means of stringing double raised thread supports from one board to the other:

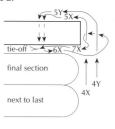

- *TYPE 6* BOARD ATTACHMENT is described on page 218. This utilizes *TYPE 1* piercing of the board. However, since a lark spur knot is used, tension of the knot is at the depth of the board. This results in an ideal hinging action similar to *TYPES 3, 4* and *5* Board Attachment.

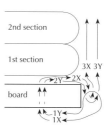

- *TYPE 7* BOARD ATTACHMENT is described on page 219. This utilizes *TYPE 3* piercing of the board. Therefore, it has ideal hinging action

TYPE 6, stringing double raised thread supports, is diagrammed on page 218.

Start at the bottom board. *TYPE 6* BOARD ATTACHMENT uses *TYPE 1* to navigate through the bottom board. The supports do not enter any of the sections, but attach the top board to the bottom, and set the tension of the supports.

Unlike the Continually Adjusted Supports on page 274, these supports must be attached only *after* the first sewing is completed. The first sewing "creates" the sewing frame, by fixing the book block and sections in position. The two boards, in effect, become the sewing frame.

Unlike stringing single raised thread supports described on page 277, an even *or* odd number of stations can be strung using double raised thread supports: A separate thread is strung from each station, using two needles, from the bottom board to the top board at the same numbered station. For digital scans of *TYPE 7* Board Attachment, see pages 279 and 285.

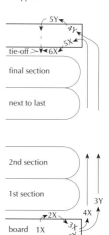

TYPE 7, stringing double raised thread supports, is diagrammed on page 219.

Start at the bottom board. *TYPE 7* BOARD ATTACHMENT uses *TYPE 3* to navigate through the boards. The supports do not enter any of the sections, but attach the top board to the bottom, and set the tension of the supports.

Alternative positioning: Stringing single and double raised thread supports described on pages 277 and 278 might suggest the second sewing will utilize the middle stations. However, the first sewing across the spine might utilize the middle stations, 3-6. Stations 3 and 4 are paired, as well as 5 and 6.

At the remaining stations which have not yet been sewn, stations 1 and 2, as well as 7 and 8 would then be used for the second sewing on raised thread supports.

This second sewing does not necessarily have to be across the spine, despite the fact that the sewing at the head, or the separate sewing at the tail have only two stations to sew.

If double raised thread supports are strung, the paired stations at the head, as well as at the tail, could be sewn with the Centipede, which is described on page 282.

If single raised thread supports are strung, the paired stations at the head, as well as at the tail, could be sewn with the Solid Pack Raised Supports, described on page 280. Or, the single thread supports could be sewn with Solid Pack with Bead, described on page 289.

The 4–DOWN LINK SEWING is sewn *across* the spine at the head and tail. The four middle stations are sewn separately, *along* the spine: Two threads are strung at each station from board to board. See: *TYPE 7* Board Attachment, page 219. ThE second sewing is solid pack DOUBLE RAISED (thread) SUPPORTS, with DOUBLE RAISED thread SUPPORTS as Change-Over.

2–Needle COPTIC SEWING I

with the second sewing on the book as frame

SOLID PACK
RAISED SUPPORTS

This first example of the Book as Sewing Frame employs *across* the spine sewings for both the first and second sewings. The Solid Pack Raised Support Sewing, described on page 41 and 75 is for sewing *along* the spine. The solid pack described for the second sewing, on the facing page, has been modified for paired stations, sewing *across* the spine.

PREPARATION

Pierce the sections and boards with 8 stations. The paired stations at the head and tail, stations 1 and 2, and 7 and 8 will be for the first sewing, the 2–Needle Coptic Sewing I. Paired stations 3 and 4, as well as 5 and 6, will be for the second sewing of Solid Pack Raised Supports.

First Sewing: 2–Needle COPTIC SEWING I

Sew the head and the tail with the 2–Needle Coptic Sewing I. Refer to page 235.

NOTE: Start the sewings at the head and tail, and proceed with both, simultaneously. Do not sew the head and tail consecutively, as you will stretch the first sewing as you sew the second.

Attaching the Raised Thread Supports: String the single raised thread supports at stations 3-6. Use *TYPE 3* Board Attachment, stringing the supports, *prior to* the second sewing. It is described on page 277. The book will then appear as in the digital scan to the right:

If you are stringing double raised thread supports, refer to *TYPE 6* Board Attachment, page 218, and *TYPE 7*, page 219.

Stations at the head and tail are sewn with the 2–NEEDLE COPTIC SEWING I. Raised thread supports, stations 3-6, are attached for the second sewing.

Second Sewing: SOLID PACK RAISED SUPPORTS

Solid Packed Raised Supports is sewn *across* the spine. It is different than Loop Pack With Climbing Pack, page 75, which is sewn *along* the spine. Start the second sewing inside the first section. A new thread exits station 3 to the outside, on the inner side of the paired supports. Exit station 4 with the needle on the other end of that thread to the outside, on the inner side of the paired stations. Do the same with another thread for stations 5 and 6.

Pack the left support (station 3) in a clockwise direction to the height of the same numbered station in the second section. Enter the second section and exit the paired station (4).

Pack the right support (station 4) in a counter-clockwise direction to the height of the same numbered station in the second section.

Enter the second section with each needle, exiting the paired station.

Continue until the final section is packed. Enter the final section and tie-off the paired threads. Do this same sewing at the remaining paired stations (5 and 6).

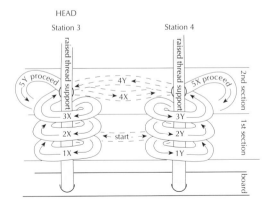

Starting the SOLID PACK RAISED SUPPORTS
for paired stations sewn across the spine

Valentine book for Scott, 1995. The second sewing, SOLID PACK RAISED SUPPORTS, has been sewn across the spine at stations 3-6.

CELTIC WEAVE
with the second sewing on the book as frame
The CENTIPEDE

This second example of the book as sewing frame employs across the spine sewings for both the first and second sewings. The first sewing is the Celtic Weave. See page 247. Then, double raised supports are strung at stations 4, 7 and 10. These are thread. The book will then appear as the digital scan to the right. Stations 3-5 will be used for one sewing of the Centipede, which was devised specifically for the book in this scan. A separate sewing of the Centipede is then sewn at stations 6-8. A third sewing is then done at stations 9-11.

PREPARATION
Pierce the sections and boards with 13 stations.

First Sewing: The CELTIC WEAVE
Sew the paired stations at the head and tail, stations 1 and 2, 12 and 13 with the Celtic Weave. Refer to page 247. Use *TYPES 3* or *4* Board Attachment, pages 216 and 217, *as you sew* the Celtic Weave.

Double raised (thread) supports will be strung at stations number 4, 7 and 10:

Attaching the Double Raised Thread Supports:
Follow the steps and diagrams on page 278 to string double raised thread supports at station 4. String the supports at stations, 7 and 10, but not at 3, 5, 6 8, 9, and 11.

The double raised supports, which are thread, rather than cord, are now ready to be sewn. See the digital scan on page 285, as well as for the completed second sewing, the Centipede,

The second sewing requires three separate sewings of the Centipede, one beginning at station 4, one at 7, and the third at station 10.

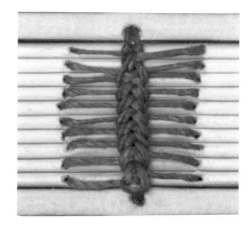

Detail of the sewing referred to as the CENTIPEDE is shown on the right. For the completed sewing, see page 285.

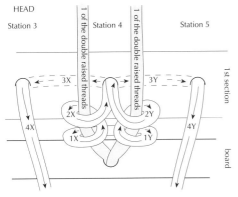

HEAD

Station 3 · Station 4 · Station 5

1st section · board

Starting the CENTIPEDE SEWING

Step 1 loops the double raised threads. Each needle wraps a support again before entering the section.

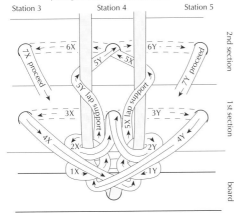

Station 3 · Station 4 · Station 5

2nd section · 1st section · board

Sewing the first section

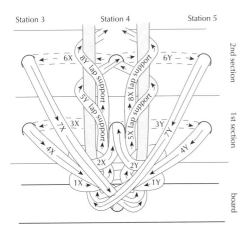

Station 3 · Station 4 · Station 5

2nd section · 1st section · board

Continuing the CENTIPEDE SEWING

Second Sewing, The CENTIPEDE:

1. Start the second sewing with a new thread which loops the double supports between the bottom board and the first section at station 4. The two needles will extend outward from the book. See diagram on the left.

2X. Take the left thread and pack the left raised support twice in a counter-clockwise motion. Enter the first section at station 4.

3X. Exit station 3.

2Y. Take the right thread and pack the right raised support twice in a clockwise motion. Enter the first section at station 4.

3Y. Exit station 5.

4X. Drop, angle, lap both raised supports. Link under between the board and the first section.

5X Climb, lapping the right support. (The climb would be a span, but it laps a support to strengthen the sewing: It anchors prior to entering and travelling on the inside to exit either station 3 or 5.)

6X Enter station 4 of the second section. Exit station 3.

4Y. Drop, angle, lap both raised supports. Link under between the board and the first section.

5Y. Climb, lapping the left support.

6Y. Enter station 4 of the second section. Exit station 5.

7X. Drop, angle, lap both raised supports. Link under between the first and second section.

8X. Climb. Lap the right support.

9X. Enter station 4 of the third section. Exit station 3.

7Y. Drop, angle, lap both raised supports. Link under between the first and second section.

8Y. Climb. Lap the left support.

9Y. Enter station 4 of the third section. Exit station 5. The double raised supports and the two climbs with the *X* and *Y* threads create a core of four threads.

Each drop at an angle starts to build up thick chevrons over the supports. It is a rope pattern. The structure is reminiscent of the sewing I call The Rope, page 159 in Volume II.

Remaining Sections: Continue in this manner: drop at an angle, lapping the double supports. Link under the previous section. Climb, enter next section. Exit the left or right station, respectively.

After entering the final section, exit station 3 with the *X* needle. Lap both supports. Pack the left support once clockwise and enter. Exit station 5 with the *Y* needle. Lap both supports. Pack the right support once counterclockwise and enter. Tie-off on the inside. Sew the Centipede at the remaining raised double supports.

The Centipede could be the sole sewing for a book, with two or more sewings on the spine. Each Centipede across the spine would require three sewing stations, with the center station having double raised supports.

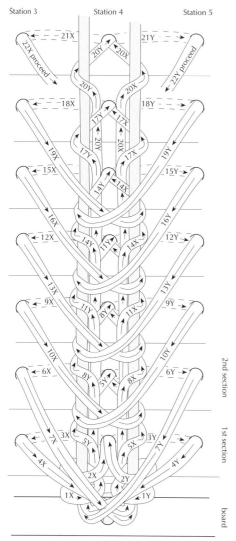

The CENTIPEDE

In the actual sewing, the climbs and the double raised supports
will be hidden by the linking threads.

Stations at the head and tail are sewn with the CELTIC WEAVE. The second sewing, the CENTIPEDE, in progress, is being sewn on double raised thread supports.

Paired stations at the head and tail are sewn with the CELTIC WEAVE. The middle sewings are now completed, sewn with the CENTIPEDE.

2–NEEDLE COPTIC SEWING I

with the second sewing on the book as frame

ISOLATED PACK & WEAVE

This example of the book as sewing frame employs across the spine sewings for both the first and second sewings.

First Sewing: 2–Needle COPTIC SEWING I
The first sewing, at stations 3-6, is the 2–Needle Coptic Sewing I, described on page 235, which locks the link stitch, in the manner of a true kettle stitch, as opposed to not locking with the 2–Needle Coptic Sewing II.

If you wish, substitute any of the 1– or 2–Needle Coptic Sewings here.

The second sewing is on the following page.

Book as Sewing Frame: In this example, the first sewing is in the middle of the book, rather than at the head and tail. Stations 3 and 4 are paired, as are stations 5 and 6. The 2–Needle COPTIC SEWING I is made across the spine at these stations. Then, Stations 1, 2, 7 and 8 are strung in preparation for the second sewing. Make sure not to string the supports too tightly, or the boards will be distorted at the head and the tail.

Second Sewing,
ISOLATED PACK &
WEAVE

Single raised thread supports are strung at stations 1, 2, 7 and 8. See page 277.

The Isolated Pack & Weave, described on page 174, is sewn at stations 1 and 2. A separate sewing is made at stations 7 and 8.

The completed book will then appear as in the digital scan to the right.

Utilizing the book as sewing frame, makes possible combinations of sewings, as well as the use of thread as supports—without the need of a sewing frame. The second sewing, at the head and tail, is the ISOLATED PACK & WEAVE.

The first sewing at stations 3 through 6 is the 2–NEEDLE COPTIC SEWING I.

CELTIC WEAVE

with the second sewing on the book as frame

THE SPIRAL BINDING

This example of the book as sewing frame employs across the spine sewings for the first sewing, followed by sewing along the spine.

First Sewing: The CELTIC WEAVE
Sew the paired stations at the head and tail, stations 1 and 2, and 8 and 9 with the Celtic Weave. Refer to page 247.

Second Sewing, THE SPIRAL BINDING
Refer to page 86 for the second sewing, THE SPIRAL BINDING.

Single raised thread supports are strung at stations 3 through 7. See page 277.

THE CLIMB: The change-over will be at stations 3 and 7, which will serve as the "head" and "tail" for the second sewing. The completed book will then appear as in the digital scan to the right.

The CELTIC WEAVE is sewn at the head and tail. Then stations 3-7 are strung in preparation for the second sewing, along the spine, using the *book as sewing frame.* The second sewing is THE SPIRAL BINDING.

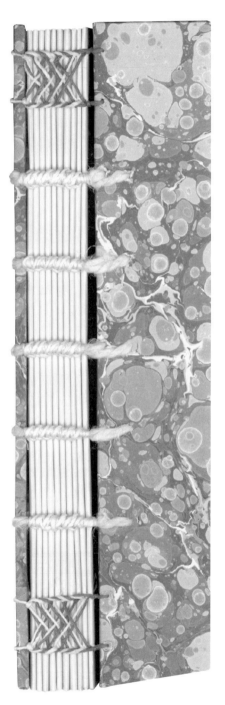

4–DOWN LINK SEWING

with the second sewing on the book as frame

SOLID PACK WITH BEAD

This example of the book as sewing frame employs across the spine sewings for the first and the second sewing.

First Sewing: 4–DOWN LINK SEWING

Use *Type 3* Board Attachment, page 216, *as you sew* the 4–Down Link Sewing, at the paired stations at the head and tail, stations 1 and 2, 7 and 8. The 4–Down Link Sewing is described on page 263:

Second Sewing, SOLID PACK WITH BEAD

The second sewing is across the spine, sewn at paired stations. It is a variation of the Solid Pack Raised Supports, described on page 280.

Use *Type 3* Board Attachment, stinging the supports, *prior to* the second sewing. The second sewing is diagrammed below, and description the following page.

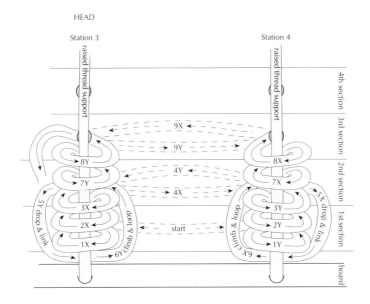

Starting the SOLID PACK WITH BEAD
for paired stations sewn across the spine

Proceed as if sewing the Solid Pack Raised Supports, described on page 280.

After packing each section to the height of that section, the bead will be added. See diagram on the previous page.

Start. Exit on the inner side. Set on the second section.

1-3. Pack to the height of the middle of the second section. Enter the second section on the outer side of the support.

4.   Exit the paired station.

5.   Steps 5 and 6 are the bead: Drop on the outer side. Link under the last two connected sections. (The first link is between the board and the first section.)

6.   Climb on the inner side. Slip behind the support, directly above the top of the packing, to the outer side.

7, 8. Pack to the height of the middle of the next section (3). This time the packing will be in the opposite direction. Direction of the packing alternates after each bead is formed. Enter the section (3) on the outer side of the support.

9.   Exit the paired station.

10 Exit on the outer side of the paired stations. Drop and link under.

11. Climb on the inner side. Slip behind the support, directly above the top of the packing, to the outer side.

Continue in this manner until the final section is packed. Form the bead. Link under, climb and enter the final section on the inner side. Tie-off with the paired thread.

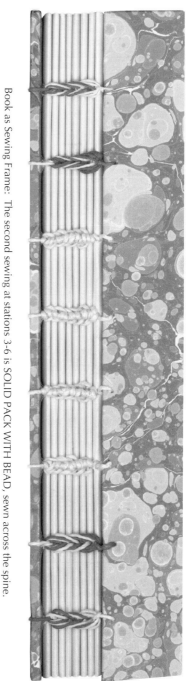

Book as Sewing Frame: The second sewing at stations 3-6 is SOLID PACK WITH BEAD, sewn across the spine.

2–NEEDLE COPTIC SEWING II

with the second sewing on the book as frame

LOOP PACK, PACKED CLIMB WITH BEAD

This example of the book as sewing frame employs across the spine sewings for the first sewing, followed by sewing along the spine.

First Sewing: 2–NEEDLE COPTIC SEWING II
Sew the paired stations at the head and tail, stations 1 and 2, 7 and 8 with the 2–Needle Coptic Sewing II. Refer to page 239.

Single raised thread supports are strung at stations 3-6. See page 277.

Second Sewing, LOOP PACK, PACKED CLIMB WITH BEAD
The second sewing, described on page 81, is along, rather than across the spine. Threads, rather than cords are strung as single supports. See page 277.

THE CLIMB: The climb will be at stations 3 and 6, which will serve as the "head" and "tail" for the second sewing. The completed book will then appear as in the digital scan to the right:

Utilizing the book as sewing frame, makes possible combinations of sewing *along,* as well as *across* the spine on the same book. The first sewing at the head and tail is the 2–NEEDLE COPTIC SEWING II. Then stations 4-6 are strung in preparation for the second sewing. The second sewing here, at stations 4-6 is along the spine, using the LOOP PACK, PACKED CLIMB WITH BEAD.

First sewing is the 2–NEEDLE COPTIC SEWING II. The second sewing is LOOP PACK, PACKED CLIMB WITH BEAD.

2–NEEDLE COPTIC SEWING IV

with the second sewing on the book as frame

SOLID PACK RAISED SUPPORTS

This example of the book as sewing frame is sewn across the spine for both the first and second sewing.

First Sewing: 2–NEEDLE COPTIC SEWING IV

Sew the paired stations at the head and tail, stations 1 and 2, and 7 and 8 with the 2–Needle Coptic Sewing IV. Refer to page 242. All eight stations are pre-pierced. In this example, *Type 1* Board Attachment is used. It is described on page 212.

Second Sewing, SOLID PACK RAISED SUPPORTS

Sew both of the paired stations in the middle of the spine with Solid Pack Raised Supports. Refer to page 281.

Book as Sewing Frame: The first sewing at the head and tail is the 2–NEEDLE COPTIC SEWING IV.

The second sewing at stations 3-6 is SOLID PACK RAISED SUPPORTS.

GREEK SEWING

with the second sewing on the book as frame

2–NEEDLE COPTIC SEWING III

This example of the book as sewing frame employs across the spine sewings for the first and the second sewing. In this *TYPE 1* Board Attachment, the thread goes through the board and locks twice, rather than the usual single attachment and lock.

First Sewing: GREEK SEWING
Sew the paired stations at the head and tail, stations 1 and 2, and 7 and 8 with the Greek Sewing. Refer to page 258.

Second Sewing, 2–NEEDLE COPTIC SEWING III
Sew both of the paired stations in the middle of the spine with the 2–Needle Coptic Sewing III. Refer to page 240.

This example of the 2–Needle Coptic Sewing III is sewn with two colors of thread: The two threads are tied together, and one color exits one of the paired stations, while the other color exits the remaining paired station. The knot is inside the first section to be sewn.

The boards are attached. Then, the linking begins. This results in one color making the span, while the other color forms the link which surrounds the span. At the other paired station, the color of the span and the link is reversed. This results in a lovely link sewing.

Book as Sewing Frame: The first sewing at the head and tail is the GREEK SEWING.

The second sewing at stations 3-6 is the 2–NEEDLE COPTIC SEWING III.

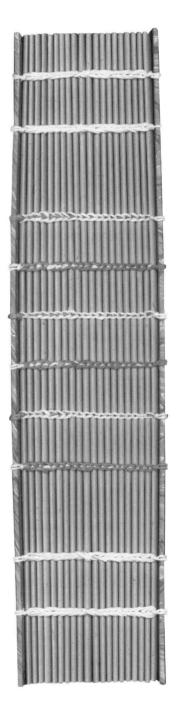

Kim, Myoung Soo, (Ivary) *Suicide*, 2005. Sewn on raised cords. 19.5 x 15 x 3.2cm.

Kim, Myoung Soo, (Ivary) *Suicide,* 2005. 19.5 x 15 x 3.2cm. This elaborate book goes through a series of annimations, from getting out of bed, to shaving, to a roof top chase of the person by his id, trying to aid him. The young man jumps off the building while his id grabs him by his tie in an attempt to save him.

Ivary is one of many young Korean book artists who are doing exciting work. There is a phenomenal amount of activity in the book arts world in Korea, spear headed by Na Rae Kim (no relation).

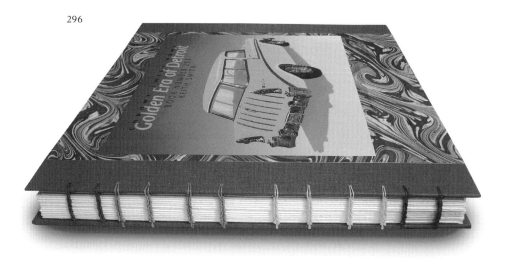

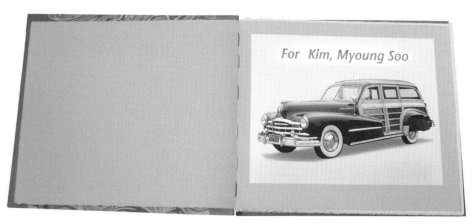

Keith Smith, *Chrome Sweet Home, Golden Era of Detroit.*
Book Number 233, 2006,
34.4 x 38.6 x 3.4 cm. Edition of 5.
Over 40 prints of cars from the 1940's and 1950's are digitally layered into landscapes. The images were constructed with about a dozen layers each in PhotoShop.

The book is sewn using twelve needles and six colors of thread with a 2–Needle Coptic Sewing II, described in this manual.

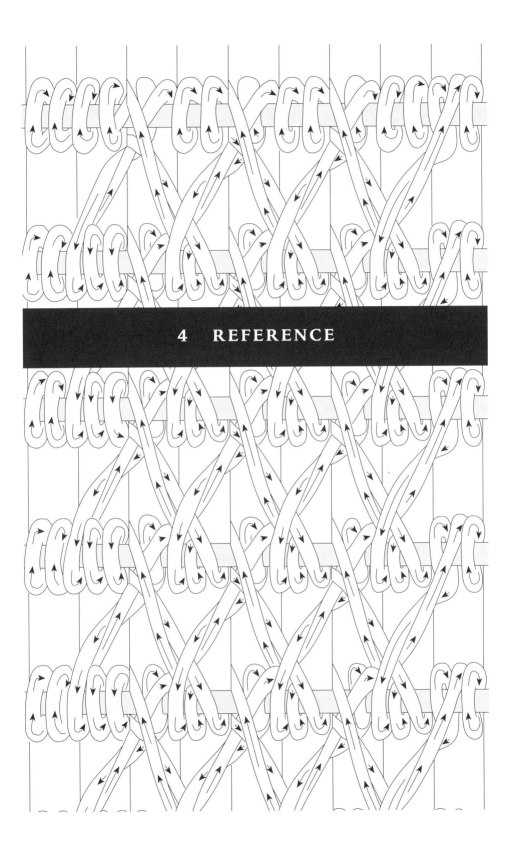

4   REFERENCE

CONCLUSION

Over the last six years I have written five books-on-books. For thirty-two months now, all day long, seven days a week, with few exceptions, I am sewing prototypes on the bench or on the computer. The endeavor kept growing; I broke it into two volumes—Books 169 and 170.

…making up sewings to please myself, but also, to offer to others.

> In and out
> along the spine
> my heart, my mind
> lovingly, literally in the gutter—
> as I become the sewer.

Is this the end? Do I write more books, or return to making ones-of-a-kind and limited production books? I have made few picture books since 1988. I miss the language of vision. But I do not consider my so-called textbooks as a separate endeavor. One is not "art" and the other something less.

In my art and my life, I have never drawn a line.

Whether making pictures, or writing a technical manual, both require imaginative invention, both confront and express that day's needs.

Some say they have no time to make their art. Do they see it as a separate reality, divorced from their living?

> I know
> only a handful
> will ever hold one of
> my ones-of-a-kind
> in their hand.
> The textbooks have the largest audience I have ever reached,
> in pictures,
> books,
> or the classroom.
> This is a joy, and, a consolation.

Do I say, "good-bye?"
I do not think so. We will speak again, pick up where we left off.

Why, there is no need to even complete…

GLOSSARY OF TERMS

accordion pleat 1. Several parallel, alternating, and closely placed folds. Pleats are usually not pages, but an additional hinging device between the backbone and the attached folios or sections. Very often the pleat *is* the backbone, with separate side-covers, rather than a flat back. Pleats also expand the depth of the backbone to accommodate additions to the book block. 2. Also known as the *concertina fold.*

across (*also referred to as* **all across**) 1. Perpendicular to the folds, cover to cover.† 2. Sewing which proceeds from section to section, generally in two or more separate sewings, using paired stations. Examples are Blanket Stitch with Slit Strap, 2–Needle Coptic Sewing and the Celtic Weave. Sewing across the spine is always more secure than sewing along the spine. If a thread breaks, only the sewing at those paired stations is affected. If the thread breaks sewing along the spine, the entire binding is compromised.

adhesive Generic for glue and paste. Glues used for binding remain pliable, and are used on the backs over the sewing of most bindings. Glue on the backbone may be a heat glue, made from animals. It is archival, in that it may be easily removed, but not in the sense it attracts insects which eat it. Another pliable glue is a poly-vinyl-acetate.Plastic based, it does not attract animals, but is not archival, inasmuch as it is not removable, and thwarts attempts at book restoration. Pastes are used to adhere leather to spines, paper to paper, and paper to boards. Wheat or rice paste are commonly used.

adhesive binding single leaf binding without sewing using a synthetic adhesive consolidation on the back.* Referred to as *perfect binding.*

against the grain Folding paper at right angles to the grain.

along (*also referred to as* **all along**) Parallel to the folds, head to tail.†

angle To move diagonally.†

Asa-No-Ha Toji Japanese name for the stab binding also known as the Hemp-Leaf Binding.

back or backbone 1.The binding edge of a text prior to sewing or adhesive consolidation.* Note: The *back* differs from the *spine,* which is part of the cover which overlays this.

back saw Moulding saw or tenon saw used to cut the sewing stations when the book block is held in a finishing press.

backward (reverse) Counter to the direction of the sewing.†

bead 1. Top edge of the book (when viewing the book upright). 2. The little

---

* *A VOCABULARY of TERMS for BOOK CONSERVATION PRACTICE,* by Gary Frost

† "*GLOSSARY of TERMS,* based on the work of Pamela Spitzmueller and Gary Frost," a handout in a workshop by Betsy Palmer Eldridge.

roll formed by the knot of an endband (see: *spine-bead* and *inside bead*).

beeswax   Cake of wax purchased in a small block from a binder's supply. It is used for waxing all unwaxed thread, prior to sewing.

blind   A type of book (see: *venetian blind).*

blind embossing   Stamping type into leather, without gold or foil.

board or **book board**   A layered stock specifically for side-covers.

bodkin   A sewing tool which is a type of awl. Unlike an awl which has a shaft which graduates in thickness, a bodkin has a thin metal shaft which remains constant in diameter except for narrowing at the point. It is similar to a *bradawl,* which is a carpenter's tool. An awl is inferior for piercing sewing stations, as it is difficult to obtain proper size of the opening in the paper. Choose a bradawl or bodkin which will give a hole slightly less than the diameter of the needle which will be used in the sewing.

book block or **text block**   Total of the collated signatures, sections, folios, or sheets, constituting the body of a book.

book block pleat   See: *concertina guard.*

booklet   1. A one-section binding. 2. A pamphlet. 3. A magazine.

bostrophedon   A Germanic term meaning *as the ox plows.* In a single word, it graphically describes moving across a field, back and forth in a continuing *S* fashion. It is as if a page of text were read, the first line from left to right, the second from right to left, and continued in this alternating manner. This movement, and thus his term, describes the Scott McCarney binding. He also calls this the *snake format.*

bone or **bone folder**   A flat, polished tool, made of bone or plastic. Paper is folded by hand to a temporary fold. The bone is used to score the fold to a permanent position, and to flatten the fold. This is done in a single stroke, as burnishing the paper will scar or make it shiny.

bradawl   A straight shafted awl with chisel edge used to make holes for brads or screws. Like the bodkin, a bradawl is ideal for piercing sewing stations in paper in bookbinding. Either tool is superior to an awl for piercing sewing stations.

butterfly sewing   An across the spine sewing which utilizes paired stations. Each needle spans, enters the next section, then cross inside to exit the other station. It is also called the Japanese 4–Needle Sewing, not to be confused with the stab binding called the Japanese 4–Hole Sewing. This 12th century binding is known as Yamato Toji.

catch-word   In early printed books, the last word on a page was positioned at the foot. The same word was repeated at the top of the next page. Perhaps this served as a bridge in reading from page to page, but its purpose was a guide in collating signatures.

chain stitch   "Chain stitch" is an embroidery term, not actually a stitch in bookbinding. In binding, the chain is a result of a succession of link stitches. *Link* is a stitch; *chain* is the resulting pattern.

to change over   To continue sewing in the different section.†

clamshell A box for storing a book. It has a bottom and a lid, hinged to open like covers.

climb To move upward.†

codex (plural: **codices**) A book, bound along one edge. One of the four types of books, the others being the *fan, blind,* and *the fold book.* Note: Many binders do not agree with this definition.

compound binding A hybrid book structure of two of the same or differing *types of books.* There are 4 types of books: the fan, the blind, oriental foldbook and the western codex. Creating a structure of two or more of these types of books is a compound binding. Examples: 1. Sewing sections onto an accordion pleat for a concertina binding. 2. Including a foldbook as a unit, along with sewing sections into a single spine.

concertina 1. A type of binding, utilizing the concertina fold. 2. The concertina fold is also called an *accordion pleat.*

concertina guard A form of construction securing sections to folded stubs with a pamphlet sewing and, in turn, sewing the stubs together to form a text block.*

content Statement within the book of text and/or pictures. In a no-picture book, it is the cast shadows, cut shapes, holes, et cetera. Note: To avoid confusion in this text, *content* is never used to mean *satisfied.*

continuous support sewing Use of a single support, as opposed to sewing onto cords or tapes. The paperback sewings in Volume II of *Non-Adhesive Binding* are examples. It is important to reinforce the spine on the cover. Folding or pasting a second ply of paper in this area strengthens the sewing.

to continue on To continue sewing in the same section.†

core A support. It might be a cord, or rolled material to form a cylindrical support, generally out of leather. The endband is formed on a core.

cover stock or **cover weight** Heavy paper used for covers as opposed to text weight used for book blocks. Commercial printing papers generally come in both cover weight and text weight.

crease A fold induced by pressure marking or die debossing, not cutting. * Other binders refer to this procedure as a *score.*

creep The successive protrusion from the outermost folio to the innermost within a section or signature.

crossbar The wooden dowel held above and parallel to the base of the sewing frame by threaded posts. The crossbar is often slotted to accept threaded hooks.

curl The distortion of a sheet due to differences in structure, coatings, or moisture from one side to the other.

deckle In papermaking, the width of the wet sheet as it comes off the wire of a paper machine.

deckled-edge The untrimmed feathery edges of paper formed where the pulp flows against the deckle.

digital scan Half-tone photographic images created on a computer scanner. I do not use the term *photograph,* reserving that dear term for silver prints.

display   Presentation of the object, generally through turning pages. Books with one-sided display, the fan, blind, and fold book might be displayed fully extended on a table, or wall displayed. Books with unusual formatting may be presented in the round as sculpture, the pages not meant to be turned. Note: To avoid confusion in this text, *display* is never used as a verb.

dos-à-dos   A specific traditional format of two connected codices which have a back cover in common.

drop   To move downward.†

duodecimo   aka **12mo**   A sheet folded down to create a section of 12 sheets, or 24 pages (see: *folio, quarto, sexto, octavo,* and *z fold).*

end paper   In tradition binding, the sheet which is glued down on the inside of the cover board, extending across the gutter as the first page.

endsheets   The first (and last) folio or section of a book may be blank and perhaps a nice laid paper in a particular color different from the bulk of the book block. Endsheets function as a mat surrounding a drawing. It is blank space to clear the mind before the introduction of the content of the opus.

enter   To pass from the spine side to the fold side.†

exit   To pass from the fold side to the spine side.†

F&G's   (Folded and Gathered)   The F&G's are the assembled signatures ready for sewing.

fan   A book, bound at one point. One of the four types of books, the others being the *blind, codex,* and the *fold book.* Fans and blinds are used by South Sea Island cultures.

first section   In the sewing procedures, the term first does not necessarily mean the beginning of the book. On the bench, you may very well start sewing from the back, towards the front of the book. In that instance, the "first" section to be sewn is the final section of the book.

flap   An single extension on each side of the spine at the hinge-fold. The flap is usually one piece, crossing the spine, and included in the sewing. Covers are attach to the flap.

flatback   Sewing without rounding the spine.

flatback cover   Paper cover with two folds which delineate the spine from the side-covers. These folds create the hinging action of the cover, and are called *hinge-folds.*

flush cover   1. A cover whose front and back panels are the same dimensions as the pages. 2. In commercial binding, a cover that has been trimmed with the text block, so that cover and text block are the same size (see: *overhang cover).*

fold   see: *accordion, hinge-fold, fold out, gate fold,* and *thrown out.*

fold book   A book, whose binding is mechanical; the sheet is folded back and forth upon itself to create pages. One of the four types of books, the others being the *fan, blind,* and the *codex.*

fold-out   See: *throw-out.*

folio aka **fo** A sheet folded in half to yield a section or signature of 4 pages, and two leaves (see: *quarto, sexto, octavo, duodecimo,* and *z-fold).*

foredge 1. The front edge of a book. (pronounced *forrej*). 2. The edge of the side-cover and book block opposite the spine.

format The size, style, type page, margins, page set-up, etc.

forward In the direction on the sewing.†

gate fold Two facing fold outs in a codex. Each fold out is hinged on the foredges of an opened folio. When the gate fold is opened, or thrown-out, there are four facing pages, the two at each extreme extend beyond the book block.

gathering Assembling the folded signatures into the proper order for binding (see: *F&G's).*

grain The direction in which most fibers lie which corresponds with the direction the paper is made in commercial production machinery. Note: To avoid confusion, this is the only definition of *grain* used in this text.

gutter 1. The blank space or inner margin, from printing area to binding. Note: To avoid confusion, this is the only definition of *gutter* used in this text.

head and **tail** The top and bottom of a book when stood upright. They are at right angles to the backbone and foredge. Note: Only definition of *head* or *tail* used in this text.

head band/tail band Wrapping and beading decorative thread, usually of colored silk or cotton, at the head and tail of codices. Thread is wrapped around a core and periodically stitched into the book block. "Imitation" machine-made head bands are sold by the yard and pasted onto the backbone of commercial hard cover books.

hinge-fold The folds on either side of the spine, delineating the side-covers from the spine-cover (see: *flatback cover).*

horizontal wrapper See: *wrapper*

implied compound binding A inventive folding of pages or itinerary through a book that suggests a hybrid book structure of two of the same or differing *types of books.*

imposition The laying out of pages on a sheet, so that they will be in numerical order after the sheet is folded down as a folio or section or signature.

inner Between paired sewing stations. The approach to a station which is towards the center of the spine, rather than to the outer, which is near the spine-hinge. Inner should not be confused with the term inside.

inside The position on the valley side of a section, as opposed to the mountain peak, which is called the outside.

to the inside Toward the head or tail.†

inside bead In sewing Endbands as Change-Over, the sewing procedure results in beads on both sides of the packing. The bead on the spine side is referred to as the *spine-bead.* The bead facing the foredge is called the *inside bead* (see: *Two-Sided Beading,* page 139, Volume III).

Japanese 4–Needle Sewing See: *butterfly sewing.*

jog To knock up and level to an edge, preferably at the head to keep text in registration.

Kangxi Binding Japanese name for the stab binding known as the Noble. This binding is also referred to as Koki.

kerf cuts made with a back saw across the section folds of an unsewn text. *

kettle stitch sewing procedure of ending one section, changing direction of movement in adding the next. The sewing drops backwards and links, slips and climbs.

key a 2-pronged metal unit, about the size of a key. A key for each cord rests under the slot in the base of a sewing frame temporarily tying the cord while the sewing proceeds.

Kikko Japanese name for the stab binding also known as the Tortoise-Shell Binding.

Koki Japanese name for the stab binding known as the Noble Binding. This binding is also referred to as Kangxi Binding, after its reputed originator.

lap To pass over a support or sewing thread.†

leaf 1. A sheet. 2. Two pages, back to back; a recto/verso.

link To pass under another thread.†

loop To circle around a support or sewing thread.†

moulding saw Backsaw or tenon saw used to cut the sewing stations when the book block is held in a finishing press.

octavo aka **8vo** A sheet folded in half three times, to yield a section or signature of 16 pages, with 8 leaves. A *sextodecimo*, or *16mo*, has 32 pages with 16 leaves (see: *folio, sexto, octavo, duodecimo* and *z-fold*).

one-of-a-kind A book conceived and executed as a single copy. I do not use the word *unique*, meaning "special" to define a single copy item, as the term applies to production work as well. Note: Some librarians define a book as an item which must have more than one copy. Consequently, they do not recognize or purchase ones-of-a-kind.

open ended Open ended stations refer to the use of the head and the tail as sewing stations. The support is not pierced. It is a *passive station,* that is, the thread wraps around the head or tail, marking the change-over.

opened folio The two facing pages at any point to which the codex is opened.

Oriental fold book See: *fold book.*

outer Towards the outside of paired sewing stations, rather than centrally, between. Outer should not be confused with the term *outside.*

outside The position on the mountain peak of a section, as opposed to the valley, which is called the inside.

to the outside Away from the head or tail.†

overhand knot Half a square knot. For instructions how to tie, see: *Knots,* page 50 in Volume I.

overhang cover A cover larger in size than the pages it encloses. The amount of the side-cover that extends beyond the book block, bordering the head, foredge and tail is called the *square.* (see: *flush cover).*

pack To loop several times around.†

page 1. One side of an unfolded sheet. 2.That portion of a folio or section or signature bordered by folds and/or the edge of the sheet.

paired stations Sewing directly across the spine employs two sewing stations. Other paired stations along the spine are sewn independently. Each paired station uses one thread and two needles.

pamphlet 1. A one-section text. 2. A booklet. 3. Type of sewing for a booklet.

pamphlet sewing Type of sewing used to bind a booklet (see: page 57, Volume I, and, page 16, Volume II). The term *pamphlet stitch* should be avoided, as it is a sewing. *Pamphlet stitch sewing* is correct, but awkward. The pamphlet sewing is a *"b"* stitch, as opposed to a *figure 8* stitch (see: page 132-135, Volume II).

paste See: *adhesive.*

perfect bound 1. Adhesive binding. 2. Binding of a book which has no sewing, and no folds on the backbone. The book therefore has no sections, signatures or folios, only a stack of sheets. The back is glued. Commercial paperbacks are generally (imperfectly) *perfect bound.* Thus, unfortunately there is a general low esteem for any book with paper covers. In the past, the main difference between trade books which were paperback and hard cover, was the latter was sewn. Now, many publishers are reducing the quality of their hard covers, and are using perfect binding, rather than sewing them.

pleat An Oriental fold used to attach sections, rather than as a complete book in itself. Also known as a concertina, concertina guard, or accordion fold (see: *accordion pleat).*

ply In this text, the term is used as one piece of paper, rather than the process of making paper in layers. *Two-ply* is only used in this text to mean a sheet folded back upon itself for reinforcement. This fold could optionally be sewn down. The term is never used to mean *duplex,* a type of commercially made paper with a different color on each side of the sheet.

production books A book made in an edition, whether by hand, or published (printed).

punch Metal cylindrical tool with sharpened hollow shaped end for cutting, and solid head for striking with a hammer to cut through paper. Shapes are usually various diameters of circles, and, rarely, squares, diamonds, oblongs.

quarto aka **4to** A sheet folded in half twice, first against the grain, then with the grain, to yield a section or signature of 4 leaves, or 8 pages (see: *folio, sexto, octavo, duodecimo,* and *z-fold).*

ream Five hundred sheets of paper.

recto/verso Two pages, back to back; a leaf. *Recto* is a right hand page. *Verso* is the back of that leaf, not the page facing the recto in the opened folio. Note: Recto does not mean *front;* verso does not mean *back.* A recto or a verso is a front side when it is viewed. Each becomes a back when the page is turned, and it is not in view. Recto/verso is convenient terminology for folding and collating signatures.

saddle wire or **saddle stitch**   In commercial binding, to fasten a booklet by wiring it through the fold or the side of the single section. The machine is adjusted to the thickness of the opened section, and uses a spool of wire. It is looped through the section, cut and crimped, similar to stapling.

score   1. To indent with a bone folder. 2. A light surface cut made to facilitate folding or flexing in card or board (see: *crease*).

section   1. A sheet folded down to yield eight or more pages, such as an octavo, sexto, or duodecimo. 2. Two or more loose folios compiled. NOTE 1:   To avoid confusion, *section* is never used to mean a *portion*. NOTE 2:   If the sheet has been printed, then folded down, it is referred to in printers' terminology as a *signature*. Any signature can be called a section, but only a section which has been printed is technically a signature (see: *signature*).

self cover   A cover of the same paper as the text block.

sew a set   To sew one more than one section on at a time.†

sewing stations   1. The mark, or the pierce along the spine-fold of the cover, and the backbone of the section, or folio showing the positions of the sewing. 2. Path of the needle through paper to create the sewing on the spine. If made with a saw, they are called *kerf stations* (see: *sewn vs stitched*).

sewn vs **stitched**   Sewing refers to the thread path along the valley and mountain peak, as opposed to set in from the fold. That is *stabbing*. Stabbing is *stitching*, not sewing. Path of the needle limited to the gutter is not "stitching", but sewing. S*titches* is appropriate to sewing in the fold, but *stitching* equals *stabbing*.

sexto aka **6to**   A sheet folded down to create a section of 6 leaves, or 12 pages. The sheet is first folded against the grain with a Z-fold, dividing the sheet into thirds. That is then folded in half with the grain (see: *folio, quarto, octavo, duodecimo,* and *z-fold*).

sheet   1. An unfolded piece of paper. 2. A leaf. 3. The full size of the paper before being folded down into a folio or section. 4. In single sheet bindings, a sheet is two pages back to back; a recto/verso.

side-cover   Front and back cover, as opposed to the spine.

signature   A specific type of a *section,* differing from the general term of section, in that a signature is a sheet that first has been printed, then folded to a section. *Signature* is a printer's term for the binder's word *section.*

simple/compound   Terms used only to differentiate basic bindings from hybrids constructed by combining two or more basic *types of books.*

slip   To pass under itself.†

slips   The ends of tapes, cords, or supporting straps that are attached to the covers.

slit   Slit is a severing with a knife. It has length, but no width (see: *slot*).

slot   A slot is an opening, constructed by two slits, parallel, and no more than about ⅛" apart. Slots, rather than slits, are needed to accommodate the thickness of the inserted photographs, or weaving a strap or flap, to help prevent buckling of the sheet.

Smythe-sewn   Commercial method of machine-*stitching* a book (see: *sewn vs stitched* in the Glossary).

span   To climb and change over to another section.†

spine or **spine-cover**   1. The depth of a bound book, connecting the two side-covers. The spine-covers the back, or backbone. 2. That part of the book that is visible when it is on the shelf. It is sometimes referred to as the *backstrip.*

spine-bead   In sewing Endbands as Change-Over, the sewing procedure results in beads on both sides of the packing. The bead on the spine side is referred to as the *spine-bead.* The bead facing the foredge is called the *inside bead* (see: *Two-Sided Beading,* page 139, Volume III).

spine tab   A strip woven onto the spine.

square or **square of the book**   1. The projection of the side-cover beyond the book block. 2. Only the part of the cover that extends beyond the book block and borders the head, foredge, and tail. (The total surface of the cover is referred to as an *overhang cover.*)

square knot   Reef knot (see: *Knots,* page 50, Volume I for instructions how to tie).

a station   1. A place where the sewing stops to attach a section to other sections or to a common support or to both.† 2. *Passive sewing stations* is the use of the head and tail as change-over. This is referred to as *open ended.* In diagramming sewings with endbands as change-cover, I assign the support, usually cords, at the head and the tail a sewing station number. They are not pierced sewing stations, but *passive,* that is, *open ended.* This makes for easy reference in the drawn illustrations (see: *paired stations).*

stitching   See: *sewn vs stitched* in the Glossary.

strap   Horizontal supports across the spine onto which supported sewings are made. The strap is usually separate from the cover, and attached after the sewing. In the Buttonhole binding, the straps are sections of the spine.

supported sewings   Sections sewn together around common straps, tapes or cords, which go across the back, perpendicular to it. The supports are generally attached to side-covers.

swelling   Thickness added to the backbone by the accumulation of sewing threads or any guards (see: *swelling the backbone,* page 47, Volume I and *expanding the spine pleat,* page 226 and 272, Volume I).

tab   A narrow strip woven as means of attachment.

tail   1. The bottom edge of a book when standing upright. 2. The edge opposite the head, and perpendicular to the spine and foredge.

tapes   Woven fabric supports, usually linen, onto which the sewing occurs. They are usually 1/4" wide, and always are non-adhesive.

tenon saw   Moulding saw or backsaw used to cut the sewing stations when the book block is held in a finishing press.

tension   Regulation of tautness. Uniform shape and tautness is desired. Betsy

Palmer Eldridge says that the tension varies with each sewer. It varies even if one person stops for a break. It is best to start and sew the entire book at once. The operative word is snug. Tension should not be loose, but neither should it be tight. I find that men tend to sew too tightly. Link stitches lose their teardrop shape when pulled tightly.

text block See: *book block.*

tie-off Joining two threads with a knot at the beginning or end of a sewing.

ties-down The threads which extend from the endband, in on the spine to the next station to anchor the endband. The tie-off may enter a station on the section, or link under a support at that station.

throw-out A fold-out. The action of unfolding of a fold-out or throw-out is referred to as *thrown-out.* A throw-out might be a single fold, gate fold, or any other page which is larger than the book block, and folded down for storage. Traditionally refers to a fold-out at the end of a book containing a map. The map is *thrown-out,* so that it remains visible while any other page in the book can be read and turned.

types of books There are four basic types of books, determined by how they are bound:
1. at one point is called a fan.
2. at two points is the venetian blind. The fan and blind are used by South Sea Island cultures.
3. across one edge, is the western codex.
4. alternate folds back and forth upon itself is the Oriental fold book. The other three types of books are sewn. The fold book's binding is mechanical.

unsupported sewings Sections sewn directly together, without common straps, tapes or cords.

venetian blind A book, bound at two points. One of the four types of books, the others being the *fan, codex,* and the *fold book.* Fans and blinds are used by South Sea Island cultures.

verso See: *recto / verso.*

vertical wrapper See: *wrapper.*

with the grain Folding paper parallel to the grain of the paper.

wrapped stations Head and tail of the sections used as sewing stations. Passive, as opposed to a pierced or slit stations. Open ended.

wrapper Paper covering board covers without the use of adhesives (see *Flat Back with Boards,* page 244, Volume I and *Separately Wrapped Boards,* page 246, Volume I).

Yamato Toji Japanese name for the 4–needle sewing, across the spine (see: *butterfly sewing).*

Yotsume Toji Japanese name for the 4–hole stab binding.

Z-Fold Procedure to create a 6, and a 12 page section. The sheet is first folded in thirds, against the grain (the Z-fold). Folding the Z-fold in half once, with the grain, gives a sexto. Folding the sexto in half with the grain gives 12 leaves, or 24 pages. It is called a duodecimo (see: *folio, quarto,sexto, octavo,* and *duodecimo).*

Daniel Essig

Much of Dan's work is Coptic sewings. Here, he has sewn a Coptic, but embellished it with a Coptic tailband, but a Caterpillar headband. One Caterpillar Sewing augments the sewing across the spine.

The Caterpillar is a single station sewing using paired holes. I learned this sewing from Betsy Palmer Eldridge. She had seen a fragment of an ancient sewing where the thread is packed to become a support. The ancient sewing probably was covered with a leather spine.

Betsy had made a sewing with clothesline rope onto cardboard as a 3–dimensional illustration.

Daniel Essig, untitled Ethiopian binding with Coptic endbands, 1999. On top of the headband is a Caterpillar sewing which extends along the boards at the head. This binding is also shown on pages 311 and 312. 12.5 x 10 x 4.25 cm.

Dan's caterpillar sewings which I saw at Penland in May 1999 were the first books sewn with the Caterpillar that I had seen, except for the ones I sewed as illustrations in *Exposed Spine Sewings*. I believe Dan learned this sewing from this book. It was a treat to see that others could sew this complicated procedure from the directions in my book.

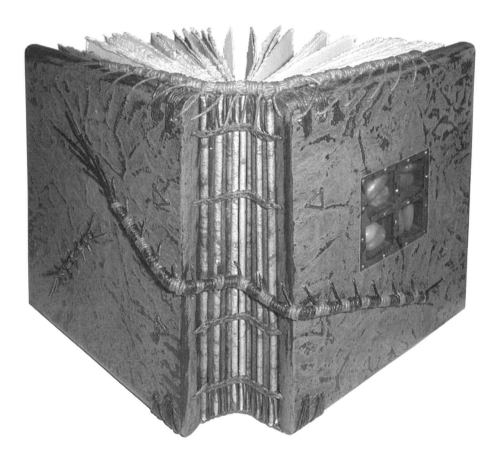

Daniel Essig, untitled Coptic sewing with Caterpillar. 1999. Examining this book at my home in April 2001, Gary Frost was impressed with the use of color, the precision in sewing, proportion of the pleat and the board transmission in opening the book. It is an exquisite piece.

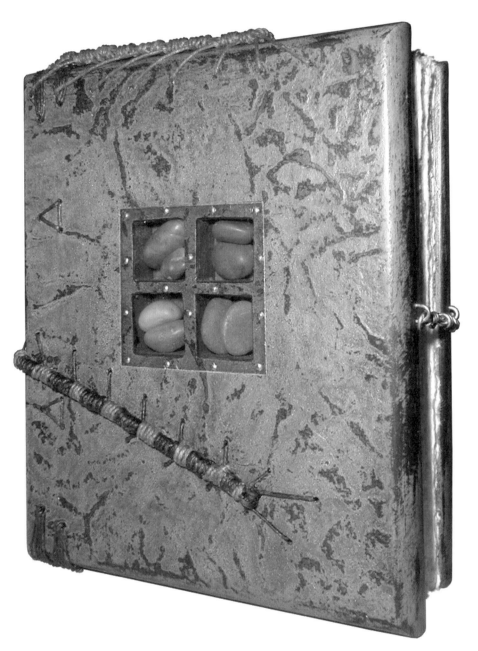

Daniel Essig, untitled Coptic sewing with Caterpillar, 1999. Collection of Keith Smith.
12.5 x 10 x 4.25 cm.

BOOKS-ON-BOOKS

CONCEPT

Structure of the Visual Book, keith smith
BOOKS, Expanded Fourth Edition,
2003. This book on ideas, not how
to bind, discusses concepts of ordering a book of pictures by means of a
group, series, or sequence. Pacing is
stressed by composing the pages as
well as the individual pictures.
Utilizing the space between pictures is
part of the awareness of time in books
that conceives the book as a visual
object, not by imposed decoration,
but through understanding and
applying structure.

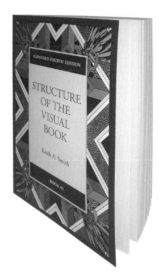

This new edition almost is double in
size from the earlier editions with
over 450 photographs of artists
books from 148 contemporary book
artists from around the world. The
illustrations, alone, are a great
resource.
432 pages.
$35
ISBN 0-9740764-0-6

CONCEPT

Text in the Book Format, keith smith
BOOKS, Expanded ThirdEdition,
2004, is conceiving text as a book
experience, not a running manuscript.
The book is revealed not by recitation
but turning pages conceived as part of
the content. Writing is not poured
onto blank pages but emanates from
the inherent properties of a book.
248 pages with 48 pages in color.
$25.00
ISBN 0-9740764-1-4

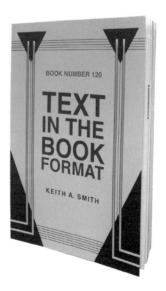

ORDER ONLINE: *www.keithsmithbooks.com*

How To Bind

Non-Adhesive Binding, Volume I: *Books without Paste or Glue,* keith a smith *BOOKS,* The Revised & Expanded Edition, 2001. Introduction covers binding, paper, sewing, knots and tools. This is followed by detailed written instructions for 32 simple to complex sewings. The procedures are also presented in 320 drawings, diagrammed step by step. 116 photographic reproductions of bindings by 37 contemporary binders and artists. 352 pages.
$30
ISBN 0-9637682-6-3

How To Bind

Non-Adhesive Binding, Volume II: *1- 2- & 3-Section Sewings,* keith a smith *BOOKS,* First Edition, 1995. Written and drawn instructions for 122 sewings which yield four, to perhaps a hundred pages imposed as one, two or three sections. Almost all of these sewings on continuous limp paper supports were devised by Smith, as the book was written. Photos of bindings by 28 contemporary binders and artists. 320 pages.
$30
ISBN 0-9637682-2-0

Keith Smith, 1115 East Main Street, Suite 219, Box 8, Rochester, NY 14609
Voice Mail or FAX: 585 482 2496

All books are available either as Smythe sewn paperback, or, in sheets, folded and gathered sections, if you wish to hand bind your own copy.

How To Bind

Non–Adhesive Binding, Volume IV: *Smith's Sewing Single Sheets,* keith smith BOOKS, First Edition, 2001. These sewings can be used to bind single sheets of paper, board, plexiglass and even metal. The bindings open flat to any page, unlike traditional post bindings and stab bindings commonly used to bind single sheets.

Pages opening flat make handsome and functional presentation of photographs. Smith devised these sewings to make one-of-a-kind books from large ink-jet prints. Seven bindings are described.

paperback or in sheets: $30
ISBN 0-9637682-8-X

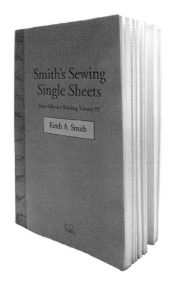

Autobiography

200 Books, An Annotated Bibliography, First Edition, July 2000, keith smith BOOKS. *200 Books* is a memoir as told through all the books made by the author.

Text and pictures describe the 199 previous books by Smith with over 550 photo reproductions. The text gives background of the author and describes why each book was made with references to other artists. Sometimes there are detailed descriptions of how the imagery was technically achieved. 336 pages.

hard cover or in sheets: $35
ISBN: 0–9637682–7–1

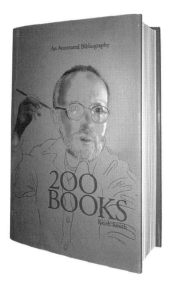

Individuals or stores can order directly:
keith smith BOOKS, 1115 East Main Street, Suite 219, Box 8, Rochester, NY 14609-6152.
Telephone or FAX: 585 482 2496   Email: keith@keithsmithbooks.com

ORDER ONLINE: www.keithsmithbooks.com

How To Bind
Non–Adhesive Binding, Volume V: *Quick Leather Bindings,* keith smith *BOOKS,* First Edition, 2003. Hard cover quarter leather bindings are constructed without paste or glue using archival pressure-sensitive sheet adhesive. No binding equipment is used, just needle, thread, scissors, metal straightedge, X-Acto knife and a self-seal cutting surface. Sections are sewn through the spine as continuous support sewings.

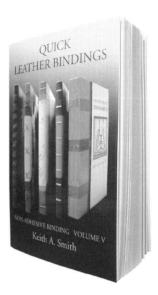

Smith devised 17 new sewings for this book. You can also sew any of the 122 bindings from Volume II as hard cover, quarter leather. This approach makes leather binding simple and—quick.
$30
ISBN 0–9637682–9–8

How To Bind
Bookbinding for Book Artists, First Edition, 1998, keith smith *BOOKS. Bookbinding for Book Artists* presents a simple approach to binding in cloth or unpared leather. Household tools are substituted for traditional binding equipment.

Three bindings are described:
• *Pamphlet Binding with Boards* gives a hard cover book with only 4 to 32 pages.
• *Flat Back* is shown as sewn onto tapes as a book of 24 to 100 pages.
• *Tight Back* and the *Hollow Back* are presented as leather bound books, rounded and backed.
Over 400 detailed drawn illustrations augment the text with 60 photo reproductions of books by 24 contemporary binders and book artists. 432 pages.
$35
ISBN 0–9637682–5–5

DISCOUNTS: Besides store discounts, there are group discounts for individuals ordering 6 or more various titles. Email keith@keith-smithbooks.com for details.

REFERENCE OF PHOTOGRAPHIC ILLUSTRATIONS

PHOTO CREDITS

Digital scans of books by Scott McCarney.

All photographs by Keith Smith, except for the following: 70, Gary Frost; 71, Gary Frost; 72, Wilber H. Schilling; 111, Bill Gedney; 112 top, Frank Margeson; 112 bottom, Paul Warchol; 128 top, Kathy Wyatt Thiele; 128 bottom, Penny Carey-Wells; 178, Catherine Hopkins; 179, Catherine Hopkins; 203, Marcia Ciro; 206, Wilber H. Schilling; 208 top, Nancy Barnett; 208 bottom, Jane Levine; 246, Jane Levine; 272, Denise Carbone.

COLOPHON

Book 170
was begun in March 1993 on a Macintosh IIcx, and completed on a
Power Mac 7100/66. There was no running manuscript. Text was format-
ted *as* it was written, using Quark XPress. Drawn illustrations were
imported from Aldus Freehand, and, later, from Macromedia Freehand.

Exposed Spine Sewings
was periodically proofed on an Apple Laserwriter II NT, and later, on a
Hewlett Packard LaserJet 4MV. The book was sent to the printer on-disk,
postscript, using SyQuest 44 megabyte removable cartridges, for negative
output: 1200 dots per inch for the type and 150 line screen for the drawings and digital scans.

Typeface is Columbus MT and Columbus Expert MT, with captions in
Optima. Drawn and photographic illustrations are by the author, except
for the photographs listed on the facing page.

Non-Adhesive Binding, VOLUME III
cover design and digital scans of the sewings and photographs are by
Scott McCarney.

This Fourth Printing of the First Edition is offset in 1000 copies on Finch
Vellum 80 lb. text and cover with matte film lamination. The book is
Smythe sewn, paperback.

Additional copies are available unbound, folded and gathered, for those
who might wish to hand bind their own copy of the book.

Keith A. Smith
October 2006

KE◉TH

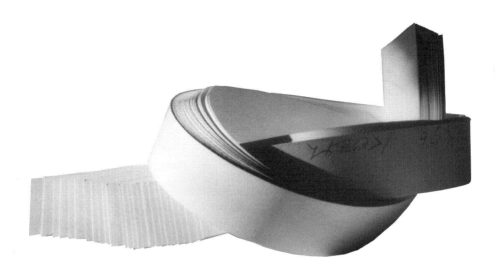

Keith Smith, Book Number 56: *The Hand-Bound Book,* 1975. 2.5 X 36.1 cm.

The book was made tongue in cheek. In that manner, I guess this could be called a *single sheet sewing,* but unlike those in Volume IV, Non-Adhesive Binding. No thread here—the sheets themselves are tied in an overhand knot, which I proudly refer to as an *overhand* K.